CRANKS, QUARKS, AND THE COSMOS

OTHER BOOKS BY JEREMY BERNSTEIN

Ascent: The Invention of Mountain Climbing and Its Practice

Einstein

Experiencing Science: Profiles in Discovery

In the Himalayas: Journeys Through Nepal, Tibet, and Bhutan

Kinetic Theory in the Expanding Universe

The Life It Brings: One Physicist's Beginnings

Mountain Passages

Quantum Profiles

The Tenth Dimension: An Informal History of High Energy Physics

Three Degrees Above Zero: Bell Labs in the Information Age

Cosmological Constants: Papers in Modern Cosmology
(with Gerald Feinberg)

CRANKS, QUARKS, and the COSMOS

WRITINGS ON SCIENCE BY
Jeremy Bernstein

BasicBooks
A Division of HarperCollins*Publishers*

Credits can be found on page 211.

Library of Congress Cataloging-in-Publication Data
Bernstein, Jeremy, 1929–
   Cranks, quarks, and the cosmos : writings on science / by Jeremy
Bernstein.
      p.   cm.
   Includes bibliographical references and index.
   ISBN 0–465–08897–X
   1. Science—Miscellanea.   I. Title.
Q173.B54   1993
500—dc20   92–53239
                                                                      CIP

Designed by Ellen Levine

93 94 95 96 CC/RRD 9 8 7 6 5 4 3 2 1

To GARY FEINBERG,
in memory, and to
WILLIAM SHAWN

Contents

Preface

READERS OF THE INTRODUCTION to this book will readily understand why William Shawn is one of the people to whom I have dedicated it. Without his help and encouragement I never would have written professionally.

As for Gary Feinberg, I first met him at a physics conference in the late 1950s, although I already knew of him by reputation. It was long before electronic mail attached physicists to each other umbilically; nonetheless, when a bright star, especially a contemporary, emerged, one got to know about it pretty fast. Before I actually met him, I knew of Gary as one of the few students of the Nobelist T. D. Lee and also as one of Columbia's brightest students. What I did not know about was his generosity. This I learned over a period of over thirty years of nearly daily phone calls and other contacts. For a while Gary and I chased each other around professionally. First he went to the Institute for Advanced Study, and then I went there. Then he went to the Brookhaven National Laboratory, and then I went there. Then he went to New York University, and then I went there. Finally, he settled at Columbia, and I at the Stevens Institute of Technology across the Hudson. We collaborated on several physics papers, joint lectures, and even a book of annotated papers on cosmology. I have never met anyone in physics with a clearer grasp of the subject. The number of questions of mine Gary answered, with patience and humor, is beyond counting. He read nearly all the essays in this book with his usual critical and generous eye. He set for me the highest possible standards for understanding, and I would like to believe that the best of this book reflects that.

Many other people have also helped me: editors, checkers, scientific colleagues, and friends. I won't name them for fear of leaving some out, but I am grateful to them all.

New York City
March 1992

INTRODUCTION

The Scientific Profile

F OR THE PAST THIRTY YEARS, principally in the *New Yorker* magazine, I have been writing what I would call scientific profiles. This is a literary form that did not exist, certainly not at the *New Yorker*, before I serendipitously found my way from the laboratory to that magazine in the fall of 1960. It is a profile in which one attempts to convey deep science—or, indeed, deep technology—by having it emerge as the experience of recognizable human beings. I act as a channel between these subjects and an audience of readers whom I do not assume to be scientists, but whom I *do* assume to have intellectual curiosity. It is a profile in which the personality serves the message—the science—and not the other way around. Prior to my arrival at the *New Yorker*, there had been profiles of scientists, to be sure; but these scientists emerged like the scientists in the C. P. Snow novels—full of odd, and often fascinating quirks, but their science of little or no relevance. The scientists in a C. P. Snow novel might as well be professors of Greek, for all that the science matters. What I would like to trace out for you, is a kind of personal history of how all of this came about, and of how I have gone about trying to carry it out.

I have the impression that, from rather early childhood, I knew that I could write. This is very odd, because in a literal sense, I almost couldn't. For a while, in the Rochester, New York, school system of the 1930s, there was a sort of tacit understanding that everyone should write with the right hand. So, although I am left-handed, I learned to write, very badly, with my right hand. This gave me an aversion to writing at all. But, when I did write, what I wrote was close to the way I spoke, since instead of writing and revising on paper, which would have been very painful, I did it in my head—and still do. Those of you who have tried to write will appreciate how hard it is to align the printed and the spoken word. Many people who converse brilliantly, write badly, because they cannot get these two forms of communication to line up. Some of the rage and frustration writers feel is, I think, caused by an inability to bridge this gap. What one reads on the paper is not at all what one has wanted to *say*. But, as a child, I became aware, somehow, that what I put down on the paper was—at least some of the time—*exactly* what I wanted to say. The first time I realized that this odd ability might actually have some commercial value, was at age nine. The Whitman Publishing Company of Racine, Wisconsin, the publishers of the Big Little Books of blessed memory, offered cash prizes for the best essay, of less than seventy-five words, describing the merits of these books. Mine read

Dear Sirs,

I enjoy big-little books. When I was sick at camp, big-little books were the only thing that kept me from going nuts. I have read many of the big-little books on your list. The reason why I like your books is because there is always something new and exciting. It always gives me a thrill when I get one.

Sincerely yours,
Jeremy Bernstein

My parents were astonished when this entry won second prize, which was seventy-five dollars—a huge sum in those Depression years—a higher word rate than is presently paid by most of the better magazines. I was not quite sure what I had done, but the results were pleasurable and the effort not excessive.

If life were logical then I would be able to trace some sort of straight line leading from this childhood realization to my arrival at the *New Yorker* in 1960. But it isn't, and I can't. The only writing of a nonobligatory nature I did in high school, was an occasional column I wrote for our high school newspaper—which I called "Seeing Stars." By this time, our family had moved to New York—then, as now, an entertainment colossus. With a good deal of energy, and even more nerve, I managed to interview people like Edgar Bergen, Duke Ellington, Tommy Dorsey, and the acerbic comedian Henry Morgan for my column. I still have a few of these high-school newspapers, dating back to the mid-1940s. In rereading my columns, I find that they have an uncanny resemblance to *New Yorker* "Talk of the Town" pieces. I think this is an example of convergent evolution, since I do not remember reading the *New Yorker* until I got to college.

At Harvard I did even less noncompulsory writing than in high school. I took just the one required freshman writing course. I am glad it was only one, since I think that if I had studied writing, I might well have lost the one thing I was able to do: to reproduce the sound of my inner voice. There was a literary circle—indeed, several—presided over by people like John Updike; but, as far as I was concerned, they might have been living in another universe. In actual fact, at least two of my classmates bridged whatever cultures there were. On the one hand, there was the late Paul Fenimore Cooper, Junior—known, I later learned, as Nikki—who had a double major in Greek and physics and was summa cum laude in both. His cousin, Henry S. F. Cooper, Jr., has been my colleague on the *New Yorker* for the last thirty years and is our man in space. On the other hand, there was Harold Furth, the former director of the Princeton Plasma Fusion Laboratory and one of my dearest friends. Furth and I both lived in Eliot House, and I knew who he was. In fact, because of his literary associations, I took him to be a sort of precious fop. I imagine that Robert Oppenheimer might have made something of this impression on people who saw him from a distance at Harvard and were aware of the fact that he contributed to *Hound and Horn*, a literary magazine. I was astonished when I learned that Furth was a physics major and that he had, in fact, like Paul Cooper, graduated summa cum laude. Furth was, I believe, the first member of the American Physical Society to have had something published in the *New Yorker*. Some years before I got on the scene, the magazine had published over Furth's initials a delightful poem, describing an extragalactic encounter between Edward Teller and his antiparticle. "All the rest was gamma rays," the poem ends. In subsequent years, I have sometimes thought that, in this case, it would have been nice if life had imitated art. For a time, Furth, Cooper, and I were all at the Harvard Cyclotron Laboratory, a delightful place tucked off in a corner of the campus out of harm's way.

One may well wonder why I was unaware of these people during my undergraduate years, since they were physics majors. The explanation is simple. I was not a physics major—and, indeed, the only two courses I can recall taking in physics during that time were freshman physics, which I took as a sophomore, and the future Nobelist Julian Schwinger's course in quantum mechanics, which I took as a senior. If eclecticism had been a possible major at Harvard, I certainly would have chosen it. I entered Harvard in 1947 with no notion what I wanted to study, but with a clear notion that I did *not* want to study either science or mathematics. I had taken one science course in high school—physics—and it had evaporated. I was reasonably good at mathematics, but it never occurred to me that this was an activity for serious people. Besides, there was the family tradition that Bernsteins were not expected to understand mathematics. Harvard offered general education courses, including a required science course. By studying the "Confidential Guide," an irreverent guide to courses put out by undergraduates, you could choose the easiest one—Natural Sciences 3. It was taught by the historian of science I. Bernard Cohen, who had the best blackboard handwriting I have ever seen. The course proceeded uneventfully, until Cohen got to modern physics. As I look back on it, my reaction to the theory of relativity and the quantum theory was a bit like that of Einstein and his contemporaries. I do not recall finding the quantum theory radical, because my understanding of it was negligible. In 1905, only Einstein realized how radical the theory was, because he understood it and his contemporaries did not. On the other hand, I was absolutely dumbstruck by the theory of relativity—which Einstein himself regarded as conservative. That measuring sticks should contract, clocks slow down, and masses become more ponderous when they are moving, seemed to me the most remarkable thing I had ever heard. While, at the time, I had no intention of becoming a physics major, I decided that I would try to understand the theory of relativity. This ambition was further fueled when Cohen said—in retrospect, it must have been a joke—that only seven people in the world understood the theory. I decided to become the eighth.

Fortunately for me, there was at Harvard, at this very time, Philipp Frank who became my first great teacher. Professor Frank had been born in 1884 in Vienna. He had studied physics in an atmosphere that included men like Ludwig Boltzmann and Ernst Mach and later Erwin Schrödinger. He was some five years younger than Einstein but, unlike so many of his scientific contemporaries, recognized early the importance of his work and began corresponding with him in 1907. In 1912, Frank succeeded Einstein at the German University in Prague. In 1938, he was fortunate enough to be able to emigrate to the United States, where he was given a modest lectureship at Harvard. During the war, he and Einstein were both employed, for a time, in problems involving the detection of submarines. The year before I first encountered him, he had written a wonderful biography of Einstein called *Einstein: His Life and Times*. He, too, was teaching in the general education program; and, by bending the rules a little, I was able to take both his course and Cohen's second semester simultaneously. Professor Frank's course changed my life. His knowledge was staggering. He was fluent in German, French, Italian, Spanish, Russian, Czech, and English and able to read Persian, Arabic, Hebrew, Latin, and Greek. He was also fluent in mathematics. This made a profound impression on me. I realized that if I was ever going to be anything but a parroting dilettante when it came to relativity, I would have to learn mathematics. I recall going with some trepidation to someone in the dean's office to learn whether my mathematical aptitude tests had shown that I had the brains to learn the calculus. I was much relieved to be told that I had. There then followed over ten years during which I was totally immersed—or nearly so—in mathematics and then theoretical physics. I say "nearly so" because, not long ago, I came across a yellowish notebook from this period containing some verse—terrible verse—I had written. One set of poems was called "Four Poems for Three Loves Now Lost." I have been trying desperately to retrieve these three young women from my memory, if only to recall which of them got the *two* poems.

The scene now shifts to Upton, Long Island. It is the fall of 1960. I have just returned from a marvelous year in France, thanks to the National Science Foundation. This has come after a two-year stint at the Institute for Advanced Study in Princeton. Before leaving for France, I had accepted a job at the Brookhaven National Laboratory in Upton and been granted a one-year leave to go to France. The summer before returning, I had taught at a summer school on the island of Corsica: the leisure of the theory class. It was a heartbreakingly beautiful place. Glowing red cliffs cascaded into the incandescent blue of the Mediterranean. It was also very funny: deeply serious, bearded students of theoretical physics mingling with the native Corsicans. Whatever actual labor was performed on the island was done by the

Corsican women. The men could be found in the local cafés settling the affairs of the world. There was also an astonishingly beautiful local girl with whom we were all in love, called Annie.

This was all fresh in my mind as I contemplated the scrub pines of eastern Long Island, from the windows of my room in the wooden officers' barracks—part of the old Second World War camp Yaphank. I had brought back with me some Juliet Greco records and would listen to them at night. Occasionally, the late Sam Goudsmit, then my boss at the lab, who had been the subject of a *New Yorker* profile of the type I have described, would come in to listen to the records. I never found out why he, too, had a nostalgic torch lit for France. I had been telling people—Goudsmit was certainly one of them—about Corsica; and after I had told this story a few times, some atavistic instinct led me to write it down. By this time, I was a devoted reader of the *New Yorker,* so I decided to write it as a "Letter from Corsica"—in line with the magazine's "Letters" from Washington and other places around the world. For several nights, after work, I wrote down what I had been saying, and that old childhood ability resurfaced—that is my spoken voice.

I showed my "Letter" to a few people at the laboratory, including Goudsmit and Ed Purcell. They said, Why don't you send it to the *New Yorker?*—something I had decided to do anyway. I put my badly typed manuscript into an envelope bearing the lab's return address and then went back to work calculating whatever it was that I was then calculating. I had no idea what to expect. I thought that perhaps the *New Yorker* was like the *Physical Review;* and that, in short order, I would receive a postcard, or something, acknowledging the receipt of my manuscript. Weeks, even months, went by. Nothing at all was forthcoming. By this time, I was getting ready to go back to Europe to finish the rest of my fellowship. I decided to call the *New Yorker* offices to see whether I could find out what had happened to my manuscript. At first, I chanced on someone in the fiction department who cheerfully informed me that they "lost a lot of manuscripts," but he would look around. A second call was made, and this time I was switched to "fact." When I gave my name, the person at the other end of the line said, "Oh, you must be back from Corsica." I pointed out that I had been back from Corsica for over six months, and was told I would be hearing something shortly. A few days later, the phone rang, and a man identifying himself as William Shawn was on the line. To be honest, I had never heard of a

William Shawn. I may have asked him who he was, and in the tentative way he sometimes appeared—and it was appearance, I can assure you—to reply to inquiries, he explained that he was the editor of the *New Yorker*. Before I could say anything, he added, "We liked your piece, and we wonder if it would be all right with you if we published it?" I said that it would be all right. He then asked if I could stop by the office sometime to talk with him. I explained that it would have to be soon, since I was on my way back to Europe, and we made a date for a day or two later.

Years afterward, I discovered the sequence of events that led up to this remarkable call. My Corsica article arrived at the magazine and was read by a first reader. All manuscripts sent to the *New Yorker* are read by someone. It had been judged of sufficient interest so that it had worked its way up to Edith Oliver who, besides being one of the magazine's theater critics, was also functioning as a reader of fact manuscripts. She had just finished reading my article, when William Shawn walked into her office with a problem. The problem was that there seemed to be all this exciting science going on—especially physics—but no one was able to write about it in a way he wanted to publish. Miss Oliver, she later told me, held up my manuscript and said, in effect, This may be the solution to your problems. Hence the phone call. Now you see why I don't view life as logical.

A few days later, I paid my first visit to the offices of the *New Yorker*. I don't know what I expected. I have always noted a kind of inverse proportionality between the elegance of the offices of physics departments and their quality. I think this may often be true of magazines. The *New Yorker* offices had, at the time, the shabby lived-in quality of some of the better physics departments. I was ushered into Shawn's office. He turned out to be a smallish, balding man, with a deceptively timorous manner. Over the years, I was always impressed by how rapidly, and directly, Mr. Shawn could get down to business once the initial, and inevitable, polite exchanges were over. On this occasion, he ushered me into his office and offered me a wide variety of reading matter, while he completed, over the telephone, some essential business of the magazine. Since I was much more interested in studying him and the office, I declined the various magazines and newspapers. After some minutes on the phone, he turned his attention to me. Among his many other attributes as an editor, Mr. Shawn had a genius for listening. He gave one the impression that what you were saying was the most interesting thing that had happened to him that day, or even that week. In his presence, thoughts spilled out of one's head, like jelly beans from an overturned bowl. In this case, he seemed to want to know what it was like to be a young physicist—the very thing I was. I told him, as best I could, for nearly an hour. At the end of it, he said that he thought I could do a kind of writing that had never been done for the *New Yorker,* which was to write about science as a form of experience—my experience and the experience of people I knew. There were no instructions about how I might go about this. There was no mention of writing profiles of scientists or anything like that. I was just to write about science as a form of experience.

I walked out of the office in a sort of euphoric trance. Here was the editor of my favorite magazine conferring upon me this awesome literary responsibility. The kid from Rochester, New York, had suddenly been called on to play the lead. The trouble was that the only script available was one I would have to write. For one year, during which I was working at my primary job as a theoretical physicist, I tried to write about science as a form of experience. Nothing worked. It was not a matter of writer's block. It was rather a matter of writer's compulsion. I felt compelled to write about everything, filling notebooks. This was the exact opposite to what had happened when I wrote about Corsica. I had not been looking for a subject; rather, the subject had come looking for me. I was telling myself a story about Corsica, and what emerged was that inner storyteller's voice, which was now lost. I submitted a few things to Mr. Shawn who, of course, rejected them, all the while encouraging me to keep at it.

The scene now shifts to Geneva, Switzerland, in the summer of 1961, about a year later. I have just sprained my ankle playing tennis. Arthur Clarke, the science fiction author, once said to me that nothing really bad can ever happen to a writer: however painful the experience, it furnishes, at the very least, grist for the mill. My sprain was sufficiently painful to put me on crutches. I was living in a modern apartment building not far from downtown Geneva, but rather far from the Centre pour la Récherche Nucléaire—CERN—where I was working for the summer. One of my neighbors in the building were the Lees—Tsung Dao Lee and his wife, Jeanette, and their sons. T. D. Lee and C. N. Yang were awarded the Nobel Prize in physics in 1957 for their theoretical work on what is known as the nonconservation of parity. This is sometimes called the nonconservation of mirror symmetry, since a mirror exchanges your left and your right hands. Until Lee and Yang did their work, it was generally assumed that left- and right-handed descriptions were identical. The fact that they aren't was one of the great surprises of postwar physics. It was a sensation when it was discovered in 1956. When Lee and Yang were awarded the prize the next year, Yang was thirty-five, and Lee thirty-one. They were the first native-born Chinese to win the Nobel Prize. As it happened, we had been at the Institute for Advanced Study at the same time, and I had worked with them there. But I certainly did not know them. In fact, when the prize was celebrated at the Institute in 1957, we junior members were not even invited to the ceremonial dinner. Although T. D. Lee was only a few years older than I, the professional gulf that separated us was vast.

The Lees, seeing that I was not able to walk properly, offered to help. In particular, T. D. offered to drive me back and forth to CERN, for which I was extremely grateful. During these rides, we began to talk, and he told me a good deal about his life and about the events that led up to his work with Yang. As these conversations evolved, once again my inner voice began to stir. I began telling myself the story of these conversations and rearranging them editorially in my head. Pianists talk about a piece lying under the hand. In the same way, I felt almost as if I had already written the profile. There was, however, a gigantic obstacle: I had not told Lee, to say nothing of Yang, that I wanted to write about them. The obstacle was both personal and institutional. On the personal level, I had a modest reputation as a young physicist and no reputation at all as a writer. I do not even think that my piece on Corsica had been published, although many people knew that I had had something accepted by the *New Yorker*. It was generally assumed that this had been an amusing diversion and I had now returned to more serious things. I may have told a few close friends about my "assignment" from Mr. Shawn, but I doubt that they took it seriously. I had, therefore, an enormous feeling of inhibition about asking Lee for permission to write down parts of what had been, after all, a series of private conversations. To compound matters, there was an institutional obstacle that was much more subtle but, nonetheless, serious. The *New Yorker* had a reputation then among many of my colleagues for making fun of science, and scientists. There was some basis for this. James Thurber had, for example, published in the *New Yorker* a series of delightful drawings that illustrated his notion of the war between the sexes. There was one I have never forgotten: a posse of those unspeakably formidable Thurber women is shown capturing some cowering, bearded individuals who are identified as physics professors. Indeed, E. B. White had been quoted as saying that a "gentleman should not understand anything more complicated than a Model-T Ford." When I heard this, the operative word seemed to me to be "understand." All Sadi Carnot wanted to do, was to understand the workings of the steam engine which is, God knows, simpler than a Model-T Ford; and he invented the science of thermodynamics. But somehow I don't think that this was what White had in mind.

By the end of the summer, I got up my courage to ask T. D. Lee whether I could write a profile of him based on my conversations with him and, possibly, on some future conversations I might have with him and Yang. If Lee had said no, it is quite possible that my writing career would have ended then and there. But, with some well-deserved scepticism, he agreed. During the following winter, I wrote what became my first profile for the *New Yorker*. It was a joint profile of Lee and Yang, to which Mr. Shawn gave the title "A Question of Parity." In putting things this way, I make it sound as if I pressed some sort of a button and—Presto!—a profile appeared in the *New Yorker*. It wasn't that way at all. To my great regret, I do not have a copy of the manuscript I submitted to the magazine. For many years, I never kept a copy of anything I wrote. I cannot believe now that I took my work so lightly that I made no copies, but that is a fact. (A few years after I began writing regularly for the *New Yorker*, one of the editors gave me a stern lecture on the irresponsibility of this practice, and I began making copies.) But what I *do* have, is the original of a remarkable four-page typewritten document, dated 8 January 1962, from Mr. Shawn. The yellow pages are now a bit shopworn and coffee-stained; but each time I look at them, I am still awed. It was Mr. Shawn's practice to edit himself some of the new writers, and he had decided to edit my profile. The four pages consisted of *forty-seven* questions and comments. I recall vividly the occasion on which I was given them. He had asked me to come to his office to work on my profile. When I walked in, I found my profile on the floor of his office chopped up into paragraphs and sections. Mr. Shawn appeared to be moving them around physically—rearranging them like pieces in a puzzle. He asked me a certain number of questions and then gave me the four sheets to take home and think about.

The first thing I read on top of page 1 was: "Your piece on Yang and Lee is beautifully done, and stirring. Below are some questions and suggestions that I hope may be helpful."

That out of the way, Mr. Shawn then got down to business. Query 7, for example, reads: "Indirection. *What* annual visit? Has not been established that he made annual visits. How long had he been making them? And for what purpose? And for what length of time. Mean he just paid a brief call once a year, or he put in a period of some length doing research there? Or what?"

By the ninth query, Mr. Shawn had apparently decided that a few general principles were in order. He wrote:

Ah! They *had* been collaborating. But, again, comes in here by indirection . . . the word "their," we'd feel, is over-burdened. Just as "his" is, above, in phrase "his teaching duties." Our feeling is that, in factual writing (though often not in fiction), indirection should be avoided, for the sake of clarity, grace, structural strength, and so on. We believe in not backing into things. Also, a few more concrete details would help, wherever can be supplied without vulgarity. Piece now tends here and there to be too abstract and skeletonized.

Finally, in the forty-seventh, query he summarized: "Well, piece could certainly stand a little more on the personal lives of the two men, and what they are like personally, but perhaps there's good reason to keep the piece as impersonal and rarefied as it is. At any rate, we can discuss."

I would say that this four-page document was the first, and only, writing lesson of any value I have ever received. In any event, I went back to Brookhaven and attempted to answer Mr. Shawn's questions as best I could. During the next several months, we had many discussions about the piece—some in his office and some over the telephone. Two occasions in his office stand out. On one of them, he questioned my use of the word *dialogue,* as in the "dialogue between theory and experiment." He said that the use of the word *dialogue* in that way had become sort of chic. "Even the Kennedys," he added, "are using 'dialogue.' " I was somewhat mystified by this reference, but the sentence in the published profile reads, "In all the good work in physics, a perpetual colloquy goes on between experiment and theory." The other occasion in Mr. Shawn's office was a matter of the artwork. *New Yorker* profiles are generally accompanied by a drawing of the subject, or subjects. However, part of my understanding with Lee and Yang was that neither I nor the magazine was going to bother them. They were wholly engrossed with their physics. This, incidentally, was one of the reasons the piece was as "rarefied" as it was. I didn't have much more to say about their personal lives than I had written. It also meant that the artist had to work from photographs. Since I was the only one of us who had actually *seen* Lee and Yang in the flesh, I was called in from time to time to comment on the drawings. I noted that while they were certainly, as far as I could tell, excellent drawings, they did not really resemble either Lee or Yang. After this process had gone on for a while, Mr. Shawn said, "Mr. Bernstein, do you draw or paint?" I was not sure where this question was leading, but I replied that I did not. "If you did," Mr. Shawn went on, "you would know that artists are not like writers; you can't *talk* to them." In the event, the artist must have gotten permission to sketch Lee and Yang, because the final drawing that appeared with the profile looks very much like them. I recently looked at it again, and noticed that in the background there is a representation of a blackboard covered with equations. Studying them, I remembered that the handwriting is mine. Somehow, it got incorporated into the drawing.

My profile of Lee and Yang appeared in the *New Yorker* of 12 May 1962. It was sixty pages long, or one third of that issue of the magazine. Its publication changed both my life and, I think it fair to say, that of the magazine. It was the most technically complex piece of science writing that had ever been done for the *New Yorker*, and probably the most technically complex piece of science writing that had ever been done for a general-circulation magazine. It could only have been written by a physicist; and, I may add, it benefited enormously from the help of many of my colleagues who were fantastically generous in reading drafts, making suggestions, and pointing out mistakes. Thanks to Mr. Shawn, it was also readable. I did manage to inject some personal details, especially those connected to Lee and Yang's affection for their Chinese cultural heritage. Both men had, by the time of my profile, become American citizens. In particular, I was able to describe their consultations with the *I Ching*. For example, they asked the oracle whether there was going to be an imminent breakthrough in elementary particle physics. The last four lines of the response read:

The wild goose gradually draws near the summit.
For three years the woman has no child.
In the end nothing can hinder her.
Good fortune.

As Lee commented to me, "The prophecies sometimes set your mind off into new directions."

But, in my profile, the personal lives of the two men were secondary to their science. There was, I felt, just enough of—in Einstein's haunting phrase—the "merely personal"—to give the reader some sense of personal identification with Lee and Yang, but not enough so that this became the central issue of the profile. To my taste, a good deal of contemporary science writing appears to have reversed these priorities. The trouble is that, viewed this way, scientists are not any more interesting than anyone else. Marital infidelity is marital infidelity whether it is practiced by Erwin Schrödinger or your neighborhood grocer. What makes Schrödinger special is that he invented wave mechanics and thus transformed twentieth-century science and technology. "Seek the source and not the shapes," as one of the Hindu masters wrote.

At some point during the editorial process, Mr. Shawn called me into his office and handed me a one-page typewritten document—single-spaced—over the signature of one R. Hawley Truax, then vice president of the *New Yorker*. Mr. Shawn explained that if I signed it, he would be able to pay me more money. It was the first of thirty annual contracts I have signed with the magazine. These contracts do not oblige the writer to write or the magazine to buy anything, but spell out what would take place in case such a transaction were to be completed. The one I signed on 25 January 1962 had an exceedingly arcane paragraph involving a cost-of-living index. Mr. Shawn, in attempting to explain it to me, got hopelessly lost. Finally he said, "Mr. Bernstein, you are a mathematician. You understand these things." Neither of these statements were true. The *New Yorker* is one of the few magazines to have a free-lance staff like this. We even got codified by law in the 1970s when the Internal Revenue Service attempted to disallow a pension program the magazine had set up for us. A special bill was passed, naming all ninety of us, artists and writers, individually. The *New Yorker* staff became an act of Congress.

It will not have escaped notice that what I have done in this essay is to present a profile of myself learning to write a profile of myself. I have become—as Yeats might have put it—both the dancer and the dance. Curiously, there was a serious possibility in the beginning that the two might be separated. Sometime before my "Letter from Corsica" was published, I had decided not to use my real name as its author. There was a certain vogue for this at the *New Yorker* then. What was rumored to be a conglomerate of priests and nuns was signing "Letters from the Vatican" as Xavier Rynne, and the magazine's racing correspondent signed *his* column Audax Minor. But my motivation was not fashion. Some intuition told me that having a dual career could be a problem. I might find myself caught in some no man's land between physics and writing and end up not being taken entirely seriously as either. In fact, I had already chosen a writing name, "Jay Amber"—*bernstein* (burning stone) being German for "amber." I had even spoken to Mr. Shawn about doing this. He was perfectly agreeable—and sympathized with my reasons—but said that I might eventually come to regret it. I am glad I followed his advice. While being a writer-physicist—or a physicist-writer—has had its share of problems, the rewards have far overshadowed the difficulties. It has been a fascinating life.

CHAPTER 1

How Can We Be Sure That Albert Einstein Was Not a Crank?

FROM TIME TO TIME I entertain myself with the following fantasy:

The year is 1905. I am a professor of physics at the University of Bern. For many years, I have been teaching, probably from the same set of notes, respectable courses based on what is for me the familiar and comfortable physics of the nineteenth century. I teach the mechanics of Newton, the relatively modern theories of electricity and magnetism of James Clerk Maxwell, along with good solid nineteenth-century thermodynamics. I believe that atoms exist although I am troubled occasionally by the question that, around the turn of the century, Ernst Mach asked Ludwig Boltzmann: "Have you seen one?" All in all, it is a good, comfortable life. Then, with no warning at all, a series of physics papers begins arriving in the mail. They carry the return address of the Swiss National Patent Office in Bern. The covering letter identifies their author as a patent examiner—a technical expert "third class"—of whom I have never heard. He does not even have a doctoral title. Upon browsing through the papers, I discover that this doctorless unknown is claiming—using totally unfamiliar kinds of reasoning—that essentially all of the physics I have been teaching is wrong. Not just wrong in a few minor details, but fundamentally wrong. What would my reaction be? What should it have been? In short, how could I then have known that the author of these papers—the twenty-six-year-old Albert Einstein— was not a crank?

Before responding to this question, let me note that, as a matter of historical fact, at least one contemporary individual did receive these papers in more or less the way I just described. He was a young man named Conrad Habicht. Einstein had met him in 1901 in Schaff-hausen, in a private school where Einstein had gone to teach since no proper university would hire him. Habicht was studying mathematics and later taught it in high school. But in 1903, he, Einstein, and a third young man named Maurice Solovine founded an entity in Bern they called the "Olympia Academy." Solovine had answered an ad in a Bern newspaper—placed there by Einstein—offering physics lessons for three Swiss francs an hour, and in this way became Einstein's lifelong friend. The so-called academy met every week to discuss intellectual matters—principally philosophy. In later life, Einstein recalled that, when he founded the theory of relativity, their readings of Hume had as much influence on him as anything else. On one of Einstein's birth-days, Habicht made an attempt to introduce him to caviar. The experi-ment came to naught since on that particular evening Einstein was lecturing to the "academy" on Galileo's principle of inertia and was so absorbed that he paid no attention to what he was eating. In 1905, the "academy" broke up. Its three members went their separate ways, but continued to communicate by letter. That year Einstein sent Habicht a letter that began, "I promised you four papers. . . ." It was these four papers that laid the foundations of twentieth-century physics. The only one of the four that Einstein considered, in his words, "very revolution-ary" led eventually to the discovery of the quantum theory. The last of the papers—"employing," as he said, "a modification of space and time"—created the theory of relativity. One can only wonder about Habicht's reaction to this letter.

Now back to my fantasy. It is the year 1905, and I, Jeremy Bern-stein, have just received a copy of this letter and the four papers contained therein. Not having any hint of who this Einstein might be—after all Habicht *knew* who he was—what will I do with them? Will I even bother to look at them at all? Most physicists, and espe-cially those of us who write about science for the general public, re-ceive crank papers all the time, which we routinely throw away with-out reading or, at least, without reading carefully. How can we be sure that we have not thrown away a paper written by another Ein-stein? How can we know? What criteria can we use? As I describe my answer to these questions, I think that you will see that they apply to science and not to art. They will not, I think, help you to decide what to make of Marcel Duchamp's *Nude Descending a Staircase,* James Joyce's *Finnegans Wake,* or John Cage's *Four Minutes and Thirty Three Seconds.* If you have been exposed to the last, you will know that during the specified time interval, a pianist sits at a piano in front of an audience and does nothing. I think, however, my criteria will help you to distinguish between a theory of relativity and an idea for making a perpetual-motion machine. I also think that exploring this matter will take us deep into the nature of science itself.

I would propose two criteria to help us distinguish between crank science and the real thing: "correspondence" and "predictiveness." The term *correspondence* I have stolen from Niels Bohr, who used what he came to call the "correspondence principle" to help him construct the first quantum theory of the atom (on Bohr, see also chapter 3). He began working on it in 1911 when he was a visitor at the University of Manchester. Bohr pictured the atom as consisting of a tiny, massive, positively charged nucleus (the atomic nucleus had been discovered by Bohr's mentor at Manchester, Ernest Rutherford, a year or two earlier) around which circulate the negatively charged electrons of much smaller mass. Bohr's novel suggestion was that these electrons are allowed to circulate only in selective orbits—"Bohr orbits," we call them. The picture of these circulating electrons has become one of the defining symbols—logos—of the atomic age. If one studies the Bohr orbits for, say, hydrogen, one discovers that the various ones closest to the nucleus have distinctive energies. The energy difference between the electrons in one orbit and those in another is substantial. According to Bohr, when this energy difference is given up as an electron transits from orbit to orbit, it reappears as the energy of the light quanta given off by the atom. These orbital transitions account for the beautiful spectra that are characteristic of these elements. For the orbits in which the electron is far removed from the nucleus, however, the energies merge into each other, creating a kind of continuum of energies. The quantum nature of the electron's motion becomes unimportant. We say that the motion has become "classical," in that, for all practical purposes, it obeys the laws of classical physics. That there is a well-defined classical limit to Bohr's theory is crucial. Otherwise, we could not understand why quantum effects are imperceptible to us. Nothing in our daily experience suggests that the orbits we move in are restricted in any way by the quantum theory. If we whirl a stone around our heads, the size of the circle is up to us. It is true that there are Bohr orbits for this situation as well, but they are so close together that we are never aware of them. The melding of quantum and classical concepts in a well-defined limit is Bohr's correspondence principle. I would like to use it in a more general sense. I would insist that any proposal for a radically new theory in physics, or in any other science, contain a clear explanation of why the precedent science worked. What new domain of experience is being explored by the new science, and how does it meld with the old?

To me, this is such an important benchmark for distinguishing real science from its imitations that I would like to illustrate it with another example. I would like to compare some of the proposals in Einstein's 1905 relativity paper with a hypothetical paper I might well also have received in that year in which the author claims to have discovered a perpetual-motion machine. This marvelous device, the author assures us, will, once started, continue to operate indefinitely without any additional infusion of energy. (A cynic might say that this is a fairly decent description of academic life.) Let me contrast this with one of the outré proposals in Einstein's paper: namely, that the mass of an object *increases* with its velocity. In fact, Einstein's claim goes even further: when an object approaches the speed of light—186,320 miles a second—its mass becomes *infinite!* When I first learned of this as a freshman at Harvard in 1948, I thought it the most astounding thing I had ever heard of—although, if pressed, I would have had a hard time explaining what was meant by the term *mass.* At first sight, this proposal of Einstein's seems to be entirely mad. We know that mass is a measure of the resistance of an object to an attempt to change its momentum. Nothing in our common experience gives us any hint that this resistance has anything to do with the speed at which the object is traveling. Why, then, am I not allowed to dismiss Einstein's paper out of hand as a violation of the generalized correspondence principle—as crank science? If we study it, we notice that all the novel relativistic effects—the ones that defy common sense—vanish in a world in which the velocity of light is infinite as opposed to simply being very large. The order of magnitude of these effects depends on the ratio of the velocity in question to that of light—squared in the case of the increasing inertial mass. The familiar pre-Einsteinian world is one in which light is transmitted instantaneously. The correspondence principle, applied here, means that we can make a smooth transition from the relativistic to the classical worlds by considering velocities that are very small compared with that of light.

One may well wonder how large these relativistic effects are in practice. It is amusing to contemplate what sort of speeds were available in 1905 for terrestrial vehicles. I believe that the fastest speed anyone had traveled around the time of the publication of Einstein's paper was about a hundred miles an hour. This is the speed an expert racer can get using one of the special sleds—luges—that run the Cresta ice chute in Saint-Moritz. On my first and only try, I, as an absolute novice, got going at fifty miles an hour. Experts were doing a hundred easily. The ratio of a hundred miles an hour to the speed of light is about 1 in 10,000,000. But the relativistic correction to the mass goes as the square of this: that is, in this case the correction is an effect of one part in ten raised to fourteen powers. It is little wonder that these effects play no role in our daily experience. It takes all the refinements of a physics laboratory working with high-speed particles to show them up. Einstein himself was fully aware of the importance of correspondence. Indeed, of the four papers he sent to Habicht, he begins the one that he described as "very revolutionary" with a discussion of how correspondence applies to his new and radical views on light. Traditional optical phenomena, Einstein notes, were wonderfully well described by a theory in which light is thought of as a smooth wave. But, he argues, these phenomena involve the average behavior of light over time. However, when light is emitted and absorbed, as in the Bohr atom, this is an instantaneous process, and the old ideas need not apply to it. This was the first hint of the duality between particles and waves that is the heart and soul of the modern quantum theory. Einstein's paper, as radical as it was, clearly spelled out why it was not in conflict with what one already knew.

Let me contrast this with the way a typical crank paper—say, on perpetual motion—presents itself. Cranks tend to use a lot of exclamation points and capital letters, but that is the least of it. To a professional physicist, it is immediately clear that any perpetual-motion machine violates what is known as the second law of thermodynamics. This law states that in any realistic process entropy—the measure of disorder—increases. Machines stop because the production of entropy by friction slows them down. Of course, like any law of physics, the second law of thermodynamics must, in the last analysis, be based on experience. But all our experience, academic life aside, is consistent with its validity. At the very least, the crank must explain why his device (all the crank papers I have so far seen have been written by men) alone of all the machines ever constructed violates this law. What has everyone overlooked? Where is the correspondence? Whoever actually takes the trouble to read these papers will find that this question never occurs to the crank. The crank is a scientific solipsist who lives in his own little world. He has no understanding nor appreciation of the scientific matrix in which his work is embedded. I would gladly read a paper on perpetual motion which began by explaining why we had all been overlooking something about entropy, something that makes a correspondence with the science we know. In my dealings with cranks, I have discovered that this kind of discussion is of no interest to them. If you find a specific flaw in their machine, they will come back the next day with a new design. The process never converges.

The second criterion that genuine science should satisfy is predictiveness. Real scientific ideas cry out to be tested in laboratories. Einstein's 1905 papers are, as I will discuss, full of predictions. This, too, is in complete contrast to the typical crank paper. Papers on perpetual-motion machines only predict that a given machine will run perpetually. One wonders how even *that* is supposed to be tested. (There are, of course, crank papers that predict the end of the world, which—considering the way things are going—may give one pause.) I would like to discuss two of the predictions in Einstein's 1905 relativity paper. They are fascinating to me because one of them was actually tested and found to be in *disagreement* with the theory; and the other, if it had been tested, would also have been in disagreement with the theory. The reasons are quite different and tell us a good deal about the scientific method.

I have already noted that one of Einstein's predictions was that mass will increase with velocity—an absurdly small effect, as I have said for terrestrial vehicles. But even in Einstein's day, there were objects that moved with speeds comparable to that of light. In 1896, the French physicist A. H. Becquerel discovered that uranium is radioactive. By the turn of the century, he had identified one component of this radioactivity as consisting of electrons. These had been identified a few years earlier by the British physicist J. J. Thomson. Becquerel's radioactively emitted electrons are rather energetic and move with speeds comparable to that of light. If Einstein was right, these electrons should show, by modifications in their trajectories, the dependence of their masses on their velocities.

Around the turn of the century, the German physicist Walter Kaufmann began a series of experiments designed to measure the mass of the electrons emitted—in this case, by the electron decay of radium. His idea was to force the electrons to follow curved paths in a magnetic field. By measuring the curvature, he could indirectly measure the mass. Measuring the mass of an electron by putting it on a scale is hopeless: it takes 10-raised-to-30 powers' worth of them to weigh 1 pound.

The idea that the mass of the electron might depend on its speed was actually in the air even prior to Einstein. A contemporary German theorist named Max Abraham had proposed a theory—now long forgotten—that predicted such a dependency but one different from Einstein's. As far as I know, the first reference to Einstein's 1905 relativity paper in a physics journal is to be found the following year in the same journal, *Annalen der Physik,* where Einstein had published. It is in Kaufmann's paper which states categorically that his experimental results disagree with Einstein's prediction but do agree with those of Abraham. Einstein's reaction to this paper was extremely interesting. He dismissed the experimental results. He was certain that they *had* to be wrong since he had more confidence in the overall coherence of his theory than he did in the experiments. A decade later, it turned out that he was right when the experiments were shown to be wrong. Einstein clung to this Platonic view of the relation between theory and experiment for the rest of his life. A remarkable instance occurred in 1919, a few years after he had produced his scientific masterpiece—the general theory of relativity and gravitation. One of the predictions of that theory is that light can be bent by gravity. An extreme example of this is where, in the interior of a black hole, the light is bent back on itself and never gets out. The idea of curved light rays was first carefully tested in 1919 during an eclipse of the sun. Astronomers were able to observe light from stars that passed close to the rim of the occulted sun. The small shift found agreed almost exactly with Einstein's prediction. When the news— which made Einstein an international celebrity—came to Berlin, he happened to be with a young student named Ilse Rosenthal-Schneider. She later reported what happened: "When I was giving expression to my joy that the results coincided with his calculations, he said quite unmoved, 'But I knew that the theory is correct'; and when I asked what if there had been no confirmation of his prediction he countered, *'Da könnt mir halt der liebe Gott leid tun—die Theorie stimmt doch'* 'Then I would have been sorry for the dear Lord—the theory is correct.' "

The second example of a prediction in Einstein's relativity paper is also remarkable because it is wrong. He states it in so many words: "Thence we conclude that a balance clock at the equator must go more slowly, by a very small amount, than a precisely similar clock situated at one of the poles under otherwise identical conditions." This is Einstein's colorful way of describing one of the most disturbing features of the theory of relativity: what is known as "time dilatation." The theory predicts that a clock in motion keeps time at a slower rate than an identical clock at rest. My teacher Philipp Frank used to say apropos of this, "Travel and live longer." Time dilatation effects depend on the ratio of the square of the velocity in question to that of light. We now have atomic clocks so accurate that this prediction can be tested directly. I suspect that when Einstein put the bit about clocks on the equator and clocks on the pole into his paper, he was making a bit of a joke. A clock on the pole does not rotate with the earth, while a clock on the equator is moving at about a thousand miles an hour. Using the 1905 version of relativity—we call it the "special" theory of relativity as opposed to the "general" theory—predicts that the equatorial clock lags its polar twin by about a hundred and two billionths of a second per day! Einstein was then living in the nation of watchmakers—but billionths of a second? It is probably just as well that this experiment was not carried out in 1905 because it would have given a null result in total disagreement with Einstein's prediction. What Einstein did not know in 1905 was that two effects act on the clock: the velocity effect which he discussed, and a gravitational effect which he did not fully understand until a decade later. The two effects conspire in the following way. The experiment takes place at sea level. Sea level is determined by balancing the force of gravitation which holds the sea down, with the centrifugal force that is trying to eject it from the spinning earth. The net force at sea level is zero. If one puts this into Einstein's formula for the time dilatation, one finds that there is a time dilatation but that it is independent of latitude. The clock at the pole runs at the same rate as the clock at the equator. This was actually tested in 1977 when the physicist Carroll Alley of the University of Maryland led a team that flew three cesium clocks from Washington, D.C., to the Thule Air Force Base in Greenland. The clocks are also affected by the motion of the flight itself. But when that is subtracted out, the resulting null result is in perfect harmony with Einstein's combined special- and general-relativity predictions.

What would Einstein have made of this disagreement with his 1905 paper had he been confronted with it then? Assuming that he did not simply dismiss it, as he had the Kaufmann mass experiments, he would have come to the conclusion that something was missing from his original theory. Perhaps he would have been driven by experiment instead of by purely aesthetic considerations to the discovery of the general theory of relativity. Einstein never believed that constructing fundamental theories in physics is a matter of simple extrapolation from experiment. It involves, he felt, a creative leap. He once wrote that "the creative principle resides in mathematics. In a certain sense, therefore, I hold it true that pure thought can grasp reality, as the ancients dreamed." He felt that if the equations are beautiful enough they *have* to be right. This is one of the reasons many of his contemporaries had such a hard time accepting his work. Not only were the results counterintuitive, but they had been arrived at by completely unfamiliar thought processes.

A case in point is the matter of the "luminiferous aether." This ghostly medium made its way back into the physics of the nineteenth century because experiments performed at the beginning of the century had persuaded physicists that light consisted of waves. The ether, or "aether," had first found its way into physics at the hands of Newton's contemporaries who could not accept the idea that gravitation propagated across empty space. Newton thought that light consisted of particles—an idea that went out of fashion after experiments performed in the nineteenth century seemed to show that it was a wave phenomenon. Beams of light could be made to interfere with each other, even pass through each other—something that, it was thought, only waves could do. But the only sorts of wave motion people were familiar with, were waves that oscillate in a medium such as water or air. The electromagnetic theory of light propagation invented by Maxwell in the middle of the century allowed, however, for the possibility of light waves propagating in a vacuum. This notion was too much for Maxwell and his contemporaries, so they invented a medium—the aforementioned aether—which, as someone later observed, became the subject of the verb "to oscillate." As Maxwell himself put it in 1865, "We have therefore some reason to believe, from the phenomena of light and heat, that there is an aethereal medium filling space and permeating bodies, capable of being set in motion, and of transmitting that motion from one part to another, and of communicating that motion to gross matter so as to heat it and affect it in various ways." Indeed, a cottage industry developed among theoretical physicists and applied mathematicians in the nineteenth century which produced more and more complex models of the aether. The models became so complicated and even self-contradictory that it is a wonder the enterprise lasted as long as it did. In its defense, I should point out that while it was going on, a number of the mathematical tools we still use in theoretical physics were created. No doubt, as a knowledgeable professor of theoretical physics in Bern in 1905, I would have been familiar with the latest aether literature; probably some of my work would have been devoted to aether-related problems. Imagine, then, how I would have reacted to the one and only reference to the aether found in Einstein's 1905 relativity paper. It is in a sentence that occurs in the third paragraph and reads in part, "The introduction of a 'luminiferous aether' will prove to be superfluous because the view here to be developed will [not] require an 'absolutely stationary space.' " There it is! My life's work dismissed as superfluous in a single sentence written by a twenty-six-year-old who did not even have an academic job. No wonder I would have been inclined to dismiss Einstein as a crank.

How, then, was Einstein's early work actually received—before he was famous—by his contemporaries? This is a fascinating subject in its own right, and much has been written about it—country by country. All things considered, I think the report card is surprisingly good. After being rejected in 1907 by the University of Bern where he had applied to be a *Privatdozent*—a kind of privately paid instructor—he was accepted a year later when he produced the thesis report he had failed to produce the previous year. This was fairly typical of the young Einstein. When it came to such formalities, he did pretty much what he felt like doing. A year later—1909—he was made an associate professor at the University of Zurich. What is more remarkable, that same year, he was given the first of his many honorary degrees—this one by the University of Geneva. I was so struck by this that I decided to investigate it further. I was fortunate to have the aid of Professor Pierre Speziali, a historian of science now retired from the University of Geneva. It was Professor Speziali who uncovered and put together the magnificent collection of letters exchanged for over fifty years between Einstein and his best friend Michele Besso. Professor Speziali informed me that the proposal to grant Einstein this honorary degree came from a professor of physics at the University of Geneva named Charles-Eugène Guye. In Zurich, he had taught a course in electricity and magnetism that Einstein had taken while an undergraduate prior to the turn of the century. In 1900, Guye received an appointment in Geneva. He read Einstein's relativity paper in 1905 and was immensely impressed by it. Indeed, in 1907 he began a series of experiments to confirm Einstein's relation between mass and velocity. It was these experiments—completed in 1915—that gave the most precise verification of this aspect of the theory. Professor Speziali informed me that the original documents concerning Einstein's honorary degree—including the citation—appear to have been destroyed.

As one might imagine, the comprehension and acceptance of Einstein's early work broke down along generational lines. Physicists—at least the good ones—of about Einstein's age understood almost immediately the importance of at least some of what he had done. Leopold Infeld, who came from Poland to work in the 1930s with Einstein at Princeton, wrote:

> My friend Professor Loria told me how his teacher Professor Witkowski in Cracow . . . read Einstein's paper [on relativity] and exclaimed to Loria, "A new Copernicus has been born! Read Einstein's paper." Later when Professor Loria met Professor Max Born at a physics meeting, he told him about Einstein and asked Born if he had read the paper. It turned out that neither Born nor anyone else there had heard about Einstein. They went to the library, took from the bookshelves the seventeenth volume of *Annalen der Physik* [now a collector's item worth many thousands of dollars!] and started to read Einstein's article. Immediately Max Born [who was a few years younger than Einstein] recognized its greatness.

It is ironic that twenty years later, when Born introduced the now generally accepted probability interpretation of the quantum theory, Einstein became its most powerful opponent. Indeed, many people have argued that Einstein's refusal to accept the quantum theory itself bordered on crankiness. Another young physicist who immediately understood the importance of Einstein's paper was Max von Laue. (He, like Born, was later, in 1914, to receive the Nobel Prize.) Von Laue was then in Berlin, but Einstein's paper made such an impression on him that he made a special trip to Bern just to meet him. He may well have been the first professional physicist Einstein actually met after his student days. In the 1930s, von Laue, who remained in Germany, showed extraordinary courage when he publicly opposed the Nazis' attempt to disassociate Einstein's name from his theory—to turn relativity in some sort of "Aryan physics." My teacher Philipp Frank began corresponding with Einstein in 1907 and, soon after, was publishing papers on relativity.

With the older generation the situation was more complex. At one end of the spectrum were physicists who understood absolutely nothing and were proud of it. A representative of this genre was one W. F. Magie who appears to have been a professor of physics at Princeton. In 1911, when delivering the presidential address to the American Association for the Advancement of Science, he chose to express his views on relativity. He remarked, "I do not believe that there is any man now living who can assert with truth that he can conceive of time which is a function of velocity [the time dilatation discussed earlier] or is willing to go to the stake for the conviction that his 'now' is another man's past." This, despite the fact that in 1911 the special theory of relativity had almost become a part of classical physics. Indeed, that very year, von Laue had published his great monograph, the first comprehensive text on the theory—*Das Relativitätsprinzip,* a book that can still be read with pleasure.

A much more complex case is that of Max Planck. Planck, who was born in 1858 and died in 1947, would certainly be on the list of the greatest physicists of the twentieth century. He was awarded the Nobel Prize in physics in 1918 for his work on what is known as "black body radiation." This is the radiation produced in the interior of a heated metal cavity. It is also the kind of radiation left over from the photons produced in the Big Bang. His work paved the way for Einstein's radical 1905 paper on the nature of light. In this paper, as I have mentioned, Einstein postulated that light has a particulate nature. He noted that this could be tested by shining light on metal surfaces and studying how the electrons were ejected—what is known as the photoelectric effect. It was for this work that Einstein received the Nobel Prize in 1922 and not for the relativity theory, which the Swedish Academy found too speculative.

Planck was an immediate convert to the theory of relativity. In fact, von Laue, who was his assistant, first learned the theory in a series of seminars Planck gave about it soon after Einstein published his first paper. It was Planck, it appears, who published the first theoretical paper on the new theory. But he simply could not deal with Einstein's paper on the quanta. He was sure it was wrong in the same instinctive way that Einstein later decided that the probabilistic quantum theory was wrong. Indeed, Planck spent a decade trying futilely to derive his radiation formula from classical physics. Einstein spent the last fifteen years of his life trying to derive the results of quantum mechanics from classical physics. Planck's feelings about the quantum were so strong that when in 1913 he proposed Einstein for the Royal Prussian Academy of Science, he felt obliged to write that Einstein "sometimes may have missed the target in his speculations, as for example, in his theory of light quanta, cannot really be held against him." It is unlikely that Einstein knew of this when, in 1928, he nominated for the Nobel Prize Erwin Schrödinger and Werner Heisenberg, the two original creators of the modern quantum theory. To qualify his recommendation, however, Einstein felt obliged to add that "it still seems problematic to me how much will ultimately survive of [their] grandiosely conceived theories."

Wolfgang Pauli occasionally used to say that there were physics papers so bad they were not *even* wrong. That is the trouble with most crank papers. Of course, there are some that are *simply* wrong. But to me these are more like bad science than vintage crank. The vintage crank paper has no correspondence and no predictiveness. That is why it, and its author, are, as a rule, so hard to deal with. It is as if the crank is speaking in tongues. Furthermore, the authors of these papers do not want to be instructed: they want to be *affirmed.* All of us who have tried to work in a deep science know just how hard it is to get to the frontier—just how much devoted training is involved. Even Einstein went through this apprenticeship. The notes he took in H. F. Weber's 1887–88 lectures at the Swiss Federal Polytechnic School in Zurich still exist. They are the notes of a conscientious student with a clear understanding of the physics that preceded his own. The typical crank appears to regard all this apprenticeship as beneath his intellectual dignity. He wants to go right to the head of the class. No apprenticeship for *him.* By now, having been at it for many years, I feel that I can spot a crank paper in physics after reading a few lines. Nonetheless, I am made cautious by my fantasy. Will I be able to spot the next Einstein if he or she sends me, out of the blue, the equivalent of Einstein's four papers in the mail—art unframed. I hope so. But sometimes I wonder.

CHAPTER 2

Ernst Mach and the Quarks

For over thirty years I have been an Ernst Mach buff. This is not because Mach was taught in the Rochester, New York, public school system where I received my primary education, and even in the New York City private school where I "prepared," as they say, for Harvard. It happened, rather, that the first real course I took in physics, in the spring of 1948, was taught by Philipp Frank, who had, as Einstein once remarked, "imbibed Mach with his mother's milk." Professor Frank had even talked with Mach personally on at least two occasions that I know of. One of them occurred sometime after Einstein had invented the special theory of relativity in 1905. I would guess that it must have taken place in 1910. As Professor Frank explained it to me, he was summoned to see Mach in Vienna, where they both lived and where Professor Frank was then a *Privatdozent* in physics at the university, to explain to Mach the mathematician Hermann Minkowski's then brand-new—and quite radical—four-dimensional formulation of the theory of relativity. I recall Professor Frank's telling me that Mach was not very enthusiastic about it. He also told me that Einstein, after studying Minkowski, remarked that now that the mathematicians had gotten hold of his theory he couldn't understand it himself any more. The second encounter with Mach took place a few years later and also involved Einstein, but this time in person. The subject of that meeting had more to do with the main subject at hand: why Mach, for most of his scientific working life, denied that atoms exist.

But before I get into all of that, I should say, for the benefit of the non-Mach buffs, just a little about who Ernst Mach was. I might say, parenthetically, that, as far as I know, there is only one full-scale Mach biography, *Ernst Mach: His Life Work and Influence* by John T. Blackmore. Mach, who died in 1916, did not want a biography written of him, and his son Ludwig, who had collected material for one, apparently destroyed it during the Second World War. Blackmore, however, was able to interview some of Mach's living relations as well as a few of the men of Professor Frank's generation who had had some direct contact with Mach. Mach is, at the present time, I think, not even one of those figures who is "oft quoted but rarely read." He is not much quoted and almost never read.

Mach is known to most of us, if at all, because of the so-called Mach number, which is the ratio of the speed of, say, an airplane to the speed of sound. It is so named because of Mach's work on supersonic projectiles. He managed to photograph the shock waves caused by such a projectile—a speeding bullet—in 1886. Physiologists have likely encountered Mach bands, which have to do with shaded bands that appear if one looks at, for example, white and black rotating discs and that represent neurological inhibitions, rather than objective optical phenomena. Cosmologists continue to discuss Mach's principle but rarely can agree as to exactly what it is, let alone whether Einstein's general theory of relativity and gravitation fulfills it. But it is unlikely in the extreme that many of them have read Mach's historical polemic, *The Science of Mechanics*, first published in 1883, in which Mach attacks the foundations of Newtonian mechanics. This book, Einstein wrote near the end of his life, "exerted a deep and persisting influence on me." It helped to liberate Einstein from the Newtonian idea that space and time are absolute; and Mach's ideas about the relativity of acceleration, which are connected to what has become known as Mach's principle, surely influenced Einstein when he began to think about acceleration and gravity.

Be that as it may, Mach was not really a great physicist—compared with such of his contemporaries as Einstein, Max Planck, and Ludwig Boltzmann. He was even less a mathematician. He once wrote, "Set theory [for example] has long been beyond me. The reason goes back to the weakness of my youthful training in mathematics which, unfortunately, I have never found the opportunity to correct." Nonetheless, Mach had a profound impact on the scientific and intellectual life of his day and on the people he met. For example, William James encountered Mach in Prague in 1882, where Mach was then teaching in the German University. After hearing Mach lecture, James wrote to his wife: "I don't think anyone ever gave me so strong an impression of pure intellectual genius. He apparently has read everything and thought about everything, and has an absolute simplicity of manner and winningness of smile when his face lights up that are charming." Professor Frank, who certainly regarded himself as a Machian, took great pleasure in pointing out that Lenin had written an entire book, *Materialism and Empirio-Criticism,* to refute Mach's brand of positivism. It appears that one of Lenin's objections to Mach was that in certain situations in physics he was prepared to eschew the notion of force.

Mach, who was born Ernst Waldfried Joseph Wenzel, on 18 February 1838, in the Austro-Hungarian town of Chirlitz near Brunn, the capital of Moravia, was not exactly a child prodigy. At the age of nine, he was enrolled in a Benedictine gymnasium near Vienna. His performance was sufficiently bad for him to be invited to leave a year later. Mach was, it appears, singularly mediocre in Latin and Greek grammar. He recalled having particular difficulty with the sentence *"Initium sapientae est timor domini"* (The beginning of all wisdom is the fear of God). The Benedictine fathers classified him as *"sehr talentlos"*—more or less hopeless. Fortunately, Mach's father, Johann, functioned professionally as a tutor, and proceeded to tutor young Mach at home, occasionally shouting at him such imprecations as "Norse brains" or "Head of a Greenlander."

About this time, Mach decided that he would like to become a cabinetmaker and move to America. For two years, he was apprenticed to a cabinetmaker in a nearby village and acquired a lifelong fondness for making things. His book *The Science of Mechanics* is full of drawings of odd machines, which, one imagines, were constructed by Mach or his assistants. At the age of fifteen, he returned to the gymnasium. Of that time he later wrote:

With respect to social relations and the like I must have seemed extremely immature and childish. Apart from my slight talent in this direction, this is to be explained to some extent by the fact that I was fifteen years old before I ever engaged in social intercourse, particularly with students of my own age. . . . At the beginning things did not go especially well, since I lacked all of the school cleverness and slyness which first have to be acquired in these matters.

Mach was able to enter the University of Vienna in 1855 and, in 1860, took a doctorate in physics there. Then in 1861 he became a *Privatdozent*—the same unpaid lecturing position Professor Frank held a half century later. It is interesting to note the level of physics practiced at the university by Mach and others. In 1842, the Austrian physicist Christian Doppler proposed on theoretical grounds what has become known as the Doppler effect: the now well known fact that as, for example, a source of light or sound waves is moving toward a person, the pitch or frequency of the wave increases. This is so obvious to us now—we test it routinely by listening to the sound of automobile horns—that it is hard to imagine that it was once a highly controversial bit of physics, even twenty years after its invention. (The Doppler shift, by the way, was tested in Holland a couple of years after its invention by the Dutch meteorologist Buijs Ballot, who had a railroad flatcar loaded with trumpet players towed at various speeds while musicians with absolute pitch were stationed on the ground to testify if they heard any alterations in frequency. This was done, it appears, for two days, and the Doppler shift was confirmed.)

One of Mach's own professors, Joseph Petzval, even claimed the Doppler shift was impossible since it violated what Petzval had called the "law of the conservation of the period of oscillation." In 1860, Mach built a simple device to demonstrate the Doppler shift in sound. In essence Mach's apparatus consisted of a long tube that was free to rotate around a central axis. A whistle, or reed, was made to sound in the tube by forcing wind through it. The Doppler shift became evident if one stationed oneself in the plane of rotation of the tube, and it would disappear if one stationed oneself on the axis of rotation. This became a standard bit of teaching apparatus in central Europe. Yet even in 1878, eleven years after Mach had moved to the German university in Prague, the Doppler shift was still the subject of controversy. That winter Mach persuaded a group of students and professors to sit on a hill overlooking the train tracks and to listen to the whistles of moving trains. Afterward, they signed a document testifying to what they heard.

None of this is great or, indeed, even very important physics. The true importance of Mach was in his skeptical attitude toward much of the received wisdom in the physics of his day, combined with his ability to write and lecture about such matters with extraordinary clarity. It is also true—and this I will try to make clear—that this skepticism when applied to the atomic theory, while certainly reasonable in its origins, eventually caused Mach to run somewhat amok. Before indicating how Mach got into the atomic question, it is worthwhile to recapitulate briefly the status of the atomic hypothesis as it stood in the middle of the nineteenth century. The first thing to be clear about is that the atomic hypothesis was just that—a hypothesis. No one had ever seen an atom; indeed, various arguments had convinced physicists and chemists that atoms, if they existed, would have to have the incredible size of about 10^{-8} centimeters—which we believe to be about the size of a typical atom. In fact, there were at the time really two kinds of atom, the physicists' atom and the chemists' atom; and most of the mid-nineteenth century physicists and chemists believed that these were distinct. In his *Principia*, Newton had declared himself an atomist when he wrote: "The extension, hardness, impenetrability, mobility and iner-tia of the whole, results from the extension, hardness, impenetrability, mobility and inertia of the parts." By "parts" he meant the indivisible atoms. This concept of matter, and in particular of gases, was used by Newton's younger contemporary Daniel Bernoulli to explain how gases exert pressure—namely, by the random collisions of the invisible gas particles with the sides of a gas container. The chemists, especially beginning in the nineteenth century with the work of John Dalton, were interested in using the atomic hypothesis to explain certain regularities observed in chemical reactions: the fact, for example, that when carbon and oxygen combine, they do so in definite proportions by weight that can be explained if we think of individual carbon and oxygen atoms, or molecules, hooked up to one another. In this picture, the actual sizes and masses of the atoms are irrelevant; Einstein commented on this in his *Autobiographical Notes* when discussing Mach's views: "In chemistry only the ratios of the atomic masses played any rôle, not their absolute magnitudes, so that [for the chemists] atomic theory could be viewed more as a visualizing symbol than as knowledge concerning the factual construction of matter."

To earn his living at the University of Vienna, Mach gave lectures on physics to medical students. These were published in 1863 under the title *Compendium of Physics for Medical Students*. Some years later, he de-scribed what happened. "In the year 1862, I drew up a compendium of physics for medical men, in which, because I strove after a certain philosophical satisfaction, I carried out rigorously the mechanical atomic theory. This work first made me conscious of the insufficiency of this theory, and was clearly expressed in the preface and at the end of this book, where I spoke of a total reformation of our views on the foundations of physics."

In his *Compendium*, Mach had taken the atomic hypothesis as a given and, in terms of it, had attempted to give a unified explanation of the several branches of physics. He had run into trouble—trouble that he kept more or less to himself—especially when he tried to use the classical atomic theory to explain the spectral lines, the discrete colors of light, given off by heated gases. Of this work he later wrote: "My attempts to explain mechanically the spectra of the chemical elements and the divergence of the theory with experience strengthened my view that we must not represent to ourselves the chemical elements in a space of three dimensions. I did not venture, however, to speak of this candidly before orthodox physicists." In actual fact, Mach did not have a prayer of explaining the line spectra before the invention of the quantum theory. Niels Bohr's work, which did provide an explanation of many of the features of the spectra of at least the simple elements, was done fifty years later in 1913. Exactly what Mach meant by giving up the three-dimensionality of atoms I am not sure, but I am sure that it had nothing to do with the modern quantum theory in which atomic sizes and shapes are discussed in terms of wave functions that are not, in general, functions in three dimensions.

After 1863, Mach more or less abandoned original research in physics for his work in physiology and psychology, although he continued to think and write about the philosophical and historical foundations of physics, and he produced the books that caught the attention of Einstein and his generation. As if often the case in these matters, there was an almost inevitable intellectual collision between Mach and this new generation of physicists—Einstein, Boltzmann, and Max Planck among them. These people began to take the atomic hypothesis extremely seriously as an essential foundation for their work in statistical mechanics. In 1895, Mach returned to the University of Vienna, but in a chair of philosophy. The year before, Boltzmann had been given a chair of physics there, so the stage was set for an intellectual confrontation. Boltzmann's general temper and wit can be gauged by the title of a lecture he proposed to give to some philosophers—namely, "Proof that Schopenhauer Was a Degenerate, Unthinking, Unknowing, Nonsense Scribbling Philosopher, Whose Understanding Consisted Solely of Empty Verbal Trash." (I am indebted to my colleague the late John Bell for calling this splendid lecture to my attention.) Boltzmann wrote: "I once engaged in a lively debate on the value of atomic theories with a group of academicians, including Hofrat Professor Mach, right on the floor of the academy [of science] itself. . . . Suddenly Mach spoke out from the group and laconically said: 'I don't believe that atoms exist.' This sentence went round and round in my head."

In debates like this, Mach was fond of asking, "Have you seen one? [Haben Sie einen gesehen?]"—an interesting and not entirely trivial question. It is sometimes said that Boltzmann's suicide at the age of sixty-two in 1906 was caused by Mach's criticisms of his work on statistical mechanics and of his use of the atomic hypothesis. Professor Frank, who knew Boltzmann—and often told me that he thought that Boltzmann was the most mathematically brilliant theoretical physicist he had ever known—thought that this was complete nonsense. "It is said that Boltzmann was so desperate about the rejection of atomic theory by physicists, resulting from Mach's attacks on it, that he took his life," Frank wrote.

> As a matter of fact this could hardly be true, since Boltzmann was himself, philosophically speaking, rather a follower of Mach. Boltzmann once said to me, "You see it doesn't make any difference to me if I say that the atomic model is only a picture. I don't mind this. I don't require that they have absolute real existence. . . . 'An economic description,' Mach said. Maybe the atoms are an economic description. This doesn't hurt me very much. From the viewpoint of the physicist this doesn't make a difference."

Toward the end of his life, Boltzmann, who had been afflicted by recurrent fits of depression, nearly lost his vision and was suffering from excruciating headaches; and when he became convinced that he could no longer work, he took his life.

Mach's relations with Einstein are rather more complex. From all accounts, Einstein began his career as a convinced Machian positivist. Einstein's analysis of space and time as being defined by operations with clocks and rulers—the analysis he presents in his 1905 paper on the special theory of relativity—seems, at first sight, to be a quintessential exercise in Machian positivism. But when one looks at things more closely, one begins to wonder. The clocks and rulers of the relativity paper are highly idealized. They are like clocks and rulers, but no actual clocks and rulers are exactly like them. In later years, Einstein said that the fact that these clocks and rulers were not, themselves, treated as moving atomic configurations rather than hypothetical fundamental entities was a "sin" that one had the obligation to "eliminate at a later stage of the theory." One wonders whether Mach soon understood just how un-Machian Einstein's analysis really was. In any case, he surely must have understood that one of Einstein's other papers in the "miracle year" of 1905 was credited with being an important proof of the "existence" of atoms. This was Einstein's paper on what is now known as Brownian motion—after the nineteenth century Scottish botanist Robert Brown. Brown had observed that microscopic pollen grains, when suspended in water, appear to dance around indefinitely in an agitated random way. Einstein interpreted this as the result of the constant bombardment of these objects by the invisible water molecules; and, what was more important, he was able to make quantitative predictions about the nature of the "random walk" of the suspended particles—predictions that were soon experimentally verified. This convinced many of the skeptics that atoms indeed existed, but it did not convince Mach. No one, as far as he was concerned, had seen one.

The first contact between Mach and Einstein appears to have been in 1909. Mach, in the second edition of his book on the conservation of energy, written in 1909, adds a note in which he says, "I subscribe then, to the principle of relativity." In fact, he sent Einstein a copy of the book; and in his reply, Einstein gratefully refers to himself as "your devoted student [*Ihr Sie verehrender Schüler*]." Sometime around 1912— Professor Frank remembered 1913, but the dates don't appear to be consistent—a meeting between Mach and Einstein was arranged in Vienna. It may well have been Professor Frank who arranged this meeting, since he knew both men. Mach had had a stroke in 1898 that had permanently paralyzed the right half of his body, but he continued to work, even doing laboratory science with the aid of his son Ludwig. "At the University of Vienna," Frank wrote:

Mach had lectured on the history and theory of the 'inductive' sciences. . . . For more than twelve years [before this meeting], however, Mach had suffered from a severe paralysis and had retired from his position. He lived in his apartment in a suburb of Vienna, and occupied himself only with his studies and receiving occasional visitors. On entering his room one saw a man with a grey unkempt beard and a partly good natured, partly cunning expression on his face, who looked like a Slavic peasant and said: "Please speak loudly to me. In addition to my other unpleasant characteristics I am also almost stone deaf."

At the time of this meeting, Mach was over seventy, while Einstein was just over thirty, and Professor Frank was in his late twenties.

The conversation concerned atoms. Einstein tried to persuade Mach to accept the atomic hypothesis on the ground that with it properties of gases could be predicted that could not be predicted without atomic theory. He argued that the fact that such predictions might require long calculations did not mean that this theory was not "economical." Mach's position had always been that theories are merely economical descriptions of observed facts. According to Professor Frank, Mach seemed willing to concede that such a theory could be economical in a logical sense, and it was Professor Frank's feeling that there had been a meeting of the minds. If there was, it didn't last long. After Mach's death on 19 February 1916, his son Ludwig found the following passage among his father's papers: "I do not consider the Newtonian principles as completed and perfect; yet in my old age, I can accept the theory of relativity just as little as I can accept the existence of atoms and other such dogma." Einstein wrote a eulogy to Mach in which he noted, "Even those who think of themselves as Mach's opponents hardly know how much of Mach's views they have, as it were, imbibed with their mother's milk." But in 1922 in a lecture in Paris, Einstein let his true feelings show when he said that Mach was *"un bon mécanicien"* but a *"déplorable philosophe."*

There are two footnotes to all of this. First, in 1903 an assistant of Boltzmann named Stefan Meyer invented an instrument called a "spinthariscope," a device that produced scintillations when struck by an alpha particle. An alpha particle is a nucleus of helium and is emitted when some of the heavy nuclei, such as uranium, spontaneously decay. An alpha particle is, then, a helium atom that has been stripped of its electrons, and so one could argue that this detector is responsive to individual helium atoms. According to several sources, Mach was shown this device; and, according to Meyer, who showed it to him, Mach then declared, "Now I believe in the existence of atoms." God knows what Mach actually said to Stefan Meyer, but for the next thirteen years he expressed his views on the reality—or nonreality—of atoms in an entirely unambiguous way. For example, in 1910, seven years after this alleged conversion, Mach wrote: "The results of the atomic theory can be just as manifold and useful if one is not in such a hurry to treat atoms as realities. Therefore all honor to the beliefs of physicists! But I myself cannot make this particular belief my own." What could be clearer?

The final footnote has to do with the title of this essay, "Ernst Mach and the Quarks." In some sense the quark is the modern physicists' atom. Quarks are the hypothetical constituents out of which are made the so-called elementary particles. A neutron, or a proton, for example, consists of three quarks of various kinds. One may ask what the word *consist* means here. In old-fashioned nuclear physics when one said that a nucleus consisted of neutrons and protons, one meant that, if one whacked the nucleus hard enough, out came neutrons and protons, like the beans out of a bean bag. This is not what is meant, if current ideas are correct, when one says that a proton consists of three quarks. If these ideas are right, then no amount of thumping of the proton will reveal three bare quarks. It will only reveal new particles that are themselves made of quarks. However, in many experiments, protons and the like behave just *as if* they were made up of three discrete quarks. Modern physicists are, by and large, not very philosophical, so I have not heard any Boltzmann–Mach-like debates on whether the quark exists. My guess is that it will continue to exist as long as the theory keeps working. We have, for better or worse, long stopped worrying about finding a positive answer to Mach's question, "Have you seen one?"

CHAPTER 3

Niels Bohr's Times

IN LATE JANUARY 1958, I witnessed one of the most remarkable scenes I have ever experienced as a physicist. A little background is in order. By 1958, new elementary particles were appearing, in both cosmic rays and accelerator experiments, in a bewildering profusion. These were the pre-quark days, so there was no theoretical model within which to fit this unexpected data. Things were so desperate that J. Robert Oppenheimer—I *think* he was kidding—suggested that a Nobel-like prize be given to an experimental physicist who did *not* discover a new particle. In the midst of this miasma, a rumor arrived at the Institute for Advanced Study in Princeton, where I was then located, that Werner Heisenberg and Wolfgang Pauli had discovered a Theory of Everything. Each generation of theoretical physicists thinks it has discovered a Theory of Everything. By this time, Heisenberg's physics were thought to be a bit over the hill, but there was the matter of Pauli. Pauli, who died in 1958, was one of the most brilliantly skeptical theoretical physicists who ever lived. When Pauli said, as he occasionally did, that a paper was so bad that it was not *even* wrong, it generally sank without a trace. That Pauli had taken part in this enterprise, gave one pause.

In any event, Pauli was invited to lecture on his and Heisenberg's work at Columbia University in late January. A group of us came to New York from Princeton to hear him. I recall coming in with Freeman Dyson and sitting next to him during the lecture. Not long after it began, Dyson said to me, "It is like watching the death of a noble animal." He had seen, at once, that the new theory was hopeless. What none of us knew was that Pauli was to die of cancer a few months later. Before his death, he, too, had turned against the theory and was circulating a cartoon, of his own devising, with a blank canvas and a caption in Heisenberg's voice which read, "I can paint like Titian— only a few details are missing."

Now to the scene. Niels Bohr was also at the lecture. I recall him as a large, almost Saint Bernard–like presence, dressed in an elegant dark suit with a vest. After Pauli had lectured, Bohr was called upon to comment. I believe it was Pauli who remarked, perhaps in jest, that the theory might, at first, look "somewhat crazy." Bohr then replied that the problem with it was that it was not crazy enough. Unlike quantum mechanics, say, it did not have the divine madness of great physics. At this point, Pauli and Bohr began stalking each other around the large demonstration table in front of the lecture hall. When Pauli appeared in front of the table, he would say to the audience that the theory *was* sufficiently crazy; and when it was Bohr's turn, he would say it *wasn't*. It was an uncanny spectacle involving two of the giants of modern physics. I have never forgotten it.

I was reminded of it once again when I read the first chapter of Abraham Pais's biography of Bohr, *Niels Bohr's Times*, in which Pais gives a somewhat different, and more personalized, version of this event. In the introductory overview, entitled oddly, "A Dane for All Seasons," Pais raises, again in the guise of an anecdote, one of the most fascinating questions a biographer of Bohr must confront: namely, what was the lasting significance of Bohr's actual work in physics? Pais recounts a conversation he had with someone he describes as "one of the best and best-known physicists of my own generation." This, otherwise unidentified individual, said to Pais, " 'You knew Bohr well,' " to which Pais replied, " 'I did.' " " 'Then tell me,' " Pais's interlocutor went on, " 'What did Bohr really do?' "

It is inconceivable that this same physicist would have asked the same question about Einstein, the subject of Pais's splendid biography, *Subtle Is the Lord*, or that an Einstein biographer would even raise such a question. The simple answer would be that Einstein created twentieth-century physics. But apart from that, one can read Einstein's original papers written at the beginning of this century and later, with enormous pleasure, awed at the sheer genius of the man, to say nothing of learning physics that is *still* relevant and valid. Einstein's 1905 relativity paper, for example, written when he was twenty-six, seems as fresh and clear and correct as when it was first written. Only last spring, I read for the first time the three papers Einstein wrote in the mid-1920s on certain kinds of quantum-mechanical gases. As I read them, I kept marveling that anyone could see that far—and thinking that if Einstein had written *only* these three papers, he would have still been one of the greatest physicists of this century. On the other hand, I cannot imagine anyone but a historian of science reading Bohr's original papers. Not only are they stylistically dense—as Pais, and others, have pointed out, writing for Bohr was a terrible anguish; but they also seem dated, antique. The philosophical papers, of which Bohr was, it seems, especially proud, are almost unreadable. When I once asked the late I. I. Rabi what he thought of Bohr's philosophical contributions to quantum mechanics, he replied, "This work was his life. There was no point in trying to tell him that I thought it was irrelevant to the sort of things that an experimenter actually does in the laboratory. I felt that in this he was very profound about things that don't really matter. But one was not going to tell him that."

There is something very ironic and peculiar about all of this. Einstein was, in the deepest sense, a "classical" physicist, his sensibilities formed in the nineteenth century, and he never was able to accept the quantum-mechanical view of reality. Bohr, on the other hand, was the guiding hand in creating this reality—the sounding board and mentor for Heisenberg, Pauli, Dirac, Schrödinger, and the rest of the inventors of quantum mechanics. Yet, when one reads Bohr on quantum mechanics, he seems, with rare exceptions, almost totally obscure, as compared with Einstein. No one put this more clearly than my friend John Bell, who, of all the present generation of physicists, had thought most deeply about quantum theory. Bell once said to me, "I feel that Einstein's intellectual superiority over Bohr in this instance [the quantum theory of measurement], was enormous; a vast gulf between the man who saw clearly what was needed, and the obscurantist. So for me, it is a pity that Einstein's idea [of classical, causal reality] doesn't work. The reasonable thing just doesn't work."

This having been said, what did Bohr really do? What makes him, in many people's reckoning, after Einstein, the most important physicist of this century? On this, Pais is especially good. As he showed in his Einstein book, he is skilled at describing both the physics and the

surrounding historical context. This should not be confused with popular science writing. I do not believe that Pais's historical vignettes can
be read with much understanding by the nonphysicist. The problem
here is more acute than the one that confronts the Einstein biographer.
Einstein was dealing with fundamental issues of space and time, while
much of Bohr's work was highly technical, and the quantum mechanical aspects of it immensely subtle. Not only that, but some of what Bohr
published turned out to be totally wrong. While one may argue that
some of Einstein's very last work came close to the "not even wrong"
category, for close to thirty years everything the man published was
pure gold. This means that Pais is forced, in Bohr's case, to explain not
only Bohr's right physics but also his wrong physics. I cannot imagine
the lay reader getting much out of this exercise.

Bohr's great work was done in 1913, when he was twenty-eight. He
had just returned to Denmark from England after a postdoctoral appointment in Manchester. His mentor there was the great New Zea-
land–born experimental physicist Ernest Rutherford. Rutherford and
his young collaborators had, a few years earlier, discovered the atomic
nucleus. Two of them, Hans Geiger—he of the counter—and Ernest
Marsden, had been set the task of scattering so-called alpha particles—
actually helium nuclei—produced in radioactive decays, from thin foils
of gold. Much to their astonishment, some of the alpha particles were
scattered backward, as if they had struck something hard within the
gold atom. They had—the gold's atomic nucleus. Prior to this, the most
common view of the atom was that it was a fuzzy ball of electric charges.
The alpha particles were predicted to pass straight through it, like
bullets through fog. Instead, some of them bounced backward. It took
some twenty-five years before it was established that the nucleus consists
of relatively massive neutrons and protons with the lighter electrons
circulating outside it. But, almost from the beginning, it was realized
that the nuclear model was in serious trouble with classical physics. An
accelerated electron radiates, and hence loses energy. How then could
matter be stable? Why didn't the atoms simply collapse? Moreover, on
the classical picture, the electron radiation would be entirely chaotic.
But, in fact, it was emitted in beautiful spectral lines which were, in the
simplest cases, interrelated by elegant mathematical formulae, which
had been discovered empirically.

Bohr resolved these two problems with the same master stroke. In
our present language, he quantized the electron orbits: that is, he

hypothesized that the electron, as it moves around the nucleus, can move only in special orbits. The orbit with the least energy, the so-called ground state, was assumed to be absolutely stable. The notion of such a stable orbit was itself radical. When an electron transits from one orbit to another—makes a quantum jump—quanta of radiation are given off, with an energy determined by the energy difference between the orbits. Since the allowed orbits follow discrete patterns, so does the radiation. All of this might have been dismissed as so much speculation, if Bohr had not been able to make it quantitative. (In this I am reminded of Kepler, who was saved from the worst sort of Pythagorean mysticism by his determination to produce a quantitatively accurate description of the orbit of Mars.) Using his quantization, Bohr was able to compute the magnitude of the frequencies emitted, as well as their interrelations. When a tiny discrepency between Bohr's predicted values and the measured values showed up, he was also able to account for this, as an effect of the relatively slow motion of the ponderous nucleus. Upon hearing of these results, Einstein remarked, "This is an enormous achievement. The theory of Bohr must be right."

Bohr's atom, with its classical orbits, quantized in space, has become one of the metaphors of the atomic age. Yet it does not correspond at all to the modern quantum-mechanical understanding of the atom. It is part of what is now known as the "old" quantum theory—an uneasy marriage between classical pictures and quantum conditions. From the time Bohr published his papers until the mid-1920s, when the "new" quantum theory was invented, this ungainly structure was elaborated ad infinitum. One is reminded of Ptolemy's attempt in the second century A.D. to save the geocentric cosmology by adding more and more epicycular planetary orbits, all of which were replaced nearly fifteen hundred years later, when Kepler introduced a single elliptical plane-tary orbit around the sun.

Volumes have been written about the invention of the new quantum theory. Pais gives a useful summary, with many references. From every-thing I have read, I am persuaded that it was Heisenberg who had the first truly quantum-mechanical mind. He recognized that Bohr's orbits were, in a certain sense, irrelevant. One cannot observe an electron in its atomic orbit. The uncertainties in the act of observation destroy the notion of an orbit. This realization was later canonized by Heisenberg into his uncertainty principles. What one *can* observe are the spectral lines. Heisenberg focused on these, making a kind of calculus which became known as "matrix mechanics." It was a Faustian bargain, since to accept this calculus was to give up the visualization of the orbits. About the same time, Schrödinger invented what appeared to be a second quantum theory in which the electron is described as a packet of waves. At first, people like Einstein, who wanted to cling to classical realism, were very pleased with this version of the theory, since the waves appeared to be visualizable. This hope faded when the Heisenberg and Schrödinger theories were shown to be mathematically equivalent. Max Born then demonstrated that the Schrödinger wave packets had to be interpreted as packets of probability. The Bohr orbits become regions of space where the presence of the electrons is highly probable.

Bohr's role in all of this was, in a certain sense, Socratic. By this time, the mid-1920s, he had been given his own institute for theoretical physics in Copenhagen—it was officially opened in 1921. So he was in the position of inviting the new breed of quantum theorists to Copenhagen to work out their ideas. In these sessions, Bohr was relentless. On one occasion, the exhausted Schrödinger was forced to take refuge in his bedroom, only to be followed there by Bohr, still arguing. Out of this came what is known as the "Copenhagen interpretation" of the quantum theory, which, curiously, does not seem to have been written down systematically anywhere. Two key elements were "correspondence" and "complementarity." Correspondence refers to the requirement that the quantum theory have a classical limit. Once again, Bell:

> I disagree with a lot of what Bohr said. But I think he said some very important things which are absolutely right and essential. One of the vital things that he always insisted on is that the apparatus [the measuring instrument] is classical. For him there was no way of changing that. There must be things we can speak of in a classical way. For him it was inconceivable that you could extend the quantum formalism to include the apparatus.

One can always attempt to describe an individual measuring instrument using the quantum mechanics of its atoms and molecules, but then this description must be referred to another classical apparatus on the next level in the hierarchy. At the end of the day, the language we use is classical, Bohr would argue. It is the only language we know.

Complementarity, which became for Bohr a general philosophical principle, arose because of the particle-wave duality of matter. An object like an electron can exhibit both particle and wave characteristics depending on the experimental arrangement used to measure its properties. On their face, these properties appear to exclude each other. Waves can pass through each other—modifying the patterns—while particles, as usually understood, cannot. Bohr noted that these properties are not really contradictory, but rather complementary, since they can never be realized conjointly in a single apparatus. Each experimental setup reveals a distinctive facet of the electron. The Heisenberg uncertainty principles, it turns out, prevent contradictory facets from being realized simultaneously. But Bohr was not satisfied to limit the idea of complementarity to physics. He saw it everywhere: instinct and reason, free will, love and justice, and on and on. Pais remarks that he finds this way of viewing things "liberating." I have always found it to be a dead end.

I have also found, no doubt because of John Bell's influence, the Copenhagen interpretation increasingly obscure. The question that is unanswered within quantum mechanics itself is, To what is it supposed to apply? It is all very well to talk about "classical" apparatuses—but what are they? How many atoms does it take before one has constructed one? As Bell put it:

> It is very strange in Bohr that, as far as I can see, you don't find any discussion of where the division between his classical apparatus and the quantum system occurs. Mostly you will find [in Bohr] that there are parables about things like a walking stick—if you hold it closely it is part of you, and if you hold it loosely it is part of the outside world. He seems to have been extraordinarily insensitive to the fact that we have this beautiful mathematics, and we don't know which part of the world it should be applied to.

Most physicists of Pais's generation, especially those who were exposed directly to Bohr—people like Victor Weisskopf, Robert Oppenheimer, Rudolf Peierls, John Wheeler, and Pais, himself—do not appear to have much sympathy for these issues. They tend to believe that, in so far as these questions are interesting, they were settled in the 1930s in Copenhagen. I once witnessed Oppenheimer reduce a young physicist nearly to tears by telling him that a talk he was in the process of delivering on the quantum theory of measurement at the Institute for Advanced Study was of no interest, since all the problems had been solved by Bohr and his associates two decades earlier. In his book, Pais writes, "By 1960 the non-relativistic quantum mechanics of a few particles in an external potential was a closed chapter to Bohr, as to most physicists." Given this attitude, clearly Pais's book is not the place to turn to learn about why more and more physicists are becoming dissatisfied with the conventional formulation of quantum mechanics. A reader who has the technical background to follow Pais's book, would do well to supplement it with, for example, John Bell's *Speakable and Unspeakable in Quantum Mechanics.*

This does not mean that there are ineluctable problems in applying the quantum theory to actual physical systems. Quantum theory has, so far, given us the answer to any question we have asked of it. I am constantly reminded of a story Dyson told me, many years ago, concerning his then young children. The older daughter was explaining to her younger brother that she could now row a boat because she understood how the "rowers" worked. To this, her sibling replied, that he did *not* understand how the "rowers" worked, but could row the boat anyway.

Bohr's early success in physics made him a celebrated figure in Denmark. He rapidly became, in Yeats's phrase, a "smiling public man." Unlike Einstein, he established a school, and was successful in raising the money to keep it running. One cannot imagine Einstein applying for grants or heading scientific associations. Nor can one imagine Einstein seeking out world leaders like Winston Churchill and George Marshall to discuss his ideas about an open world in which knowledge of nuclear weapons would be freely exchanged. At first, Bohr got a sympathetic hearing from Roosevelt, and a very unsympathetic one from Churchill, who decided that Bohr was a dangerous subversive. Oppenheimer once told me that he had thought of writing a play that he was going to call "The Day That Roosevelt Died." His point was that if Roosevelt had lived a little longer, some of Bohr's ideas about an open world might have gotten further. In particular, the nuclear arms race with the Soviet Union, from which we just emerged, might have been averted. I wonder. From what I have read, including Andrei Sakharov's memoirs, I have the feeling that no amount of good will on the part of Roosevelt would have persuaded Stalin not to try to build the bomb. Sakharov wrote, "the Soviet government (or, more properly, those in power: Stalin, Beria, and company) already understood the potential of the new weapon and nothing could have dissuaded them from going forward with its development. Any U.S.

move toward abandoning or suspending work on a thermonuclear weapon would have been perceived either as a cunning deceitful maneuver or as evidence of stupidity or weakness."

I think Pais's discussion of this and several other matters suffers, as I have tried to suggest, from the common pitfall of biographers. We fall in love with our subjects. Pais is more honest than most. In the beginning of his biography, he remarks that "it may be well to state that I loved Bohr. I have tried to exercise restraint in regard to these sentiments, which may or may not shine through in what follows." One of Bohr's complementary antinomies was love versus justice. In this book, love tilts the scales. Bohr was such a complex figure that, as good as this biography is, there is still room for a further evaluation, with a different tilting of the scales.

Feet of Clay

THEIR SCIENTIFIC GENIUS ASIDE, the creators of the quantum theory—Max Planck, Einstein, Niels Bohr, Louis de Broglie, Werner Heisenberg, Wolfgang Pauli, Max Born, P. A. M. Dirac, and Erwin Schrödinger—were all extraordinary and often eccentric human beings. When I began studying the theory, in the 1950s, almost all of them were still alive. (The exception was Planck, who introduced the notion of quantized emission and absorption of radiant energy in 1900, and *he* lived until 1947.) This was at a time when scientific biographies were rather decorous, and the little that had been written about the personal lives of these men left most of the details between the lines. By now, however, they have all died; and meanwhile a new genre of scientific biography, which leaves little or nothing between the lines, has emerged. A remarkable example of this is *Schrödinger: Life and Thought*, a detailed and controversial study of the Austrian polymath by the physical chemist Walter Moore.

Professor Moore traces Schrödinger's ancestry on the maternal side back to the end of the eighteenth century. His first recorded ancestor is one Franziska Zickler, a "love child" of unknown parentage, who was born in a convent around 1780. She is said to have been a temperamental beauty, and she married into the Austrian nobility. Her daughter, Josepha, although from a strict Catholic family, fell in love with a Protestant, whom she was not allowed to marry. She was instead forced to marry the Catholic family doctor, with whom she had three children.

When he died, she married her father's secretary; and their eldest son, Alexander Bauer, became Schrödinger's grandfather. I mention all this because when it comes to Schrödinger's own tangled matrimonial situation, one sees that there are familial tendencies. While genes may not strictly determine personality, they undoubtedly give it a nudge. Schrödinger's maternal grandmother was English. Her name was Emily Russell, and she was born in Leamington. Her brother was a chemist working in Paris, and he became a friend of Alexander Bauer, who was also working as a chemist in Paris. Emily, on a visit to her brother, met Bauer, and they fell in love. They were married and settled in Vienna, where they had three daughters. In 1874, shortly after the birth of the third, Emily died; and after a brief period of mourning, Alexander married a seventeen-year-old girl, Natalie Lechner—shades, again, of the future Schrödinger. The marriage came apart ten years later; and a few years after that, Natalie became, in Professor Moore's delicate phrase, the "constant companion" of Gustav Mahler—an attachment that lasted until 1902, when he married Alma Schindler.

Upon the departure of Natalie, Alexander undertook to raise his three daughters by himself, and the middle one, Georgine—known as Georgie—married one of his former students, Rudolf Schrödinger, who had abandoned research in chemistry to manage an oilcloth-and-linoleum factory he had inherited. Professor Moore writes, "About three months after their marriage, Rudolf and Georgine effected that fortuitous combination of genes that produces an individual of genius, and on August 12, 1887, the boy"—Erwin Rudolf Josef Alexander—"was born at home, Apostelgasse 15, in Erdberg, Vienna 3." The Schrödingers had no other children, and young Erwin grew up basking in the adoration of his aunts and a variety of housemaids. This may, as Professor Moore suggests, help to account for the nature of his relationships with women, of which more shortly. Even before he could read or write, he began keeping a kind of diary—he later called them *Ephemeridae*—by dictating his reflections to his Aunt Minnie. I was struck by one of the entries, which has the special flavor of cynicism I have always associated with fin-de-siècle Vienna. He dictated to his aunt, "This says Mama, and that says Aunt. They are both only people. They could just as well say the opposite."

Schrödinger was tutored at home until he was eleven, and then he was admitted to the Akademisches Gymnasium, the most secular *Gymnasium* in Vienna. The *Gymnasiums,* which were noted for their classical

education, gave European scientists of Schrödinger's generation a certain intellectual patina. (In this matter, as in most others, Einstein was
a conspicuous exception, since he dropped out of school at the age of
sixteen.) The Nobelist Max von Laue once wrote, "I doubt that I should
ever have devoted myself entirely to pure science if I had not at that
time come into that inner harmony with Greek language and culture,
which the humanistic Gymnasium and no other kind of school provided." Schrödinger, who was always first in his class, acquired a love
of ancient Greece which stayed with him all his life. Of his mathematical facility a fellow student later wrote, "Schrödinger had a gift for
understanding that allowed him, without any homework, immediately
and directly to comprehend all the material during the class hours and
to apply it." Apart from schoolwork, Schrödinger developed a fondness
for the theater, which was flourishing in Vienna at the time, and he kept
a notebook of plays he had seen.

In 1906, Schrödinger entered the University of Vienna. Professor
Moore writes:

> He brought with him his reputation from the Gymnasium as an outstanding
> student, in fact something of a genius, and his reputation was soon con-
> firmed by his brilliant performances in mathematics and physics. Hans
> Thirring, who entered in 1907, recalls his first encounter with Erwin in the
> library of the mathematics department. A student entered, steely gray-blue
> eyes and a shock of blonde hair. Another student nudged Hans and said
> *Das ist der Schrödinger*—the Schrödinger. All the students regarded him as
> something special, but he was not cold and aloof, he often helped them with
> difficulties in maths or physics.

As it happened, in 1906 the faculty of the university's Physics Institute
was fairly thin. Both Ludwig Boltzmann and the philosopher Ernst
Mach had taught at the university. Boltzmann, who was one of the
greatest physicists of the nineteenth century, committed suicide in the
summer of 1906; and Mach, who had had a stroke in 1897, had
formally retired in 1901. Schrödinger's most important professor was
Friedrich Hasenöhrl, who had been Boltzmann's best student and had
succeeded him as the professor of theoretical physics. The only research
for which Hasenöhrl is now known is some work on radiant energy in
a cavity which was a vague precursor of Einstein's formula $E = mc^2$.
Beginning in the 1920s, the Nazis used this as "proof" that the theory

of relativity—which was published in 1905, the year after Hasenöhrl published his work—had been invented by Aryans. Hasenöhrl was not available for comment, since he was killed early in the First World War. In any event, he appears to have been a marvelous teacher. His course in theoretical physics ran eight semesters, five hours a week, and he gave all the lectures without notes. They had a terrific impact on Schrödinger, who later said that "no other person has had a stronger influence on me than Fritz Hasenöhrl, except perhaps my father."

In the Austrian universities of that time, the first degree a student could take in physics was doctor of philosophy, which was roughly equivalent to a present-day master's degree. In 1910, Schrödinger took his degree, in a purely experimental and what seems (at least to me) an extremely dull subject. By then, Einstein's theory of relativity had revolutionized our ideas of space and time, and people were beginning to wrestle with the problems brought about by the introduction of the quantum. There is no evidence that any of this had penetrated Schrödinger's curriculum. His thesis could have been written in the nineteenth century, as far as I can tell.

After earning his degree, Schrödinger was appointed an assistant in experimental physics at the university; however, he first had to fulfill his military obligation. In Austria-Hungary, young men were required to do three years of military service; but if they had sufficient educational and social standing, they were allowed to volunteer for a year of officer's training instead. This is what Schrödinger did, serving in the fortress artillery. After that, he was free to return to the university, where he began teaching and doing research in theoretical physics, none of it of particular distinction. He was mobilized in July 1914, and sent to the South Tyrol. It was for the time being a peaceful frontier, and Schrödinger was able to continue his research for a while. It was at the front that he read Einstein's great paper on the general theory of relativity and gravitation, which was published in 1916. But by then Schrödinger was in the thick of the war. A photograph of him taken at the time shows him looking like a very tough young officer. He took part in the battles of Isonzo, and was cited for outstanding service. In the bloodiest of these battles, two hundred and eighty-six thousand Italian soldiers were lost, and about half that many Austrians. Fortunately for Schrödinger, and for us, he was transferred back to Vienna in 1917, to teach an introductory course in meteorology for anti-aircraft officers; he also resumed his teaching duties, in uniform, at the university, and he moved back in with his parents, who were living in a fifth-floor apartment rented from his grandfather. The economic situation in Austria was perilous. Schrödinger's father's business had failed; and after demobilization, Schrödinger himself was earning only two thousand crowns a year from the university, at a time when it cost three thousand crowns a month to feed an average family.

E VERYONE who has ever studied Schrödinger's life, including Professor Moore, has come to the same conclusion: namely, that if his scientific career had stopped before he reached the age of thirty-eight—and it might well have—Schrödinger would have been a minor footnote to twentieth-century physics. By contrast, nearly all the other founders of the quantum theory made their mark as young men. Einstein did his great work at the age of twenty-six. In the annus mirabilis of 1925–26, when the quantum theory was invented, Heisenberg and Dirac were twenty-four, and Pauli was twenty-six. At forty-one, Bohr was already (to use Pauli's terminology) a "quantum elder." Indeed, after the war Schrödinger was quite prepared to give up physics for philosophy. He later wrote:

> In 1918, when I was thirty-one, I had good reason to expect a chair of theoretical physics at Czernowitz. . . . I was prepared to do a good job lecturing on theoretical physics . . . but for the rest, to devote myself to philosophy, being deeply imbued at the time with the writings of Spinoza, Schopenhauer, Ernst Mach, Richard Semon, and Richard Avenarius. My guardian angel intervened: Czernowitz soon no longer belonged to Austria. So nothing came of it. I had to stick to theoretical physics, and, to my astonishment, something occasionally emerged from it.

In 1925, the year before he created wave mechanics, which was his version of the quantum theory, he wrote a long essay—published in 1961, just after his death, in a book entitled *Meine Weltansicht* ("My View of the World")—that reflected his deep interest in Eastern religion, particularly the Vedanta. Since it has become fashionable in some circles to find parallels between quantum theory and Eastern religious thought, it is worth pointing out that Schrödinger, who did as much as anyone to create the theory, and whose world view became more and more Vedantic, found none.

Before describing what Schrödinger did in 1926, I must make a divagation into his *vie sentimentale*. I use the French locution because I think it renders the flavor in Schrödinger's case better than "sex life" or "love life"—although, God knows, Schrödinger had a surfeit of both. From the time he discovered women, in his teens, until almost his last days, he was obsessed by them. We know more about this than is arguably necessary, because Schrödinger took little or no pains to hide anything, leaving a paper trail of love poems, letters, and journal entries. (Among other things, in his *Ephemeridae* he recorded the names of his loves with a code to indicate the various outcomes.) Since this is the first full-scale biography of Schrödinger, Professor Moore is obliged to tackle broadside the wash from Schrödinger's love boat. He bears up manfully, occasionally retreating to Freudian explanations involving the cosseting by aunts, and citing the amours of a number of writers and artists past and present by way of rationalization.

Schrödinger met his future wife of forty-one years, Annemarie Bertel, in the summer of 1913, in the mountain community of Seeham, near Salzburg. He was studying atmospheric electricity at a lakeside observation station, and "Anny" was there to look after the children of one of his colleagues. She was sixteen, dressed in a dirndl, and wore her hair in pigtails. Schrödinger was twenty-six and recovering from the breakup of a love affair. He was only mildly interested in Anny, but she fell in love with him. During the war, she was the only one of Schrödinger's female friends to visit him at the front. They were married in the spring of 1920. Moore has a curious description of the bride: "She was considerate and kind-hearted, with an outgoing personality . . . not extremely feminine, a bit of a tom-boy as a girl, and becoming distinctly mannish in appearance as she grew older." However, there is no reason to believe that the marriage was not a romantic one, at least for the first year. Thereafter, it is best described by a verse of Hilaire Belloc's:

> *The Husbands and the Wives*
> *Of this select society*
> *Lead independent lives*
> *Of infinite variety.*

In 1921, the Schrödingers moved to Zurich, where Schrödinger had taken a position as professor of theoretical physics at the university; and by that time, the conjugal side of their marriage had apparently ended. Schrödinger had various liaisons, and Anny began a long-standing affair with his distinguished mathematical colleague Hermann Weyl. Why this bizarre marriage, which became even more peculiar as it went on, endured for forty-one years is one of those mysteries of the human heart.

Of the genesis of wave mechanics Hermann Weyl later remarked that Schrödinger "did his great work during a late erotic outburst in his life." This much is known: During the Christmas holidays of 1925, Schrödinger retreated to the Alpine resort of Arosa with a woman. Arosa had been chosen because three years earlier Schrödinger, suffering from a severe bronchial infection, had gone there for a rest cure. His muse of the wave mechanics—if that is what she was—remains unidentified, since his daybook for that year is missing. By 27 December, Schrödinger had enough of the new theory in hand to write to a colleague, Wilhelm Wien, in Munich, "At the moment I am struggling with a new atomic theory. If only I knew more mathematics!" Some of the missing mathematics would be supplied to him by Weyl. "I am very optimistic about this thing and expect that if I can only . . . solve it, it will be *very* beautiful." He was right. One doubts Weyl's assessment of the proximate cause, however, for at no time in Schrödinger's adult life did he lack for "erotic outbursts." These continued for thirty years after what Weyl misidentified as "late" in Schrödinger's life. Of eroticism there was plenty, but wave mechanics was invented *once,* and that in 1926.

W HAT, then, did Schrödinger create? In 1905, Einstein had realized that some aspects of electromagnetic radiation can be described correctly only if light is assumed to have a particulate as well as a wave character. No explanation was offered for this; it was just the way things were. Then, in 1923, the French nobleman Louis de Broglie, for his doctoral thesis, proposed (essentially on the ground of symmetry) that particles—electrons, say—have wave properties as well. (He also proposed how this might be tested; and four years later, his idea was confirmed when a stream of electrons was made to produce wavelike interference effects.) Einstein went on to apply this idea to the statistical mechanics of molecules. De Broglie's work was published in 1923 and 1924, and Einstein's in 1924 and early 1925. By the fall of 1925, Schrödinger had mastered those papers and written one of his own on molecular statistical mechanics, using what he referred to as the "de Broglie-Einstein" wave theory of moving particles.

To understand what Schrödinger did next, a historical analogy may be useful. At the beginning of the seventeenth century, the German astronomer Johannes Kepler proposed that the planetary orbits are ellipses. Until then, it had been assumed that planetary motions had to be circular, but actual observations of the planets had raised all sorts of problems, which the geometry of ellipses solved. But there was no dynamic explanation—no explanation in terms of forces—of why such an orbit should be an ellipse until half a century later, when Newton proposed his laws of gravitation and motion. De Broglie's thesis was like Kepler's astronomy. It gave no equation for how forces influence the waves, what shape the waves have, and how they propagate in time. It was this equation that Schrödinger discovered. Using it, he was able to reproduce and generalize results that Niels Bohr had found more than a decade earlier by using "Keplerian" reasoning: Bohr had invented a model of the atom—an odd mixture of classical and quantum physics— in which electrons move around the atomic nucleus in prescribed, discrete Bohr orbits (see chapter 3); the virtue of the model was that it accounted for the observed features of the light spectrum of hydrogen. Schrödinger supplied the underlying theory of the Bohr orbits; he was to Bohr and de Broglie what Newton had been to Kepler. In rapid succession, he wrote six monumental papers in which the entire subject was laid bare. One could argue that the Schrödinger equation has had more to do with the evolution of twentieth-century science and technology than any other discovery in physics. It explains, among other things, chemical bonding, the structure of nuclei, the workings of the transistor, and the generation of stellar energy. Its importance was evident immediately. Einstein called it a discovery of "genius." Schrödinger's six papers were in such demand that before the year was out he was obliged to collect them in a small book. He supplied a foreword, which Moore quotes:

> With reference to the six papers, whose present republication was caused solely by the strong demand for reprints, a young friend of mine recently said to the author: "Hey, you never even thought when you began that so much sensible stuff would come out of it." This expression, with which I fully agree after suitable discounting of the complimentary adjective, may recall the fact that the works united here in one volume emerged one after the other. The knowledge of later sections was often still unknown to the writer of the earlier ones.

The young friend was a fourteen-year-old girl named Itha Junger, from Salzburg. Three years later, she became Schrödinger's mistress.

A certain number of second thoughts soon began emerging about the Schrödinger equation. For one thing, in 1925, Werner Heisenberg had discovered what appeared to be an entirely different quantum formulation, which became known as "matrix mechanics." This, too, reproduced the Bohr results; but from Einstein's and Schrödinger's point of view, it had the disadvantage of using a mathematics that described a state of affairs impossible to visualize. "Magic," Einstein called it. Heisenberg's attitude, however, was that visualization in physics is superfluous and misleading—a view Bohr agreed with and took up as a cause. There were some acrimonious exchanges among the various principals, until Schrödinger and, independently, Dirac showed that the two theories were in essence identical. Whether one uses the Schrödinger or the Heisenberg representation of quantum mechanics is purely a matter of convenience. Secondly, there was the issue of what the Schrödinger waves really *were*. Were they the particle itself, or were they somehow attached to the particle, or what? De Broglie, Einstein, and Schrödinger certainly had the idea, at least in the beginning, that these waves were real waves propagating in space. Einstein referred to them as "pilot waves." But it soon became evident that any such simple interpretation was impossible. To see the sort of thing that goes amiss, one can take as an example a free electron—an electron that is not confined to an atom. We know that we can determine its position as accurately as we like: in other words, the electron can be located, by our measurement, in as small a region of space as we want. In terms of the wave picture, this would mean squashing the wave down into this small region. Fine, but then we can ask what happens to the squashed wave after the measurement. This question is answered by means of the Schrödinger equation. The results are dramatic. Suppose, for the sake of argument, we confine the electron to a region the size of an average atom: the Schrödinger equation implies that, once the measurement is over, the electron wave will spread out again very rapidly—indeed, it will spread out over the entire solar system in about four days. If the electron were really a wave, this would mean that it had now become as big as the solar system. Clearly, something was wrong.

A way out was suggested in a brief paper, published in late 1926 by the German physicist Max Born. Born argued that the solutions to the Schrödinger equation, which are called "wave functions," should be thought of not as describing real waves but, rather, as mathematical artifacts, to be used—to take the example I have discussed—for computing the *probability* of finding the electron in a certain region of space. In his interpretation, the rapid expansion of the electron is taken to mean that if we measure the electron's position accurately by confining it to a minute region, then at any given later time there is a certain probability of finding that electron at a given distant place. According to Born, the wave function does not tell us where the electron is but only where it is likely to be. Born's paper was a watershed for the founders of the quantum theory. Bohr, Dirac, Heisenberg, and Pauli accepted the Born interpretation of the wave nature of particles as fundamental and definitive; while de Broglie, Einstein, and Schrödinger did not.

Schrödinger's six papers transformed him from a respectable working physicist into a scientific superstar. In the fall of 1927, he succeeded Max Planck as the professor of theoretical physics at the University of Berlin, where Einstein was also teaching. "Schrödinger lectured four times a week, two-hour sessions on two afternoons," Moore writes. "He was also responsible for a one-hour problem session (usually taken by an assistant), a proseminar for undergraduates, and a two-hour meeting each week on Recent Advances in Theoretical Physics." Today, this would be regarded as an extraordinarily heavy schedule for a research scientist of Schrödinger's stature. Still, none of it affected his *vie sentimentale;* that took a new turn in 1929, when, on a visit to Innsbruck to lecture, he met Hildegunde March, the recent bride of a junior colleague. Four years later, she became—with the apparent acquiescence of her husband, whom she never divorced—a kind of second wife to Schrödinger; and in 1934, they had a daughter, Ruth, who joined the Schrödinger household.

S CHRÖDINGER always maintained that he was above politics. Unfortunately, he lived at a time when and in a place where that was a luxury no one could afford. Largely because of an anecdote that my teacher Philipp Frank told me, and which is repeated with some skepticism in Moore's book, I had thought (until I read the book) that, despite his apolitical posture, Schrödinger's conduct vis-à-vis the Nazis bordered on the heroic—something like Max von Laue's, which *was* heroic. Laue simply refused to compromise with respect to what became known as "Aryan physics." The anecdote goes as follows: 31 March 1933, was declared in Germany a day of "national boycott" of the Jews.

Mobs of Germans descended on Jewish stores—or what they perceived to be Jewish stores—and prevented people from entering them, and beat up anyone they took to be Jewish. The police stood by and did nothing. Schrödinger, it is said, happened to be in downtown Berlin in front of a Jewish-owned department store named Wertheim's. He was outraged by what he saw, and began berating the storm troopers. As they were about to attack him, a young Nazi physicist recognized Schrödinger and saved him from what would surely have been a severe beating. I should like to believe this anecdote, but it is belied by the rest of Schrödinger's behavior during this period.

First, there was the matter of Einstein, with whom Schrödinger had become close friends. In 1933, Einstein went to the United States, where he remained for the rest of his life. One of the first things he did after leaving Germany was to resign from the Prussian Academy of Sciences. This did not satisfy Bernhard Rust, the minister of science, education, and popular culture, who was responsible for the academy. He pressured the members of the academy into issuing a statement to the effect that they were pleased to see Einstein gone. At this point, Laue called a special meeting of the academy to try to get the statement withdrawn. Only fourteen members out of a total of seventy attended; and of the fourteen, only two supported Laue. Schrödinger was among the absentees, and he never made any public protest about the treatment of Einstein, though he did make many private remarks about his disgust with the Nazis. One of the people he made such remarks to was an Oxford physics professor named Alexander Lindemann, later Lord Cherwell, who was to become Churchill's wartime scientific adviser. Lindemann was not Jewish—in fact, he shared the fashionable anti-Semitism of the British upper classes—but he set out on a one-man campaign to rescue all the Jewish scientists he could from Germany, and dragged along in that net was the non-Jewish Schrödinger. Lindemann was influential in getting Schrödinger elected to Magdalen College. In November 1933, the Schrödingers arrived in Oxford, along with Hilde March, then pregnant, whose husband had remained in Innsbruck. No sooner had they all settled in than Schrödinger received the news that he would be sharing the 1933 Nobel Prize in physics with Dirac. (Heisenberg was also awarded the Nobel Prize that year, but, technically, for the year 1932. This arcane arrangement was presumably related to a struggle that had been going on within the Nobel committee since 1927 over whether the quantum theory had conferred sufficient "benefit on mankind"—the term used in Nobel's will—to merit a prize. It took six years of campaigning—with Einstein, skeptical though he was of the theory, playing a leading role—before the committee found the resolve to recognize the achievement.)

Schrödinger was not happy at Oxford. He did not like its male-oriented society and, curiously, felt that he had been given too little teaching to do. His relations with Lindemann became strained when the latter discovered his unconventional marital arrangement. In 1936, Schrödinger was offered a professorship in Graz, conjoined with an honorary professorship in Vienna, and decided to return to Austria. One factor in his decision, apparently, was the academic pension he was promised at Graz. Considering what was about to happen to Austria, such a consideration seems absurd. (I. I. Rabi, who joined the Physics Department at Columbia in 1929, told me that he offered Werner Heisenberg a job there before the war, and that Heisenberg turned it down. By that time, it was clear to all that there would be a war, but Heisenberg was worried about losing his status in the German academic system. The still waters of university life run deep.) After the Anschluss, Nazis blossomed everywhere in Austria. There was a new Nazi rector in Graz, and he advised Schrödinger to write a letter to the academic senate of the university to show that he had been "cleansed" of any doubts about the new regime. Not only did Schrödinger do this, but the letter, which was published in all the German and Austrian papers under the heading "CONFESSION TO THE FÜHRER," makes one cringe with embarrassment. It reads:

In the midst of the exultant joy which is pervading our country, there also stand today those who indeed partake fully of this joy, but not without deep shame, because until the end they had not understood the right course. Thankfully we hear the true German word of peace: the hand to everyone willing, you wish to gladly clasp the generously outstretched hand while you pledge that you will be very happy, if in true coöperation and in accord with the will of the Führer you may be allowed to support the decision of his now united people with all your strength.

It really goes without saying, that for an old Austrian who loves his homeland, no other standpoint can come into question; that—to express it quite crudely—every "no" in the ballot box is equivalent to a national suicide.

There ought no longer—we ask all to agree—to be as before in this land victors and vanquished, but a united *Volk*, that puts forth its entire undivided strength for the common goal of all Germans.

Well-meaning friends, who overestimate the importance of my person, consider it right that the repentant confession I made to them should be made public: I also belong to those who grasp the outstretched hand of peace, because, at my writing-desk, I had misjudged up to the last the true will and the true destiny of my country. I make this confession willingly and joyfully. I believe it is spoken from the hearts of many, and I hope thereby to serve my homeland.

The only redeeming feature of this sad and craven document is that it did not conclude with *"Heil Hitler!"* Schrödinger offered an explanation of sorts in a letter he wrote to Einstein the following year, in which he said, "I hope you have not seriously taken amiss my certainly quite cowardly statement afterwards. I *wanted* to remain free—and could not do so without great duplicity." What Schrödinger meant by "free" in this context is not clear. When his friends in England heard of the statement, they assumed that he had written it with a gun at his head, and that his life was in danger. It therefore came as something of a surprise when one of them—W. J. M. Mackenzie, of Magdalen—encountered the Schrödingers a short time later enjoying a pleasant ski holiday in the Tyrol. One of Schrödinger's concerns, which he mentioned to Mackenzie, was whether he would get promoted to the post at the University of Vienna's Physics Institute from which his schoolboy friend Hans Thirring had just been dismissed. By late April, Schrödinger, too—despite the letter—had been summarily dismissed from his honorary professorship in Vienna, and his professorship in Graz was threatened.

Before turning to the steps that led Schrödinger from Graz to Dublin, and to his life there, I want to note one reaction to his letter which has arisen since the publication of Professor Moore's book. Schrödinger himself did not seem to think that the matter had much importance. When he returned to England, in the fall of 1938, he was asked about it by the physicist Franz Simon. According to Moore, Schrödinger replied, "What letter?" Then he became very agitated and said, "What I have written, I have written. Nobody forced me to do anything. This is supposed to be a land of freedom, and what I do is nobody's con-

cern." Recently, in a letter to the British journal *Nature*, Maurice Gold-
haber, the former director of the Brookhaven National Laboratory,
tried to put another spin on it:

> May I add some background information to P. W. Atkins' review of W.
> Moore's biography of Schrödinger. . . . In the spring of 1933, while I was
> a student at the University of Berlin taking the course in theoretical physics
> given by Schrödinger, I visited him to discuss a possible topic for a thesis.
> During that conversation, or soon thereafter, we both decided to leave
> Germany; he because he was disgusted with the political situation and I for
> even weightier reasons. [Goldhaber is Jewish, and he, like Schrödinger,
> escaped to England.] During our meeting, Schrödinger recounted an anec-
> dote that David Hilbert, the great Göttingen mathematician, had told him.
> During the First World War, in the winter of 1916, the rector of the
> university invited the professors to gather for an important announcement.
> Hilbert thought, aha, he will tell us that we will get a goose for Christmas;
> but no, the rector announced that unrestricted U-boat warfare had been
> declared. Hilbert concluded: "I realized then that they were quite mad,"
> adding, "One has to imitate them in every detail." *("Man muss sie nachahmen
> bis ins kleinste.")*
>
> After Austria was annexed by Germany in 1938 and Schrödinger felt
> trapped in Graz, he probably remembered Hilbert's advice when he wrote
> to the senate of the university. In this letter he appears to me to be clearly
> imitating the "joyous" Nazi style.

Maybe—but I do not find any evidence that this is what Schrödinger
thought he was doing. Moreover, this is not what Hilbert himself did
when he was confronted by the Nazis. In 1933, Jewish professors were
dismissed from the German universities; and shortly afterward, the
University of Göttingen was visited by the aforementioned Nazi science
minister, Bernhard Rust. At a banquet, he sat next to Hilbert and asked,
"And how is mathematics in Göttingen, now that it has been freed of
Jewish influence?"

"Mathematics in Göttingen?" Hilbert replied. "There is really none
anymore." What answer would Schrödinger have made?

That Schrödinger got to Dublin, where he remained for seventeen
years, was due to the efforts of Eamon De Valera, the prime minister
of Ireland. De Valera, if he had not gone into politics, might well have
become either a mathematician or a scholar of the Irish language; both
subjects fascinated him. As things were, he began, soon after the Insti-

tute for Advanced Study was founded in Princeton, in 1930, to think of founding a comparable institute in Ireland. In July 1939, he introduced a bill in the Irish parliament to establish his institute. It would consist of two branches—a school of Celtic studies and a school of mathematical physics. However, De Valera did not wait until the formal founding of the institute to begin his attempts to get Schrödinger to come to Ireland. The minute he heard that Schrödinger had been dismissed from his honorary position in Vienna, he made approaches. By the late summer of 1938, Schrödinger had also been dismissed from his post in Graz, and it was clear to him that remaining in Austria in any capacity had become exceedingly dangerous. On 14 September, he and Anny left Graz with a total of ten marks in their pockets. Their first stop was Rome. Schrödinger had been elected to the Pontifical Academy of Sciences, and he sought refuge there. Enrico Fermi, who was still in Rome, lent the Schrödingers enough money to get along. De Valera was then in Geneva, and the Irish consul in Rome gave the Schrödingers first-class rail tickets to Geneva, where they completed arrangements to go to Dublin. By the time they arrived, on 7 October 1939, Hilde March and Ruth had joined them, and the four again shared a household. The attitude that this curious ménage inspired in Schrödinger's Dublin colleagues was delicately expressed by one of them, Sir William McCrea, in an essay in a book entitled *Schrödinger: Centenary Celebration of a Polymath*, published in 1987:

> Outside the Institute and Trinity College, academic colleagues saw little of the Schrödingers in a social way. Most of these lived on the south side of the city, but the Schrödingers settled at Clontarf, to the north. There they enjoyed the society of artists, literary people, and people connected with the theatre. They were members of the Dublin Arts Club. Inevitably it was concluded that they had found something like the life they had known in Vienna; it was tolerant and easy-going. As seen from the other end of Dublin, Schrödinger's domestic establishment was somewhat irregular—although it was said to be entirely amicable. But he and his household were apparently made to feel accepted in Clontarf.

One wonders what the south-siders thought of the two "extra-marital" love affairs that Schrödinger carried on almost contiguously a few years after coming to Dublin, each of which produced a daughter.

SCHRÖDINGER continued to do research after the wonder year of 1926, but it was never of the same quality. It is curious to me how closely, in many ways, his post-1926 scientific career parallels Einstein's. Both men became disenchanted with the theory they had done so much to create. Both men invented what they took to be paradoxes intended to show that the theory was defective. These paradoxes generated a great deal of discussion—it still goes on—but little in the way of new physics; the quantum theory continues to pass every experimental test it is offered. Both men spent years in apparently fruitless attempts to find nonquantum unified-field theories. This work led to one of the oddest contretemps with Einstein that I have ever come across. By January 1947, both men had independently arrived at more or less the same version of yet another unified-field theory. For some reason, Schrödinger decided that his version was an epiphany, and he announced it to the press. After his initial lecture on the subject, an item appeared in the *Irish Press* beginning, "Twenty persons heard and saw history being made in the world of physics yesterday as they sat in the lecture hall of the Royal Irish Academy, Dublin, and heard Dr. Erwin Schrödinger . . ." This news story was picked up by William L. Laurence, of the *New York Times,* who confronted Einstein with it. Instead of laughing it off as a joke, which one can well imagine the young Einstein doing, the sixty-seven-year-old Einstein was furious. He prepared a statement for the *Times* in which he said:

> It seems undesirable to me to present such preliminary attempts to the public in any form. It is even worse when the impression is created that one is dealing with definite discoveries concerning physical reality. Such communiqués given in sensational terms give the lay public misleading ideas about the character of research. The reader gets the impression that every five minutes there is a revolution in science, somewhat like the *coup d'état* in some of the smaller unstable republics.

Schrödinger must have sensed, even before he saw Einstein's remarks, that he had gone too far, because soon after his lecture he sent Einstein a letter explaining that the reason he had done it was to improve his salary and his pension prospects. The effect of all this was that Einstein cut off communication with Schrödinger for the next three years.

What Schrödinger did do in his Dublin period was to produce magnificent sets of lectures, which later became books. Two of them—

Statistical Thermodynamics and *Space-Time Structure*—are technical gems, as fresh and elegant today as when they were written. Another, *Nature and the Greeks,* is a masterful distillation of everything that Schrödinger had learned about Greek philosophy and science, beginning in his days at the Akademisches Gymnasium. And yet another, *What Is Life?,* is—except for the six papers he wrote about wave mechanics—the most influential scientific work he ever published. In many ways, it is a very strange book. It is superbly written, fascinating to read, and largely wrong. Some of it was known to be wrong at the time Schrödinger wrote it, and some of it has been proved wrong since. Max Perutz, a Nobel Prize-winning biochemist, was inspired to write, in the centenary volume I quoted from earlier, "Sadly . . . a close study of his book and of the related literature has shown me that what was true in his book was not original, and most of what was original was known not to be true even when the book was written." Nevertheless, it was this book that inspired a whole generation of young physicists—for example, Francis Crick—to go into what became molecular biology. *What Is Life?* is proof that a brilliant but partly wrong idea in science can often have more of an impact than a dull but correct one.

In 1956, Schrödinger returned to Vienna to take up a professorship there. The ménage had by now been reduced to just Schrödinger and Anny, neither of them in very good health. In due course, they moved into a five-room third-floor apartment on the Pasteurgasse, about half a mile from the Physics Institute, where Schrödinger gave lectures. In 1959, its directorship passed to Hans Thirring's son, Walter. As it happened, I had come to know Walter Thirring well when he spent some time at the Massachusetts Institute of Technology while I was a graduate student at Harvard. I had helped him translate and revise a book he had written on quantum electrodynamics, and I spent part of the spring of 1960 in Vienna, at the Physics Institute. After I had been there a few days, Thirring told me that he had lunch once a week or so with the Schrödingers in their apartment, and that Mrs. Schrödinger had told him that her husband would enjoy meeting some of the young people at the institute. He asked me if I would like to go with him and another young colleague to the Schrödingers' for lunch.

I recall a number of things about that lunch. The apartment, which you reached by taking one of those ornate, rickety European apartment-house elevators, could have belonged only to a university professor. Books and manuscripts in various languages were piled everywhere. Mrs. Schrödinger—Anny—reminded me of my grandmothers; the Central European food we had was the food of grandmothers (or, anyway, of *my* grandmothers). Schrödinger seemed very frail to me, but he had extraordinary blue eyes, made more luminous by thick eyeglasses. After lunch, he showed us the 1925 manuscript that was to form the first part of *My View of the World*. I recall his putting the pages down and saying, in lightly accented English, "There is one thing the Greeks knew, and that we have forgotten." Then, pausing and looking at us with those remarkable eyes, he added, "Modesty!" I think what he meant by this sibylline remark—the theme is taken up in his preface to the book—is that science is necessary, but not sufficient, in establishing one's view of the world. On that note, the lunch ended.

Later that spring, Schrödinger's health deteriorated to the point where he was advised to go to the mountains for a complete rest. While he was there, he completed the second part of his book, a sixty-page essay, which he titled "What Is Real?" On 4 January 1961, after being taken back, at his request, from the hospital to his apartment, Schrödinger died. Anny was at his side. His last words to her were: "Anniken, stay by me—so that I don't fall down there [*Annichen, Du bleibst bei mir—auf das ich nicht hinunter stürze*]."

Three Degrees Above Zero

Darkness there was, and all at first was veiled
In gloom profound, an ocean without light;
The germ that still lay covered in the husk
burst forth, one nature, from the fervent heat.
—Vedic hymn to the creation of the universe

I N 1 9 6 5, Arno A. Penzias and Robert W. Wilson of the Bell Telephone Laboratories published their discovery of what has turned out to be the fossil radiation left over from the Big Bang explosion in which space and time were created. For many years I have been thinking about the history of this discovery. The more I think about it, the more bizarre it has become to me. It is so bizarre that if someone made it up as part of the plot of a novel, I doubt that anyone would find it believable. But there it is. Before I describe it, let me say a few words about the subject of cosmology itself.

One of the things that all the races of humankind have had in common, is an attempt to account for the universe at large—to make a cosmology. (The brewing of alcoholic beverages is another.) It is not surprising that these early "prescientific" cosmologies involved an intertwining of the supernatural and the familiar. Some examples: An early Chinese myth tells us, "First there was the great cosmic egg. Inside the egg was chaos, and floating in chaos was P'an Ku, the Undeveloped, the divine Embryo. And P'an Ku burst out of the egg, four times larger than any man today, with a hammer and chisel in his hand with which he fashioned the world." The homey vision of universe as egg persisted well into the Middle Ages. The remarkable visionary Hildegarde of Bingen—among other things, she wrote an opera—allowed, speaking of the universe, that she saw a "gigantic image round and shadowy; like an egg, it was less large at the top, wide in the middle and narrower again at the base." The illuminated manuscripts of the Middle Ages show an ovoid universe festooned like one of those Easter creations Fabergé made for the czar. The creation passages of the Birhand-aranyaka Upanishad begin: "In the beginning nothing at all existed here. This whole world was enveloped by Death—by hunger. For what is Death but hunger? And Death bethought himself, 'Would that I had a self!' He roamed around, offering praise: and from him, as he offered praise, water was born." What could be more revealing about a society than the question "For what is Death but hunger?" "In the beginning of creation," begins the Book of Genesis, "when God made heaven and earth, the earth was without form and void, with darkness over the face of the abyss, and a mighty wind that swept over the surface of the waters. God said, 'Let there be light' and there was light. . . . He called the light day and the darkness night." If the Big Bang cosmology is right, there would not have been much *visible* light around at the Creation. It would have been all gamma rays. It takes about a hundred thousand years for things to cool down to where the gamma rays become visible light.

A notable exception in the ancient world to the idea that the universe had to *have* a beginning, and hence a creator, was Aristotle. One might call Aristotle the Fred Hoyle of antiquity. He, like Hoyle, believed in something like the "perfect cosmological principle" according to which the universe has neither a beginning nor an end. It just *is* and always has been throughout eternity. Needless to say, Aristotle's cosmological ideas came into conflict with all the major non-Asiatic post-Aristotelian religions. A way out of this impasse was suggested by the twelfth-century Jewish philosopher Moses Maimonedes whose *Guide for the Perplexed* was read by Thomas Aquinas, among others. Maimonedes took the position that Aristotle had never really *proved* that the universe had no beginning. Indeed, in 1654, the Irish divine James Ussher, on the basis of a lifetime of study of biblical chronology, announced that the Creation had occurred on Tuesday, 26 October, 4004 B.C. at 9 A.M.—presumably Greenwich mean time. It is easy to make fun of this, but one wonders what our descendants will make of our claim that all the cosmological production of helium took place at three minutes after the Big Bang. Isaac Newton, whose long life overlapped that of Bishop Ussher, very likely spent at least as much time on biblical chronology—the sort of thing Bishop Ussher was doing—as had the good bishop. Newton certainly spent more time on biblical chronology and alchemy than he did on what we would call physics.

Be that as it may, Newton was responsible for the first cosmological statement in what we would think of as the modern vein. While Newton was perfectly willing to accept the idea that the universe had a finite origin in time, he realized that there was a potential paradox if it had a finite spatial extent as well. Since all matter, he noted, is gravitationally attractive to other matter, if any clumping of matter occurred in a finite universe—he must have had in mind a universe too cold for heat pressure to play a role—the effect would run away. In short order, all the matter in such a universe would collect itself in one place, a clear-cut disagreement with observation. He understood that a way out of this paradox was to make the universe spatially infinite so that there would be no "place" where matter could collect. Indeed, in 1692, in a letter written to Richard Bentley, Newton argued, "But if matter was evenly disposed throughout an infinite space it would never convene into one mass; but some of it would convene into one mass and some into another, so as to make an infinite number of great masses scattered at great distances from one another throughout all that infinite space."

By the nineteenth century, a substantial body of evidence had accumulated—the work of geologists like the Scot James Hutton—that Bishop Ussher's creation date had to be wrong. The evidence was summarized in the enormously influential *The Principles of Geology* which the Scottish geologist Charles Lyell published in three volumes in 1830. This book, the first volume of which Charles Darwin took with him on the *Beagle,* persuaded Darwin that geological processes were evolutionary. He became a member of a developing school of thought that held that the lifetime of the earth might be—if not infinite—at the very least, unimaginably long. I do not, by the way, know what date, if any, Newton fixed for the Creation, but toward the end of his life, when he was working on biblical prophesies, he concluded that the end of the world could not come before 2060. Let us hope that he was right.

During the nineteenth century, the science of thermodynamics was created, and one of its major architects, William Thompson—later Lord Kelvin—reasoning that all geological processes dissipate heat and beginning with the assumption that the earth began as a molten ball, argued that the age of the earth lay somewhere between twenty million and four hundred million years. He also concluded that the sun must have an age of a similar order of magnitude. This appeared to be in contradiction with Darwin's theory of evolution which seemed to require countless millennia for its unfolding. But by the end of the nineteenth century, radioactivity had been discovered. The energy generated by the decay of radioactive elements keeps the earth from cooling at anything like the rate Kelvin assumed. Indeed, the age of the earth was soon extended to upward of two billion years—it is now thought to be about four and a half billion years—giving plenty of time for both biological and geological evolution to take place.

Modern cosmological theory began in 1917 with the publication, in the proceedings of the Prussian Academy, of a paper by Einstein called "Cosmological Considerations on the General Theory of Relativity." (He had published his general theory of relativity and gravitation two years earlier.) In many ways, the 1917 paper is a strange one. Einstein himself did not seem entirely comfortable with it. At one point, he writes, "In the present paragraph I shall conduct the reader over the road that I have myself travelled, rather a rough and winding road, because otherwise I cannot hope that he will take much interest in the result at the end of the journey." This is a far cry from his statement to his student Ilse Rosenthal-Schneider that if the general theory had disagreed with experiment, he would have been sorry for the dear Lord. Cosmology is another matter: *only* the dear Lord may have the answers. In his 1917 paper, Einstein attempted to construct a cosmology based on a few general principles—gleaned from experience—which he took as axioms. The first of these we still believe to be correct; and, indeed, we have much more empirical evidence for it than Einstein did when he assumed it. This is the notion that the universe is homogeneous and isotropic—at least on the average. This means that wherever we stand in the universe, we will, on the average, see the same things in all directions as we would see from anywhere else. At first sight, this may seem wrong if we think in terms of such local phenomena as the planets and constellations. But there are, presumably, billions upon billions of planets, and there are surely billions upon billions of galaxies. If we average over all of these, the homogeneity and isotropy of the universe becomes plausible. Essentially all the modern cosmological theories employ this principle.

The next thing Einstein assumed reflected the limited knowledge then available to him. When he wrote his paper, it was not yet known whether any of the celestial objects we observe are actually outside our Milky Way galaxy. That fact only became certain a decade later with the work of the American astronomer Edwin Hubble, who also made the discovery that the galaxies recede from each other—the expanding universe! Not knowing any of this, Einstein made the reasonable, albeit incorrect assumption, that, apart from small proper motions of the stars, the universe as a whole is stationary. But having made these assumptions, Einstein realized that they were in conflict with his own theory of relativity. Indeed, the problem is just Newton's dilemma—the instability of a self-gravitating system—come back again in a new guise. Newton resolved the paradox by making space infinite. Einstein resolved it by changing his law of gravitation—something that, in later years, he referred to as his greatest scientific "blunder." To his original law of gravitation, he added a new term which has become known as the "cosmological constant." The presence of this term is consistent with the mathematical symmetry of the theory, but it has an ugly ad-hoc quality about it. Nothing appears to fix its magnitude. But it acts like a small repulsive force working to counterbalance the gravitational attraction. These mutilated equations have solutions in which matter is uniformly distributed and the universe stationary.

There was an additional feature Einstein liked. It appeared as if the theory satisfied at least one version of what cosmologists call "Mach's principle," although, as far as I can tell, Mach stated it only in rather qualitative terms. This was the idea that no solutions to the gravitational equations should exist in the absence of actual gravitating matter. Since matter is the source of gravitation, this seemed desirable. The trouble was that the same year—1917—the Dutch astronomer Wilhelm de Sitter produced a second solution to Einstein's equations, one that had no matter at all, which meant that Mach's principle was not an a-priori consequence of the theory. This was one of the reasons Einstein eventually abandoned it. The de Sitter model had the remarkable feature that if test particles were introduced into the empty space, they moved away from each other. Thus, the de Sitter universe appeared to expand. Indeed, when in 1929 Hubble published his data showing that the galaxies in the universe *do* expand, he called his discovery that the velocity of recession of the galaxies is proportional to their distance from us, the "de Sitter effect." Given the somewhat poor quality of Hubble's actual data, one wonders whether he found what he had decided in advance he was looking for.

Among the readers of Einstein's 1917 paper was a twenty-nine-year-old Russian mathematician and meteorologist named Aleksandr Alexandrovich Friedmann. Friedmann had been born into a musically talented St. Petersburg family in 1888. He became a brilliant mathematics student at the University of St. Petersburg from which he graduated in 1910. Soon after his graduation, he took up theoretical meteorology as a specialty. In 1914, he published a basic paper on the temperature inversion in the upper atmosphere. That year, the beginning of the First World War, he volunteered for service in an aviation detachment. By 1917, the year of Einstein's paper, Friedmann had become a section chief and later the director of the first Russian factory devoted to the manufacture of aviation instruments. But in 1920, he took up a post in St. Petersburg and taught physics and mathematics at the university. Among his students was the young George Gamow. Gamow describes his brief encounter with Friedmann in his delightful autobiography *My World Line*. The only trouble with the book is that Gamow is not much interested in precisely dating any of the events described in it. Since Gamow took his Ph.D. from the university in 1928, and since Friedmann published his great papers on relativity— the papers that excited Gamow—in 1922, one must assume that their encounter took place sometime in between.

Although not really a professional physicist, Friedmann had nonetheless gotten caught up in the wave of excitement that followed the 1919 confirmation of Einstein's prediction that the gravitation of the sun bends starlight, a phenomenon often characterized by the statement that space is "curved." Being a remarkably gifted man, Friedmann did not simply learn the theory: he improved on it. He found solutions to Einstein's *original* unmutilated equations which described an expanding space. Indeed, there are two classes of solutions depending on the matter density in space. There is one class in which the universe continues to expand indefinitely, and there is another in which the universe goes through repetitive cycles of expansion and contraction. One of the great outstanding questions of modern cosmology is in which of these universes do we actually live. Most cosmologists prefer a universe with a constantly decelerating expansion which reaches the end of time at rest. Once again, the dear Lord will decide. Einstein's reaction to Friedmann's discovery went through its own oscillations. At first blush, he decided that Friedmann was wrong, and published a brief note to this effect. He withdrew it shortly thereafter. Indeed, by 1945, when Einstein published the second edition of his classic *The Meaning of Relativity*, he devoted a whole appendix to Friedmann's work and remarked, in a footnote, that he never would have introduced what he called the "cosmological member" if Hubble's work had been available to him. In any event, sometime in 1924 or 1925—*pace* Gamow—Friedmann announced a course of lectures at the university entitled "Mathematical Foundations of the Theory of Relativity." Gamow writes, "Naturally, I landed on the bench of the classroom for the first of his lectures." It had been Gamow's intention to work with Friedmann on relativistic cosmology but, as he writes, "[d]uring one of his flights on a free meteorological balloon, Friedmann received a severe chill which resulted in pneumonia and death." The *Dictionary of Scientific Biography* states that Friedmann died of typhoid fever. In any case, at the age of thirty-seven, he was dead.

Whether Friedmann, Gamow, or the Belgian astronomer Abbé Georges LeMaître, should be called the "father" of the Big Bang theory, we can leave to the historians. In 1927, LeMaître came up independently with Friedmann's solutions. When Hubble discovered, two years later, that the galaxies were receding, LeMaître made the specific hypothesis that the whole thing had begun as a cosmic explosion. In the beginning, there was, according to LeMaître, a "cosmic egg"—again, an egg—which contained all the matter in the universe. It then exploded, and *voilà!* here we all are. I do not mean to make light of LeMaître, but as far as I am concerned, quantitative modern cosmology begins with Gamow.

For various reasons, I do not think Gamow's cosmology was taken seriously enough when he was active in it in the late 1940s. He died on 1968, so he did have the satisfaction of seeing the beginnings of the working out of the modern Big Bang cosmology which hc had done so much to anticipate. Part of the reason the early work was not taken more seriously was the state of the field. This was a time when two rival theories—the Steady State theory of Fred Hoyle and others, and the Big Bang theory—seemed as if they could account about equally well for such phenomena as there were to account for. The two theories were, nonetheless, diametrically opposed in their underlying assumptions. In the Steady State theory, the universe has no beginning and no end and remains essentially the same at all times, in all places. The Big Bang is what it says: the universe began in a completely singular state of possibly infinite temperature and density; it is a state that may never be reproduced. It is an evolutionary theory rather than a static one. When a field is in such ferment that two theories with opposite assumptions can account for the same data, it is very difficult for many people, myself included, to take it entirely seriously. Since the proponents of the two theories could not bring much convincing evidence to bear for either theory, they spent a good deal of time insulting each other—something at which both Hoyle and Gamow were expert. In his autobiography, Gamow reproduces his version of the Book of Genesis according to Hoyle. It ends, "It was so complicated that nowadays neither Hoyle, nor God, nor anybody else can figure out exactly how it was done." In his later years, Gamow was known for enjoying the odd drink. At a conference of astronomers, he was spotted in a bar, at his quaff, by a bunch of young Turks. They bribed a waitress to go up to him and say, "There is a telephone call for you, Professor Hoyle." Without missing a beat, Gamow replied, "Don't throw Hoyle on troubled waters."

Gamow was a larger-than-life genuine Russian eccentric, with an impish, irrepressible sense of humor. The fact that, on a cosmology paper, he inserted the name of Hans Bethe between his own and that of the first author, Ralph Alpher, and tried to get his other collaborator, Robert Herman, to change his name to Delter, so that he could add it after his own, was not likely to make people take the paper as seriously as they otherwise might have. (Herman, by the way, declined.) With this in mind, it comes as a pleasant surprise to reread the original papers and find out just how good they were. Not that they agree entirely with the present ideas of how the elements were formed. Gamow had a uniformitarian theory according to which *all* the elements—light and heavy—were formed by one basic series of early universe processes. The Big Bang produced, according to Gamow, something he took to calling the "Ylem"—derived, he said, from the Greek *hyle,* meaning either "wood" or "matter." The Ylem is the primordial ur-stuff out of which everything else is to be made. In Gamow's original version, the Ylem was taken to consist primarily of neutrons and very energetic electromagnetic quanta-gamma rays. In the later versions, massless, chargeless neutrinos were added and play a decisive role. After the explosion, the Ylem expands and cools in accordance with Friedmann's cosmological equations. The neutrons are unstable particles; and in a little over ten minutes, half of any sample decay into protons, electrons, and neutrinos. Gamow's idea was that all the elements were to be built up like Tinker Toys by adding neutrons one at a time. To begin with, a single neutron captures a proton, releasing energy in the form of a gamma ray. The result is to manufacture the nucleus of "heavy hydrogen"—the deuteron—which consists of a proton and a neutron. Then these deuterons can capture an additional neutron, forming a still heavier isotope of hydrogen—tritium—which decays into a light isotope of helium. By a succession of captures and decays, Gamow hoped to be able to construct the entire periodic table. It was a nice idea, but it doesn't work. It turns out that the process more or less stops at helium. The heavy elements are made, we believe, by supernova explosions, a process still going on. This star-cooking of elements was something Hoyle and his people worked on in the context of the Steady State theory. This part of their work is still valid and useful, even if one no longer takes the underlying cosmology seriously.

What concerns me here is the fate of the primordial radiation. I will begin by describing how Gamow and his co-workers, especially Alpher and Herman, predicted the present temperature of the radiation in the universe—the remnant radiation from the original Big Bang. The first step was taken by Gamow and published as a brief note in the *Physical Review* in 1948. This was an analysis of the conditions under which heavy hydrogen would be formed in the early universe. Gamow noted that no appreciable amount would be formed before the temperature dropped to about a billion degrees—that is, some three minutes after the Big Bang. Prior to this, any deuterium formed would be ripped apart by the ambient radiation. For appreciable amounts of deuterium to be formed, Gamow argued, the rate of formation should be comparable to the rate at which the universe expands. This was something he could calculate using Friedmann's equations. By equating the two rates, he was able to estimate the density of neutrons and protons when the temperature was about a billion degrees. This number turned out to be 10^{18} particles per cubic centimeter—or about a million times less dense than, say, water. In contrast, the density of the ambient radiation was comparable to that of water, so that one is dealing with matter in very peculiar state indeed. What Gamow did not do, at least in print, was to take the next step: that is, to predict at what temperature this radiation should be today. This step was taken by Alpher and Herman, whom Gamow had recruited when they were, more or less, graduate students. In a letter to the British journal *Nature*, written in 1948, they announced, without giving the argument, that the temperature of the radiation at present should be about 5 degrees above absolute zero. Keep in mind, to appreciate the prescience of this prediction, that we now know experimentally that the radiation temperature is about 2.7 degrees above zero. (In the title of this essay, I have rounded it off to 3 degrees.) In 1949, they gave the details in a paper in the *Physical Review*.

The idea is straightforward. Gamow had found the density of neutrons and protons at a billion degrees from his consideration of the deuterium reaction. (By refining his estimate, Alpher and Herman concluded that six tenths of a billion degrees was more accurate.) As space expands, the universe becomes more and more dilute. Even if particles do not disappear in inelastic collisions, their density diminishes because the space they find themselves in is blowing up like a balloon. One can readily show from Friedmann's equations that the density decreases as the third power of the temperature—the cube of the temperature. So if we can measure the present density of neutrons and protons in the universe, and then compare this with Gamow's computed density at a billion degrees, we can solve for the present temperature. But the present density is something that Alpher and Herman knew, more or less. It had been measured by Hubble when he counted galaxies. These are presumably made up out of ordinary matter—that is neutrons and protons. Hubble's number was about one nucleon per ten million cubic centimeters—not many, and a lot less than Gamow's figure at a billion degrees of 10^{18}. Doing the density numbers more accurately gives the 5 degrees. It was an astonishing prediction, and equally astonishing is the fact that it played no role whatsoever in the actual discovery of the relic radiation.

Many suggestions have been made about why this happened. Alpher and Herman think it might have had to do with the fact that they published in physics journals rather than in astronomy journals. Perhaps—but the fact is that all the people who took part in the final discovery were physicists, not astronomers. It could well have had to do with the fact that in none of the papers where they made and repeated this prediction, did they state explicitly how it could be tested. This is something that they certainly could have done. They knew perfectly well that the 5-degree radiation would have a spectrum centered in the microwave regime—wavelengths of several centimeters down to tenths of a centimeter. This region of the spectrum had received a great deal of attention during World War II, since radar detection devices use it. By 1957, Charles Townes and his students at Columbia—among them Penzias—had developed the first masers—for "microwave amplification stimulated emission of radiation"—which are very sensitive devices for detecting microwaves. It is not clear, at least to me, whether the relic radiation could have been detected prior to the invention of the maser. Alpher and Herman have said that they asked several people and were told no. But, in any case, they never put in print the problems and possibilities for detection. As I have tried to suggest, the most important reason that no one looked is that the whole field of cosmology was not taken seriously by the scientific community at large. It was one of those circular things. It was not taken seriously because of the lack of data, and there was a lack of data because it was not taken seriously.

The first clear statement that the existence of the cosmic photons might have experimental consequences—at least to my knowledge— occurs in a brief paper by the Russian scientists A. G. Doroshkevich and I. D. Novikov which was first submitted to the Russian journal *Doklady* in 1963 and then in translation here in 1964. The relevant section of the paper is the last paragraph. Here the authors note that measurements of the background radiation in the microwave regime are "extremely important for experimental checking of the Gamow theory." Curiously, they give a reference to a paper of Gamow where the background radiation is not even mentioned. The two Russians then go on to say that this radiation should have a temperature of between 1 and 10 degrees. They give no specific reference for this number nor do they present a calculation. Then comes a most remarkable sentence in which the authors note that the measurements they wish done have *already been done!* Furthermore, the authors claim, these measurements give a temperature of the radiation which is sensibly zero. This would have been in contradiction to the predicted value.

The reference for this experiment is to a paper by E. A. Ohm of what was then the Bell Telephone Laboratories; he published it in the *Bell System Technical Journal* in 1961. In fact, this paper does report such a measurement, but the Russian scientists misread the conclusions of the paper. Ohm's result, as I will explain in a moment, was perfectly consistent with the final result of 3 degrees. In any event, this Russian paper, which none of the principles read until well after the fact, had no influence on the final events leading up to the discovery that had, in fact, *already* been made by the time the Russian paper appeared here. I want next to turn to the matter of how the telephone company got itself into the business of radio astronomy and how Penzias and Wilson came upon the 3-degree radiation.

The Bell Telephone Laboratories—now the A.T.&T. Bell Telephone Laboratories—were created by the American Telephone and Telegraph Company on the first of January 1925. Its mission was to supply technology not only to the telephone system, for which A.T.&T. had a monopoly, but also other communications technologies, such as overseas shortwave radio service which had been inaugurated by A.T.&T. in the late 1920s. In addition to its main laboratories, then located in New York City, Bell Labs, as it became known, had a couple of field stations in New Jersey. It was in one of them—the one at Holmdel—that a young radio engineer named Karl Jansky was given the job of trying to measure and record shortwave static. By 1933, after four years of observation with a directional antenna, Jansky had succeeded in separating the static into three basic components; nearby thunderstorms, distant thunderstorms, and a continual hiss that varied in a regular way each day, but reached its maximum four minutes earlier each day, when a certain set of stars were due south of Jansky's antenna. Jansky had inadvertently detected extraterrestrial radio emission and thus, more or less accidentally, founded the science of radio astronomy, a field Bell Labs promptly got out of and remained out of for the next thirty years.

In 1945, the science fiction writer Arthur C. Clark, then in the Royal Air Force, conceived the notion of the communications satellite. Clarke wrote several futuristic articles about it, which did not attract any particular attention. Recall that Sputnik was not launched until 1957. However, even before Sputnik—in 1954—the noted Bell Labs engineer John Pierce—another science fiction writer under the nom de plume J. J. Coupling—re-invented the idea. He was also the man who coined the name *transistor*. Pierce, as a well-placed member of Bell Labs, was in a position to implement his idea. In the late 1950s, the National Aeronautics and Space Administration had a program to develop a large plastic weather balloon. This balloon was exploited by Pierce in 1960 to bounce microwave signals between New Jersey and California, in what became known as the Echo project. To pick up signals from the Echo, use was made of what was known as a "horn-reflector antenna." Its prototype had been designed at Bell Labs in 1942. It looks like a large Alpine horn with, at one end, an opening that admits microwave signals. If one knows what to look for, one sees antennas like this on top of the relay stations that transmit the microwave signals that are still used by part of our long-distance telephone system. One of the virtues of the antenna is that it is very directional. If you point it up toward the sky, you get next to no noise from the ground.

A large horn antenna was built in 1960 by a Bell engineer named Arthur B. Crawford and set up on what is known as Crawford Hill, the small radio laboratory near Holmdel. This was the apparatus that Ohm used when he measured the background noise. To understand Ohm's paper—which his Russian readers did not—and the subsequent developments, you must know that radio astronomers translate various noise sources into equivalent temperatures. They imagine that the telescope is in a bath of radio signals characterized by some temperature, and they then give their results in terms of that temperature that would be required to produce the equivalent noise. In Ohm's paper, there is a table of all the expected sources of noise. What is called the "sky noise" is given an equivalent temperature of about 2.3 degrees. Somehow the Russian scientists decided that this accounted for all of Ohm's result, leaving nothing left over for the Big Bang ambient radiation. Actually, when Ohm added up all his sources of expected noise, he found a total of 18.9 degrees, with an error of 3 degrees. But the actual noise he found when he *measured* it was 21 degrees, to within an error of 1 degree. He had no reason to expect that the difference of 3 degrees had any special significance. It might simply have been experimental error.

Arno Penzias joined the Crawford Hill radio research group in 1961. He had just finished his Ph.D. under the guidance of Townes at Columbia. Penzias had built a maser for his thesis and was using it to try to locate intergalactic hydrogen. He had never taken a course in cosmology. Indeed, at this time it was rare for a physics or an astronomy department to have offered a course in cosmology. Penzias took his degree in physics. He had been hired at Bell Labs by the Viennese-born architect turned physicist Rodolf Kompfner, a man of wide interests. Kompfner decided that once the large horn reflector had served its purpose in the communications satellite business, it could be used for radio astronomy—pure science. I doubt that, given the present commercial-mission orientation of the A.T.&T. Bell Labs, such a decision would now be possible. In any event, the radio-astronomy job was given to Penzias. In 1963, he was joined by Robert Wilson who had taken his Ph.D. at Cal Tech. Wilson had taken a course in cosmology—one given, ironically, by Hoyle whose steady-state theory Wilson was about to destroy. But Wilson, like Penzias, had never read any of the papers of Gamow and his collaborators. Wilson's degree was also in physics.

When Wilson joined the Bell Labs, there was only one position for a radio astronomer in Kompfner's group: thus, like Solomon, Penzias and Wilson split it in two, with each man working half-time on telephone company business. Both men were anxious to redo their theses, which they did not think very good, and to this end, began to work over the horn reflector antenna to make it into a genuine scientific radio telescope. Penzias installed what is known as a "cold load"—a liquid helium source at a known temperature, which could be used as a reference base. Wilson built an elaborate switch that could be set either to the cold load or to the antenna. When the antenna was pointed up toward the sky, they discovered almost at once that it was about three degrees hotter than they expected it to be. This was Ohm's result—but now to an accuracy that simply could not be ignored. The first data showing the anomaly was taken on 20 May 1964. If one wants, one could call that the day that the Big Bang radiation was discovered. The only problem was that Penzias and Wilson had no idea what they were seeing. To them, it appeared as if, for some unknown reason, their antenna had too much noise. They spent the next year trying to get rid of it. They tried everything they could think of. Finding that two pigeons had been nesting in the horn, they got rid of them and, in Penzias's delicate phrase, the "white dielectric material" they had left behind. They thought that perhaps New York City, less than fifty miles from Crawford Hill, might be the culprit: but at their wavelength—7 centimeters—New York turned out to be essentially noiseless. They thought the radio noise might be an aftereffect of the atmospheric atomic bomb tests of 1962, but were able to rule this out. The effect persisted night and day for four seasons—an entire year.

While this was taking place at Holmdel, some forty miles away at Princeton, an entirely independent enterprise was unfolding. Robert Dicke, now Albert Einstein University Professor of Science emeritus at Princeton, had become interested in a version of the Friedmann cosmology according to which the universe goes through alternating phases of expansion and contraction. After each contraction, there is a Big Bang. Dicke reasoned that after each Big Bang, there should be leftover radiation. He, too, had never read the papers of Gamow and his collaborators. But Dicke made his own estimate of the present temperature of the radiation by assuming that it does not contribute more to the present energy density of the universe than does the visible matter. (We now know that the energy density of the visible matter is

about a thousand times greater than that of the radiation.) This supplied
him with an upper limit on the temperature of the ambient radiation
of some forty degrees, meaning that it was in the microwave regime. He
had forgotten that in a collaboration done in 1946, just after the war,
he and three colleagues had done an experiment showing that the
background radiation had to have a temperature of less than twenty
degrees. That such an experiment had been done was forgotten by
everyone. Dicke recruited three graduate students to work with him in
Princeton: P. J. E. Peebles, a theorist; and P. G. Roll and D. T.
Wilkinson, two experimentalists.

In short order, Peebles rediscovered the deuterium arguments of
Gamow and his collaborators, whose papers he also had not read. He
concluded, at first, that the ambient temperature of the radiation should
be about ten degrees, a figure he then refined downward. In the meanwhile, Dicke, Roll, and Wilkinson were busy on the roof of the physics
building in Princeton constructing a small low-noise antenna to detect
the very radiation that Penzias and Wilson had been observing—some
forty miles away—for about a year. How long all of this might have
gone on is not clear, but in January 1965, Penzias made an incidental
phone call to a fellow radio astronomer at MIT named Bernard Burke.
Burke asked Penzias how his measurements were going. Penzias described the trouble he and Wilson had been having with the noise. As
it happened, Burke had heard from a colleague at Carnegie Tech about
a talk this colleague happened to hear when he was visiting Johns
Hopkins—a talk given, as fate would have it, by Peebles. Burke thought
that Penzias, Wilson, and the Princeton group might have some things
of mutual interest to discuss. Penzias called Dicke; and shortly thereafter, the four Princeton people came to Holmdel to see the horn and
look at the data. They, in turn, described the cosmology to Penzias and
Wilson, who were somewhat skeptical or, at least, reserved. After all,
they had measured what was supposed to be an entire black-body
radiation curve at one wavelength—7 centimeters. It took several years
before enough measurements were made by various observers to see
that there was indeed such a curve. In addition, Wilson, who had
learned his cosmology from Hoyle, actually preferred the Steady State
theory.

In July 1965, two letters, appearing in the *Astrophysical Journal*, opened
the era of modern cosmology. Dicke, Peebles, Roll, and Wilkinson
wrote a note in which they described the cosmology, and Penzias and

Wilson described their measurement without committing themselves to the cosmological explanation. In 1978, Penzias and Wilson were awarded the Nobel Prize in Physics for their discovery; and on that occasion, Wilson noted laconically, "We thought . . . that our measurement was independent of the theory and might outlive it." It hasn't. In the Penzias and Wilson letter, the work of Gamow and his collaborators was not cited: they had never read it. In the Princeton paper, the first two references are to papers by the Gamow group, neither of which mentions the prediction of the temperature of the background radiation: the Princeton group was unaware that such a prediction had been made. Thus, it has taken some time before Gamow and his collaborators got the credit for what they did. Even now, many people working in the field—most people—do not take the trouble to read these classic pre-1965 papers to see what was and was not done. By December 1965, Wilkinson and Roll had completed their measurement of the radiation sampled at three centimeters, confirming Penzias and Wilson's result at seven centimeters. The field was now wide open and rapidly turned into a scientific industry.

What the moral of this bizarre history of scientific discovery is, I am not sure—beyond the obvious one that science is done by human beings who behave like human beings. It also gives pause for thought when one reads anyone's theory about how scientific discoveries are made. Penzias and Wilson made theirs serendipitously. If Peebles had not lectured at Johns Hopkins and the Princeton experimental group had been the first to announce the discovery, it would have been hailed as a triumph for theory guiding experiment. But there is an epilogue that may illustrate what Pasteur meant when he said that in scientific discovery "chance favors *only* the prepared mind." If one asks in what year the 3-degree radiation was *really* observed a good case can be made for 1941. That year the astronomer Andrew McKellar noted something peculiar about the light coming to us from the constellation Ophiuchus. In its spectrum were a number of dark bands, indicating that some interstellar gas was absorbing the starlight at very specific frequencies. He identified one of the lines as belonging to the molecule cyanogen— one carbon and one nitrogen atom. What struck McKellar was that this line was split in three—three closely spaced lines. One of the lines belonged to what is known as a "vibrational state" of the molecule: it was a line that was to be expected if the molecule found itself at a temperature of absolute zero. But the other two lines were very mysterious. They represented states of rotation of the molecule and could appear only if the cyanogen molecules in interstellar space were somehow being agitated—if, for example, they found themselves in some sort of radiation bath. McKellar estimated that this bath, whatever it was, would have to be at a temperature of about 2.3 degrees to account for the observation. This anomaly in the stellar spectrum was fairly well known to both spectroscopists and astronomers. Indeed, in the 1950 edition of his widely read book *Spectra of Diatomic Molecules*, the Nobel laureate in chemistry Gerhard Herzberg commented on it. Of the temperature, he noted, "a rotational temperature follows [the 2.3 degrees] which has of course only a very restricted meaning." This was two years after Alpher, Gamow, and Herman had clearly spelled out just what this meaning was. He, too, hadn't read their papers, and they hadn't read his book.

CHAPTER 6

Cosmology

N EAR THE BEGINNING of *A Brief History of Time,* Stephen Hawking's hugely successful book on cosmology and astrophysics, there occurs a discussion of what are known as "the Hawking-Penrose singularity theorems." Penrose is the British mathematical physicist Roger Penrose, and the singularity in question—of which more later—refers to conditions at the center of a black hole or at the instant of the Big Bang. The scientific exposition is interrupted by the following almost casual paragraph:

> At first sight, Penrose's result applied only to stars; it didn't have anything to say about the question of whether the entire universe had a big bang singularity in its past. [Some cosmologists write "Big Bang" and others write "big bang." Hawking is of the latter school, and I am of the former.] However, at the time that Penrose produced his theorem, I was a research student desperately looking for a problem with which to complete my Ph.D. thesis. Two years before, I had been diagnosed as suffering from ALS, commonly known as Lou Gehrig's disease, or motor neuron disease, and given to understand that I had only one or two more years to live. In these circumstances, there had not seemed much point in working on my Ph.D.—I did not expect to survive that long. Yet two years had gone by and I was not that much worse. In fact, things were going rather well for me and I had gotten engaged to a very nice girl, Jane Wilde. But in order to get married, I needed a job, and in order to get a job, I needed a Ph.D.

Hawking learned of his amyotrophic lateral sclerosis when he was barely in his twenties; he is now over fifty, and the progress of the disease has been relentless. He is permanently confined to a wheelchair and retains the use only of three of his fingers. In 1985, he developed pneumonia and, to save his life, a tracheostomy was performed, which deprived him of the power to speak. Fortunately, computer-synthesized speech technology is now sufficiently advanced to enable him to use a finger-activated speech synthesizer, which is attached to his wheelchair. He notes in the acknowledgments section of his book, "This system has made all the difference: In fact I can communicate better now than before I lost my voice." The impression Hawking makes on one in a scientific meeting, or when he lectures, is complicated. One would have to be less than human not to be appalled by the ravages of his illness. There seems to be no connection between the being one sees and the sunny brilliance of his papers.

In a sense, Hawking's *A Brief History of Time* is a complement to Steven Weinberg's seminal 1977 book, *The First Three Minutes*. Both books deal with the early universe and, to some extent, with the ultimate fate of the universe—its eschatology. But Weinberg was writing at a time when the study of cosmology was not taken entirely seriously by the full community of physicists and astrophysicists. His book, although it was written ostensibly for a popular audience, helped to change that. Weinberg, who won the Nobel Prize in physics in 1979 for his work on the theory of elementary particles, had even then a reputation both as a creative scientist and as a hardheaded critic of scientific ideas. If *he* took cosmology seriously, one felt, then there must be something to it. (A parallel can be drawn between Weinberg's book and Erwin Schrödinger's *What Is Life?*, published in 1944. The fact that Schrödinger, one of the creators of the quantum theory, found deep intellectual content in certain questions of biology inspired many young people of the time to become biologists.) Weinberg focused, no doubt deliberately, on the least speculative and least outré aspects of what can be a very speculative and outré scientific discipline. Most of his book deals with the theory of the formation, in the first three minutes, of the helium that makes up about 25 percent (by mass) of the visible universe. The fact that a quarter of the visible universe appears to be made up of helium— most of the rest is hydrogen—has, as it turns out, an explanation in terms of the nuclear reactions that took place as the universe was cooling off after the Big Bang. After the first three minutes, most of the helium we find in the universe had been formed. Weinberg also made a careful study of the development of modern cosmology, taking the trouble to read the original papers, and even to seek out their authors to learn the history behind those papers. He did not hesitate to use equations when necessary, and the appendices to his book could serve as the basis of an introductory course in the subject. Furthermore, there is a marked austerity in the philosophical outlook that animates the book—an outlook summed up in its often-quoted penultimate paragraph:

> However all these problems may be resolved, and whichever cosmological model proves correct, there is not much comfort in any of this. It is almost irresistible for humans to believe that we have some special relation to the universe, that human life is not just a more-or-less farcical outcome of a chain of accidents reaching back to the first three minutes, but that we were somehow built in from the beginning. As I write this I happen to be in an airplane at 30,000 feet, flying over Wyoming en route home from San Francisco to Boston. Below, the earth looks very soft and comfortable— fluffy clouds here and there, snow turning pink as the sun sets, roads stretching straight across the country from one town to another. It is very hard to realize that this all is just a tiny part of an overwhelmingly hostile universe. It is even harder to realize that this present universe has evolved from an unspeakably unfamiliar early condition, and faces a future extinction of endless cold or intolerable heat. The more the universe seems comprehensible, the more it also seems pointless.

In many ways, Hawking's book and philosophical outlook are mirror images of Weinberg's. In the first place, there is no need to persuade anyone that the book deals with serious science, since it has been written a decade later, when cosmology is one of the most fashionable of the scientific disciplines, attracting a vast community of elementary-particle physicists, astrophysicists, and even chemists and biologists. While Hawking does treat some of the bread-and-butter cosmological problems, such as helium formation, his real interest, both professionally and in the book, is in the deep fundamentals of the subject: What conditions actually prevail at the center of a black hole or were present at the instant of the Big Bang, and are these conditions describable in terms of the physics we know? In the second place, Hawking's treatment involves almost no formal mathematics. Indeed, in the acknowledgments, Hawking notes wryly, "Someone told me that each equation I included in the book would halve the sales. I therefore resolved not to have any equations at all. In the end, however, I *did* put in one equation, Einstein's famous equation, $E = mc^2$. I hope that this will not scare off half of my potential readers."

Hawking's professional papers, too—those he has written alone—are full of ideas and relatively free of equations. They read more like prose than like mathematics. (I have often wondered if this was connected to the way he must have to work. Theoretical physicists are notorious scribblers: no piece of paper, from the back of an envelope to a place-mat, is safe. A few physicists—Hans Bethe and John von Neumann, for example—have been prodigious mental computers, but most of them scratch and scribble. What does Hawking do? He has always worked with students and assistants, who—at least in recent years, one imag-ines—write down the equations for him. One supposes that he must therefore have been forced to do a great deal of mental computation and must also constantly have had to explain his ideas orally; he does not have the option of jotting things down on pieces of paper or on a blackboard.) Finally, Hawking's book is more benevolent than Wein-berg's in its philosophical outlook. Hawking makes frequent and amia-ble references to God—somewhat the way Einstein used to do; but since he calls Him "him," one is not quite sure how to take this. Less ambiguous, perhaps, is his apparent acceptance of what he defines as "the weak anthropic principle." The regular anthropic principle (which Hawking does not seem to embrace) he defines in a glossary as the proposition that "we see the universe the way it is because if it were different we would not be here to observe it." While this appears at first to have some scientific content, the more one thinks about it the more that content slips away, like water running through one's fingers. What the principle seems to say is not that the human race has evolved so as to conform to the condition of the universe; but, rather, that the uni-verse has evolved so as to conform to the human condition. Apart from the question of how, or whether, such a principle could ever be verified (how could one distinguish it empirically from Weinberg's dictum that "the more the universe seems comprehensible, the more it also seems pointless"?), it flies in the face of the history of science, which has been a retreat from a human-centered cosmos. This point is made by Hawk-ing, who writes:

We have developed from the geocentric comsologies of Ptolemy and his forebears, through the heliocentric cosmology of Copernicus and Galileo, to the modern picture in which the earth is a medium-sized planet orbiting around an average star in the outer suburbs of an ordinary spiral galaxy, which is itself only one of about a million million galaxies in the observable universe. Yet the strong anthropic principle would claim that this whole vast construction exists simply for our sake. This is very hard to believe.

Instead, Hawking accepts the weak anthropic principle, which, as he defines it, states that

the conditions necessary for the development of intelligent life will be met only in certain regions that are limited in space and time. The intelligent beings in these regions should therefore not be surprised if they observe that their locality in the universe satisfies the conditions that are necessary for their existence. It is a bit like a rich person living in a wealthy neighborhood not seeing any poverty.

It is not clear to me that this principle has any real content either, but at least it is not absurd.

THE most original parts of Hawking's book consist of the description of his own work. Since this has been of such great importance in modern cosmological theory, and since he describes it so lucidly, the general reader has an opportunity to learn some deep science directly from the source. Hawking's first important work in cosmology grew out of his Ph.D. thesis. Roger Penrose had noted in 1965 that whenever massive stars collapsed under the weight of their own gravitation to form the objects known as black holes, the result would necessarily be what mathematicians refer to as a "singularity." The singularity, in this case, would be a point in space-time where the physical quantities describing a black hole—such as the gravitational field inside it— become literally infinite, as opposed to merely unimaginably large. This is a very important distinction. True infinities never, as far as we know, occur in nature; and if a theory predicts them, it can be taken as an indication that the theory is "sick" or, at the very least, is being applied in a regime where it is not applicable. Here the theory at stake was Einstein's theory of general relativity and gravitation—the very theory that Robert Oppenheimer and his students had used in the late 1930s to show that what came to be called black holes might indeed exist. (The term was invented in 1969 by the physicist John Wheeler.) Penrose's result suggested a potential paradox in Einstein's theory when it was applied to regimes in which gravitation was very strong. Hawking made the fundamental observation—which became the basis of his Ph.D. thesis—that the Big Bang was like a black hole in reverse. A classical black hole—the qualification *classical* is necessitated by another of Hawking's fundamental discoveries, which he describes in a chapter entitled "Black Holes Ain't So Black"—simply swallows any matter or radiation that comes near it, whereas the Big Bang, instead of swallowing everything, emits everything. It is in some sense a black hole running backward in time. This was the insight Hawking had in 1965 which, as he informs us, enabled him to get his Ph.D., so that he could get married. (The Hawkings, incidentally, had three children and now have divorced.) But the discovery had more serious consequences for cosmology.

Black holes might or might not exist. The Big Bang, however, *must* exist if modern cosmology is to make any sense at all. Hence Hawking's result suggests that when Einstein's theory is applied to the beginning of the universe, it leads to a singularity—infinite temperatures, pressures, and gravitational fields—and therefore breaks down. By 1970, Hawking and Penrose had shown that this singularity was a feature of any model of the expanding universe which used Einstein's theory of general relativity and gravitation as its basis. The conclusion that Hawking, and many others, came to was that Einstein's theory must be incomplete. Certainly one thing missing from it was quantum mechanics. That Einstein left quantum mechanics out of his thinking about general relativity is hardly surprising, since he thought that quantum theory, with its uncertainties and probabilities, was only provisional and would eventually give way to some sort of classical theory—of which general relativity is the great paradigm. As Jean Cocteau once remarked, "a true poet sings from his family tree." Einstein apart, it had been recognized by physicists since the 1930s that gravitation would have to be "quantized," but that the mathematics of this was almost hopelessly complex. (It still is.) Nonetheless, quantum mechanics is built on certain general principles, such as the Heisenberg uncertainty relations, that transcend mathematical complexities. Hawking realized in the early 1970s that the Heisenberg relation between energy and time had remarkable implications for black holes: namely, that they "ain't so black."

In essence, the Heisenberg relation between energy and time states that no measurement that takes a finite as opposed to an infinite time to perform—that is, no actual measurement—can determine the energy of a system precisely. This carries all sorts of implications for physics. In particular, it implies that space can never be quite empty. An empty space would have no energy content, but this itself is a precise measurement; hence, such a statement would violate the Heisenberg relation. Space is alive with the spontaneous creation and annihilation of particles of matter and antimatter—for example, the electron and the positron. Under ordinary circumstances, we cannot detect these virtual—"virtual" because their existence violates the principle of the conservation of energy—particles directly, since they disappear back into the vacuum just rapidly enough not to violate the conservation-of-energy principle. (They do have indirect effects—in, for example, atomic physics.) But, Hawking argues in his book, if this process goes on at the surface of a black hole, then the hole might grab either the electron or the positron and supply the negative energy needed to satisfy the principle. The remaining particle would be liberated, and the black hole, emitting particles, would appear to an observer to be glowing like an incandescent lump of coal. For arcane reasons involving entropy, the more a black hole radiated, the more it would shrink; the more it shrank, the hotter it would get; and the hotter it got, the more it would radiate. The whole process runs away with itself, and in the end, in Hawking's words, the black hole "would disappear completely in a tremendous final burst of emission, equivalent to the explosion of millions of H-bombs." Big black holes, of the kind produced when a massive star collapses, would take many billions of years to explode; but there might be, Hawking speculates, small black holes, which could explode in the present era. If this idea is right, these exploding black holes should be detectable as sudden bursts of radiation. The experimental problem is to distinguish these bursts from other sources of radiation. So far, there is no certain evidence for an exploding black hole, at least in this neck of the universe.

Making this kind of semiphenomenological prediction, which, in a way, sidesteps the need for a fundamental quantum theory of gravitation, leaves most physicists, including Hawking, dissatisfied. For this reason, much has been made of recent attempts to develop a true quantum theory of gravitation by the use of "strings." The last part of Hawking's book is devoted to a description of this activity, and to raising some probing questions addressed to the practitioners involved in it, who sometimes claim that they have constructed, or are about to construct, the Theory of Everything—TOE, in the jargon. In pre-string elementary-particle theory, particles were thought of as points in space-time. A theory of point particles makes for all kinds of singularities, which, in the case of gravitation, become ineluctable. This problem led to the idea of replacing the point particles by tiny two-dimensional structures—loops of string—which would resemble points if one were not too close to them, but which might avoid the singular behavior of points. Miraculously, if this amalgam is conjoined to gravity, then in a small number of interesting cases the resulting theory is nonsingular. This is what has led to the excitement over strings—an excitement somewhat tempered by the fact that these theories require at least ten dimensions (nine spatial and one temporal), while we exist in four. The practitioners claim that the extra dimensions in their theories are "curled up," so that they are unobservable, which puts the burden on these theories to explain how it happens that just four of the ten dimensions know enough not to curl up as well. Aside from this (and on this point Hawking is especially good), an entire philosophical Pandora's box is opened when one talks about a Theory of Everything, and the practitioners not only leave this box unopened but seem blissfully unaware of it. Here is what Hawking has to say:

> Even if there is only one possible unified theory, it is just a set of rules and equations. What is it that breathes fire into the equations and makes a universe for them to describe? The usual approach of science of constructing a mathematical model cannot answer the questions of why there should be a universe for the model to describe. Why does the universe go to all the bother of existing? Is the unified theory so compelling that it brings about its own existence? Or does it need a creator, and, if so, does he have any other effect on the universe? And who created him?

One might object that these are not really scientific questions, but the statement that one has constructed the Theory of Everything is not science either. In science, one counts oneself fortunate if one succeeds in constructing the theory of something.

WHATEVER Hawking's strengths as a scientific popularizer, they do not make him a very reliable historian. He has an impressionistic view of the history of recent science. Very few active scientists—Weinberg is an exception, and that is one of the reasons his book is so good— actually take the trouble to read the papers of their early predecessors. A kind of folklore builds up which bears only a tangential relationship to reality; and when someone with the scientific prestige of Hawking repeats these legends, it gives them credibility. This is not the place to indulge in historical exegesis, but one example may make the point. Furthermore, this example has—at least, in my view—the virtue of making the anecdote funnier than Hawking's rather garbled version of it. The anecdote has to do with the history of the discovery of the radiation left over from the Big Bang. The Big Bang produced light quanta of unimaginably high energy. In the fifteen billion years or so since that event, these quanta have cooled down to an average tempera- ture of some three degrees above absolute zero (see chapter 5). They have wavelengths of a few centimeters, which puts them in the micro- wave category; and in 1964, Arno A. Penzias and Robert W. Wilson, of the Bell Laboratories, accidentally found them while using a radio telescope connected to a microwave detector. There are about four hundred such light quanta in each cubic centimeter of the universe; their detection began the modern era in cosmology. But as early as 1948, as we have seen, George Gamow and his students Ralph Alpher and Robert Herman had predicted that such microwave radiation should exist and should have about the temperature it has turned out to have. Their prediction was ignored, since, as I have noted, cosmology was not taken altogether seriously at the time. In any event, here is Hawking's version of the history:

> This picture of a hot early stage of the universe was first put forward by the scientist George Gamow in a famous paper written in 1948 with a student of his, Ralph Alpher. Gamow had quite a sense of humor—he persuaded the nuclear scientist Hans Bethe to add his name to the paper to make the list of authors "Alpher, Bethe, Gamow," like the first three letters of the Greek alphabet, alpha, beta, gamma: particularly appropriate for a paper on the beginning of the universe! In this paper they made the remarkable prediction that radiation (in the form of photons) from the very hot early stages of the universe should still be around today, but with its temperature reduced to only a few degrees above absolute zero ($-273°C$). It was this radiation that Penzias and Wilson found in 1965.

Now to the history. It is quite true that Alpher, Bethe, and Gamow published a paper—really a brief letter—in the *Physical Review* in 1948. It was entitled "The Origin of Chemical Elements," and nowhere in it is the microwave radiation mentioned. Rather, the paper concerns the general question of where the chemical elements come from. At the time, Gamow thought that all the elements were manufactured in the first few minutes after the Big Bang. (This is not so, and within a few years he decided that the idea did not work.) Apart from the fact that the paper had nothing at all to do with the Big Bang radiation, to describe the events that led to the odd marriage of authors by saying that Gamow "persuaded the nuclear scientist Hans Bethe to add his name to the paper" is to miss the beauty of the story. When Gamow wrote the paper, he stuck Bethe's name between his own and Alpher's, being careful to keep things legitimate by adding "in absentia" after Bethe's name. The editor of the *Physical Review* must have smelled a rat, because he sent the paper to Bethe to referee. Bethe, who has always had a certain fondness for this kind of jape, checked the calculations to see if they followed from the assumptions, removed the words "in absentia" after his name, and recommended that the paper be published. The first prediction of the relic radiation from the Big Bang was actually published that same year, in a letter to the British journal *Nature*, by Alpher and Robert Herman, Gamow's other student. Hawking's retelling of this tale denies Alpher—and, more important, Herman—the proper credit for a major discovery in theoretical physics.

Stephen Hawking has been for several years the Lucasian Professor of Mathematics at Cambridge. It is the professorship that was held by Isaac Newton and by the late P. A. M. Dirac, one of the founders of the quantum theory. Hawking has been a worthy successor, and one wishes him many future years. He has a great deal to teach us.

CHAPTER 7

A Portrait of Alan Turing

I FIRST HEARD OF ALAN TURING IN 1963, when I was writing a profile of the computer for the *New Yorker*. One day that spring, before a lecture at Columbia, I happened to run into the physicist Freeman Dyson, who asked whether I was familiar with Turing's work, and explained to me the essentials of his ideas about the logical organization of computers—"the Turing machine," as his abstract computer is known—and their implications for the limits of computation. Turing had completed this work in April 1936—he was then twenty-three and a student at Cambridge University. Dyson had known about Turing's work since his own student days at Cambridge, in the 1940s. At that time, Turing was still nominally a Fellow in mathematics at King's College, but he was in fact attached to the Government Code and Cypher School, at Bletchley, which did code work of such a sensitive nature that nothing about it appeared in the open literature until the 1970s. Only then did it come to light that while he was at Bletchley, Turing had played a significant role in breaking the German "Enigma" codes. His specialty was the so-called Naval Enigma—codes the Germans used to communicate with their U-boats. The fact that those codes were broken—something the Germans never realized—allowed British convoys to avoid areas where there were U-boat packs, and may well have played as important a part in the battle for Britain as radar. Turing worked at the University of Manchester after the war. He died in 1954, at the age of forty-one.

After my talk with Dyson, I was so taken with Turing's ideas that I tried to read everything I could get my hands on about him and his work. The only book on Turing himself was one that his mother, Sara Turing, wrote in 1959. It is essentially a eulogy. A good deal of it consists of quotations from admiring letters and reminiscences sent Mrs. Turing by people like Lyn Irvine, the wife of the Cambridge mathematician Maxwell H. A. Newman, to whom in 1936 Turing had handed, with no advance notice, his independently produced paper on the Turing machine. In my profile, I described Mrs. Turing's book as "moving and lovely." But Lyn Irvine's foreword to the book, read carefully, might suggest that Mrs. Turing's account bears only a passing relation to reality—that there were profoundly dark currents in Turing's life. Turing was

> a very strange man, one who never fitted in anywhere quite successfully. His scattered efforts to appear at home in the upper-middle-class circles into which he was born stand out as particularly unsuccessful. He did adopt a few conventions, apparently at random, but he discarded the majority of their ways and ideas without hesitation or apology. Unfortunately the ways of the academic world which might have proved his refuge puzzled and bored him.

Why Turing might have sought a refuge is now clear, thanks to a monumentally detailed biography, *Alan Turing: The Enigma*, by the British mathematical physicist Andrew Hodges.

By now we have become accustomed to biographies of artists, actors, writers, and even statesmen that discuss the most intimate details of their subjects' personal lives. But there is, I think, something disturbing—or, at least, unfamiliar—about reading a comparable biography of a scientist. That is one reason James Watson's *The Double Helix*, published in 1968, came as such a shock to many people. Here a participant in one of the truly significant discoveries of twentieth-century science was revealing himself to be an all too human creature (see also chapter 10). To those of us who spend most of our lives with scientists, this was not exactly an earth-rending revelation. But there may have been among scientists a sense of betrayal: it was as if Watson had exposed a trade secret—that scientists in their everyday behavior are not especially "scientific." One of the other biographies I can think of in which the sexual life of a scientist plays a significant role is Frank E. Manuel's

A Portrait of Isaac Newton. It connects Newton's psychological breakdown, in 1693, to repressed homosexual feelings for a Swiss aristocrat named Nicolas Fatio de Duillier; and, when it came out in 1968, it created something of a storm among historians of science. Many of them thought that Manuel's interpretations of aspects of Newton's life, including the relationship with Fatio de Duillier, went beyond the actual evidence; but there also seemed to be a feeling of distaste—a feeling that a biography of perhaps the greatest scientist who has ever lived which emphasized his intimate life, and not his science, was somehow unworthy of its subject.

I bring all this up because of the character of Hodges's biography of Alan Turing. Turing was a homosexual, and to have written a biography of him without dealing with his homosexuality would have been an absurdity. Sara Turing did just that, and in many respects her biography *is* an absurdity. I wonder, however, whether there are not limits to what we should know, or need to know, about Alan Turing—or, indeed, about anyone—and whether Hodges has not gone beyond such limits. The intrusion of the question of Turing's homosexuality into areas where it seems to have no relevance threatens to capsize Hodges's fine book—to turn it from a biography into a political tract. Hodges identifies himself, in an author's note, as a member of the London Gay Liberation Front. He sees Turing—rightly—as someone who, if he was not driven to his death by public revelation of his homosexuality, had much of the last part of his life destroyed by the consequences of that revelation.

ALAN Mathison Turing was born on 23 June 1912, in London. His father, Julius Mathison Turing, was in the Indian Civil Service. Turing's mother, a Stoney, prided herself on being a distant relative of the Irish physicist George Stoney, whom she had once met as a girl in Dublin. (Stoney is known now, if at all, because in 1891 he coined the name *electron* for the fundamental unit of electricity, which he conjectured had to exist. To Turing, this distant relative was a bogus scientist, since all he was known for was naming something; the actual particle was discovered in 1897 by the British physicist J. J. Thomson.) Turing's parents met in 1907, on a ship returning from India—Sara Turing's father was an engineer who worked in India—and were married soon afterward. Turing's older brother, John, was born in 1908. In 1913, the two boys were left in England with a retired army couple named Ward while the Turings went back to India. During the First World War, the family were briefly reunited in England. Then the parents again returned to India, and the boys were sent off to school. In the 1920s, after his father's retirement from the Civil Service, Turing's parents settled at Guildford, in Surrey. His father died in 1947, and his mother in 1976.

Hodges's chapters on Turing's early education are among the most interesting in the book. Later in life, Hodges notes, Turing said, "The great thing about a public school education is that afterwards, however miserable you are, you know it can never be quite so bad again." In a footnote, Hodges remarks that in Turing's case this was "a false prophecy." At his first school, Hazelhurst, Turing did not distinguish himself as a student, but he acquired a strong interest in chemistry. (At the end of his life, he was doing research in chemistry.) His mother had an exaggerated respect for anyone with any kind of a title; it may have been inevitable for Turing to be sent to a reasonably fashionable public school. In the event, Sherborne was selected, and Turing entered it in 1926. Something of the attitude to science in such schools at the time is suggested in a letter the headmaster wrote to Turing's parents: "If he is to stay at a Public School, he must aim at becoming *educated*. If he is to be solely a *Scientific Specialist*, he is wasting his time at a Public School." This observation came when Turing, at age fourteen, had discovered for himself the infinite series that represents the inverse tangent function—something that I, at least, was taught as a college sophomore.

When one reads Hodges' account of the social order that prevailed in a place like Sherborne, one marvels that any of the boys emerged psychologically sound. Basically, all that Turing wanted was to be left alone. By the age of sixteen, he had come upon Einstein's theory of relativity, which he was happily teaching himself. His closest friend was another science student, Christopher Morcom, who was a year older. Morcom applied for and won a scholarship at Trinity College, Cambridge, in 1929, but before he could take advantage of it he died, of tuberculosis. One of Turing's schoolmates wrote to another boy, "Poor old Turing is nearly knocked out by the shock. They must have been awfully good friends." It was a loss Turing may never really have got over. For years, he and Mrs. Morcom exchanged correspondence about what Christopher had meant to them. By 1930, Turing was just beginning to find himself to some degree socially. He was made a school prefect—one of the boys in charge of discipline. Hodges quotes a letter he received from a schoolmate of Turing's which is notable for what it says not only about Turing but about the atmosphere in the public schools:

> Turing . . . was quite a lovable creature but rather sloppy in appearance. [This was a characteristic Turing never lost.] He was a year or more older than me, but we were quite good friends.
>
> One day I saw him shaving in the washroom, with his sleeves loose and his general appearance rather execrable. I said, in a friendly way, "Turing, you look a disgusting sight." He seemed to take it not amiss, but I tactlessly said it a second time. He took offence and told me to stay there and wait for him. I was a bit surprised, but (as the house washroom was the place for beatings) I knew what to expect. He duly re-appeared with a cane, told me to bend over and gave me four. After that he put the cane back and resumed his shaving. Nothing more was said; but I realised that it was my fault and we remained good friends. That subject was never mentioned again.

In the fall of 1931, Turing entered King's College, and began his formal study of advanced mathematics. He had a successful undergraduate career and in 1935 was awarded a graduate fellowship at King's. That spring, while awaiting the results of his fellowship application, he had attended a course in the foundations of mathematics given by M. H. A. Newman. It is likely that this course changed Turing's professional life. Newman's course ended up with a proof of Gödel's theorem, which says, in essence, that in systems as complex as arithmetic there must be true statements that are not provable within the context of the axioms that govern the system. There remained, however, a fundamental problem in the foundations of mathematics which was known as the "decision problem" *(Entscheidungsproblem)* and had first been stated by the great German mathematician David Hilbert in 1900: namely, is there an algorithm (a "mechanical process," in Newman's phrase) that can be applied essentially automatically to a mathematical statement so as to enable one to decide whether that statement is provable? We are now, in many ways thanks to Turing, so likely to think of these things in terms of computer analogs that it is natural for us to rephrase the question as "Is it possible to write a computer program that could decide in principle whether a given mathematical statement is provable?" What Turing did was to recast Hilbert's problem in exactly that language. To do so, he invented an abstract computing "machine" with an infinitely long tape that could be moved, read, and modified according to very simple rules. While these rules were simple, they were so well constructed that, by combining enough simple operations, one could program Turing's machine to calculate anything that could be calculated on any machine. This universal character of the machine gave it importance in settling questions of what could or could not be programmed on a computer. In particular, any number that was "computable" (such as π or $\sqrt{2}$) could be computed to arbitrary accuracy by using an algorithm—a program— on this machine. Turing discovered that there were numbers that were not computable—no possible algorithm could be devised for computing them. Here, then, was a class of examples which demonstrated that Hilbert's decision problem was unsolvable. It put an end to Hilbert's attempt to demonstrate the formal consistency and completeness of all mathematics.

Turing did this work entirely on his own, and it took him nearly a year to write it up to his satisfaction. The final paper, "On Computable Numbers, with an Application to the *Entscheidungsproblem,*" was published in 1937—Turing was twenty-four; and it remains one of the classic papers of modern mathematics. Turing first presented it to Newman in April of 1936. As it happened, at the same time the Princeton logician Alonzo Church had come up with a different treat- ment of Hilbert's problem, and he sent a copy of his result to Newman, knowing nothing about Turing's work. Newman immediately wrote to the secretary of the London Mathematical Society suggesting that Tur- ing's paper, because of its originality, be published, and to Church suggesting that Turing might come to Princeton to work with him. In September 1936, Turing came to Princeton; he took his Ph.D. there under Church in 1938. He also met the great Hungarian-born mathe- matician John von Neumann, and made such a favorable impression that in 1938 von Neumann offered Turing a job as his assistant at the Institute for Advanced Study. But Turing had decided to return to King's, where he still had a fellowship.

Hodges learned from an acquaintance of Turing's of that period, a Canadian physicist named Malcolm MacPhail, that as early as 1937 Turing had begun thinking seriously about the possibility of war be- tween Britain and Germany and about what he might contribute to the defense of Britain. While he was working on his Ph.D. thesis in Prince- ton, he was also working very hard with MacPhail on general questions of cryptanalysis. Turing even sneaked into the machine shop in the

Princeton Physics Department and designed and put together an electric multiplier—a calculator that does multiplication—with the idea of using it, somehow, for work with codes. It is not surprising, then, that he was one of the early recruits to the war-enhanced cyrptanalysis effort at Bletchley. Mr. Hodges does a fine job of explaining how the Enigma was broken. A reader who would like to learn still more about this might read *The Hut Six Story*, by one of Turing's colleagues, Gordon Welchman. It is clear that the code breaking was a collaborative effort by a number of brilliant and idiosyncratic people. The Germans made several fundamental mistakes in using the Enigma, and allowed some of the cipher material to fall into British hands. The British nearly lost whatever advantage they had by not taking seriously enough the information that was soon being produced in reams at Bletchley. Its analysis required an enormous effort, which was mounted only after Turing, Welchman, and others there wrote a letter directly to Churchill outlining what they needed. On the day he received it, Churchill instructed his principal staff officer to "make sure they have all they want on extreme priority."

In June 1946, Turing was awarded the Order of the British Empire for his cryptanalytical work. He by then had accepted a position at the National Physical Laboratory, in Teddington, with a group that was trying to build the first British electronic digital computer. It was to be called the Automatic Computing Engine, or the ACE—a reference to Charles Babbage's Analytical Engine. The ACE was an extremely ambitious project; and, dissatisfied with its slow progress, Turing withdrew from it in 1947 and went to King's. He might have stayed there except that Newman, his old teacher, was directing a computer project at Manchester and persuaded him to accept a special position at the university, which would be funded by the Royal Society. In 1948, Turing moved to Manchester, and it was there that he spent the rest of his life.

Two excerpts from these chapters illustrate Hodges's polemical emphasis on Turing's sexuality. Chapter 4 is called "The Relay Race"—an allusion partly to the fact that Turing became a high-level competitive long-distance runner, and partly to the fact that the British and the Germans were in a kind of relay race over the military codes. (Although the Germans never knew that the British had broken the Enigma, they introduced improvements and variations into it, which the British were continually racing to decipher.) This is a fascinating chapter, because it gives the reader a feeling for both the incredible technical complexity of the code-breaking process and the extraordinary atmosphere at Bletchley. In the middle of it, however, Hodges describes a week in the late summer of 1940 that Turing spent in Wales with a young Austrian student named Robert Augenfeld, who had come to Britain as a refugee in 1939 and, with Turing's help, had been accepted at a public school. Of this week, Hodges writes, "They went fishing and for long walks over the hills. After a day or two Alan made a gentle sexual approach, but Bob rebuffed it. Alan did not ask again. It did not affect the holiday. Bob perceived that the possibility had been at the back of Alan's mind from the beginning, but did not feel that Alan had taken advantage of him. He was simply not interested." Is this episode something we really have to know about? Hodges makes no attempt to relate it to any general aspect of Turing's character apart from his homosexuality. The subject changes back to U-boats, after a portentous-sounding paragraph: "None of this was quite what Churchill had in mind when calling the British people to brace themselves to their duties, or speaking of the Empire that might last a thousand years. But duty and empires did not solve ciphers, and Churchill never bargained for an Alan Turing." In a chapter describing Turing's early postwar work on electronic computers (as opposed to his prewar work on a model of computation—the Turing machine), Hodges writes, "And thus it was that in this remote station . . . working with one assistant in a small hut, and thinking in his spare time, an English homosexual atheist mathematician had conceived of the *computer.*" At least two things leap out at once from this sentence. Reading naïvely, one might imagine that Turing in fact invented the electronic computer. This is certainly not what Hodges means, since he goes on to give at some length the history of the modern electronic computer—the real hardware computer—in which Turing played a minor role. Be this as it may, what possible relevance to this discussion does Turing's homosexuality (or, for that matter, his atheism) have? Was it supposed to confer an intellectual handicap on him, which he had to overcome to create a computer? Are we supposed to feel impressed by the fact that Turing was both a homosexual and a computer designer? This sort of reference to Turing's sexuality seems to me both gratuitous and demeaning. Turing lived under an outmoded legal and moral code, and the temptation for Hodges to turn his book into a political statement must have been great indeed. His account of the facts of Turing's life—of what he suffered as a homosexual in a hypocritical society—is eloquent. The biography would have been an even more powerful statement, however, if it had left more unsaid.

It is not much use to speculate about the choices Turing made in his life, but I cannot help wondering about paths not taken. For example, in the spring of 1941, Turing became engaged to a fellow worker at Bletchley named Joan Clarke. He had told her about his homosexuality, and she was prepared to marry him. But by the end of that summer, Turing had found that he had to break the engagement. He quoted to her the lines from Oscar Wilde's "Ballad of Reading Gaol" that begin "Yet each man kills the thing he loves." He could have remained in what Lyn Irvine referred to as the refuge of the academic world. He could have remained in Cambridge, where—with John Maynard Keynes, E. M. Forster, Ludwig Wittgenstein, and G. H. Hardy, his homosexuality would not have been an object of special scrutiny; even at Manchester, he might have remained within the confines of the university environment. Instead, he made what turned out to be the disastrous mistake of having an affair with a nineteen-year-old unemployed Manchester boy named Arnold Murray, who had been sent back to Manchester on probation after being arrested in London for petty thievery. After Murray had visited him a few times, Turing found that his house had been broken into. He confronted Murray, who said that an acquaintance of his had committed the robbery. On the morning of 3 February 1952, Turing reported to the police his suspicions about the identity of the robber. When detectives called at Turing's house, he admitted to them the nature of his relationship with Murray; and he was later charged with the crime of "Gross Indecency contrary to Section 11 of the Criminal Law Amendment Act 1885." Under Section 11, it was illegal to commit any homosexual act, no matter what the circumstances. It was this law that made British homosexuals so vulnerable to blackmail. Turing did not attempt to deny the charges. Murray was also arrested, and both of them faced the virtual certainty of a public trial; the maximum prison sentence was two years. At the very least, the arrest meant that Turing's mother and brother, who knew nothing about his homosexuality (he had seen little of them during his adult years), would now learn of it. Turing decided to begin by telling his brother, who immediately came to Manchester to help him. Turing then went to Guildford to meet with his mother. She accepted what he told her, and then appears to have ignored it; in her book there is no mention whatsoever of the trial, or of the circumstances that brought it about. Turing's colleagues reacted variously, some accepting his homosexuality and some never speaking to him again. At the trial, which took place on 31 March 1952, M. H. A. Newman was asked if Turing was the sort of person he would receive in his home; he replied that he had already done so.

Both Turing and Murray pleaded guilty. Hodges notes that if the OBE had been a medal given by the War Office, Turing, upon his conviction, would have had to return it; since it was an award given by the Foreign Office, he was allowed to keep it. Murray was conditionally discharged, and Turing was given a choice of going to prison or spending a year taking "organotherapy," at the Manchester Royal Infirmary. He chose the therapy. This meant taking prescribed doses of the hormone estrogen, which rendered him impotent and caused him to develop breasts. The treatment was supposed to "cure" homosexuality, and Turing became an experimental subject. He also began seeing a Jungian psychoanalyst. In April 1953, his probation ended. By then, the hormone had been implanted in his thigh, but Turing removed the implant. In May, he was appointed to a specially created readership at Manchester in the theory of computing, and it appeared that his future was secure. He had been working for some time on problems connected with the mathematical growth patterns of plants; in 1952 he had published an important paper on that subject, and he was thought to be working on a sequel. On the evening of 7 June 1954, Turing died, an apparent suicide.

Hodges writes, "Alan Turing's death came as a shock to those who knew him. It fell into no clear sequence of events. Nothing was explicit—there was no warning, no note of explanation. It seemed an isolated act of self-annihilation." The circumstances were such that they left an aura of ambiguity which will never be resolved. The last sentence in the entry on Turing in the *Dictionary of Scientific Biography* reads, "He was at work on a general theory [of biological forms] when he died of perhaps accidental poisoning." Mrs. Turing, in her book, makes it clear that, as far as she was concerned, Turing did die by accident. Hodges presents these facts: Turing was found by his housekeeper "lying neatly in his bed." The pathologist who examined his body concluded immediately that he had died from cyanide poisoning. There were two jars of cyanide in the house. Next to Turing's bed was a half-eaten apple. No one thought to test the apple for cyanide, but the coroner's verdict of suicide went uncontested. (Hodges notes that Turing had once spoken of apples in connection with methods of committing suicide.) I have always believed that no one—psychiatrist or not—can really understand why someone commits suicide. To most of us, the idea of exiling ourselves to that distant place before we are summoned is inconceivable. Epicurus said, "Death is nothing to us, since when we are, death has not come, and when death has come, we are not." After reading Hodges's book, I believe that Alan Turing did commit suicide. He led a burdened and tormented life, and death may have seemed the better bargain.

CHAPTER 8

I Am a Camera

THIS COUNTRY HAS, at least until recently, been known for the sort of inventions that change the way people live. Edison's invention of a usable electric light bulb is one obvious example, and the invention of the transistor in 1948 by the three Bell Labs physicists John Bardeen, Walter Brattain, and William Shockley is another. To this list one could add the invention of Polaroid, the light absorbing material used in sunglasses and wherever else it is desirable to reduce glare, and the invention in 1943 of the idea of "instant" or "one-step" photography. Both of these were the creations of the American-born scientist-inventor Edwin H. Land, who died in 1991. While Land's Polaroid Corporation is well known to the general public, Land himself was almost a complete enigma. He never allowed anyone to interview him at length, never wrote an autobiography, and never participated in the writing of his biography by anyone else.

On this last matter, I consider myself something of an expert. With the encouragement of various mutual friends, some of whom I took to be speaking for Land, I tried for nearly five years to arrange with Land to do a *New Yorker* profile of him. Since he notoriously did not answer letters, these negotiations, if that is what to call them, were carried on by emissaries, with the exception of an encounter on the evening of 6 November 1982. The Science Museum of Minnesota then celebrated its seventy-fifth anniversary by inviting a small group to join it for the occasion, a group that included Land and myself.

This was my only meeting with Land, and I was immediately taken by what seemed to be his straightforwardness. I was determined not to bring up the subject of the profile, but he almost immediately pulled out his pocket diary to show me my address and telephone number entered in it, and indicated that my request had been much on his mind. In a moment of euphoria, I remarked that writing about him would give me an opportunity to learn something about the history of photography, a subject of which I was ignorant. (I did not tell him that I had never owned a camera and knew next to nothing about how one works.) He looked at me oddly and said, "Photography . . . photography . . . that is something I do for a living. My real interest is in color vision."

I did not have the slightest idea of what to make of this remarkable statement. I did not realize that the previous August he had severed, under not very happy circumstances, his connections with the company he created, and had sold the 15-percent share of stock in Polaroid that he and his family owned. But my first, naïve, thought was to compare his situation with those taxi drivers, bartenders, and elevator operators one encounters in New York who say that what they really do is act, sing, or conduct research in cosmology. Evidently color vision, about which I also knew next to nothing, would have to be an important part of the profile. However, I never again heard from Land and my letters to him were never answered.

I mention all of this only to explain how surprising it is to find that there now is a biography of sorts of Land, *Land's Polaroid* by Peter C. Wensberg. Mr. Wensberg spent twenty-four years at Polaroid, which he left two months after Land did. His work was largely in advertising and marketing; and when he left Polaroid, he was the senior vice president in charge of marketing. He was the third most important officer in the company after Land and William McCune, the president of Polaroid. As Wensberg makes clear in the prologue, and as Land has said publicly, Land had nothing to do with the book.

Wensberg is candid about his limitations: "Edwin H. Land deserves and requires a scientific biography. His career in science has been a long one, including some achievements that will last well beyond the products of his company. I am not that author and this is not that book."

What then is it? "This is a portrait of a man and a company who occupied the same space, and often, but not always, spoke with the same voice. If it is an admiring portrait, I do not apologize."

To write an admiring portrait of someone one admires—I have done it often—hardly needs an apology, providing one does, in fact, write a portrait. The trouble with Wensberg's book is not that it is admiring but that it is not a portrait. The fault seems to be both with Wensberg and with Land. Wensberg was associated with Land for a quarter of a century but does not seem to have a clue about him.

Land was obsessively private, as he had every right to be, but how can anyone claim to have written a portrait of him when the first seventeen years of his life—including his family background—are compressed into a single paragraph? We do not even learn whether Land had any brothers or sisters. *Time* magazine's 1972 cover story about Land contains more information about his early years. The *Time* reporter had the enterprise to ask Land's high-school physics teacher what he had been like as a student. The teacher, Raymond Case, reported that in his senior year Land "was already working at a level where I couldn't help him."

Wensberg also spends pages on useless digression. There is an entire chapter, for example, on the U-2 spy plane. The only connection I could find to Land was that he was, along with several other prominent scientists, a member of the President's Science Advisory Committee under Eisenhower, which advised Eisenhower to authorize the spy missions. This Wensberg briefly tells us, after pages of commentary on the plane itself. Wensberg also describes people he neither saw nor heard looking "glumly" at their wristwatches or raising their voices "above the tumult." Reading these misguided attempts to add verisimilitude to otherwise plausible scenes, one remembers that Wensberg made his career in advertising.

An adequate study of Land would have to include at least three elements. Two of them, the founding of the Polaroid company and the invention of what Land referred to as "one-step" photography, are treated somewhat perfunctorily in Wensberg's book. The third, his theory of color vision, is not mentioned at all. Yet even a cursory account should make it clear that Land is one of the pivotal figures in creating our technological society—someone whom one might compare to Thomas Edison and certainly to George Eastman, the inventor of the Kodak camera.

L AND was born in Bridgeport, Connecticut, in 1909, and entered Harvard in 1926, at the age of seventeen. One cannot get, either from

Wensberg's book or from anything else I have read, a clear idea of what he was like at seventeen, except that he must have been an unconventional young man. If the various accounts I have heard are to be believed, and I have no reason to doubt them, by his first year in college he had acquired a specific vocation. The precise circumstances of how this happened are, at least to me, vague; and Wensberg's book is, alas, only marginally helpful. On a visit to New York while a freshman at Harvard, Land—so the legend, which may even be true, tells us—had a vision. He was walking in Times Square and was troubled by the glare of all the lights, especially the lights of the automobiles and buses. He decided to do something about it—to invent a way of controlling glare.

Given his precocious interest in physics, he must have known about the use of polarizers of light to reduce the amount of light transmitted through certain optical media; this is something one would find in a freshman physics text. The study of how wave motions are polarized certainly goes back to the beginnings of the study of wave motion itself. We can imagine the creation of a wave by jiggling a jump rope up and down. When a wave is propagated, the direction of the vibration of the wave is not necessarily the same as the direction of propagation. For sound waves it is, and for light waves it is not. In fact, for light waves the oscillations of the wave take place at right angles to the direction of propagation, something that physicists refer to as "transverse wave propagation." (Sound waves are called "longitudinal.") A normal light source produces light with a random mixture of different polarization directions. Our eyes are not sensitive to these different directions of polarization and absorb light with equal ease whatever its polarization. But some materials are sensitive to it. They absorb different polarizations selectively. These materials filter out different directions of polarization, letting through, ideally, only that part of the light beam that has its polarizations lined up just right.

The use of such materials to cut down the transmission of light had been known since the early nineteenth century. Indeed, in 1808, a French physicist named Etienne-Louis Malus discovered that if two such polarizers are put back to back, the amount of light transmitted by the combined system depends on how the polarizers are positioned with respect to each other. In theory, the second polarizer, to take an extreme example, would not transmit any light from the first if its axis were at right angles to that of the first. The first substance "polarizes" the light (in Malus's term), while the second analyzes it. This is the general principle for using polarizers to reduce the transmission of light. But no one had succeeded in making such a material artificially, and no one before Land had given much thought to what one would do with such a material if one had it.

H o w e v e r much Land's vision in Times Square sounds like a publicist's dream, he quit Harvard and moved to New York, at age eighteen, to a basement apartment on West 55th Street, where, apparently supported by his parents, he lived for the next three years and worked on polarization. Why he needed to be in New York, as opposed to Cambridge, to carry out this work is not clear. Wensberg mentions that the New York Public Library had more books than the Widener Library, but this seems a little hollow as an explanation. In any event, Land, it appears, spent his days in the library reading the works of such scientists as the nineteenth-century British chemist William Herapath, who had, in fact, made small artificial crystals that polarized light. Land also found a way to sneak into the Columbia physics laboratories at night, sometimes in the company of his future wife. He also had enough money to hire a technician, Ernest Calabro, who remained with him for the next twenty-five years.

Within three years, Land had produced his first artificial polarizing material. The secret was to use microscopic grains of needle-shaped crystals, which polarize light, and embed them in a lacquer. Land called his new product "Polaroid glass." It "transmits," he said, "almost all the useful light rays," but it contains "a matrix of tiny crystals [that] combs out the tangled waves of light so that they are all vibrating on the same plane. The crystals are so small that you cannot see them. They are suspended in cellulose, all oriented in precisely the same direction."

Land, now twenty and married, returned to Harvard, where he lasted for another two and a half years. He never took his degree. By this time, he had met George Wheelwright III, a physics instructor of independent means six years Land's senior, who suggested that they open their own laboratory. It became the Land-Wheelwright Laboratories; and in 1934, Land was issued his first patent, for manufacturing sheets of polarizing material. By 1937, the name of the company had been changed to Polaroid and Land had become chairman of the board, president, and director of research. Wheelwright ended up as vice president. Wensberg does not tell us whether this transition was amiable. Ironically, in view of a bitter lawsuit Land and Polaroid eventually won in 1985 for patent infringement by Kodak on the Polaroid instant cameras, the first serious customer of the new company was Kodak, which wanted to use the material as filters for camera lenses.

The immediate future of the company had been secured by its alliance with the American Optical Company, which made sunglasses. Polaroid sunglasses became widely used and still are. However, as Wensberg reports, by 1940 the market was saturated, and Polaroid was reduced to selling its product for use in Wurlitzer jukeboxes, where it enhanced visual effects. No car manufacturer had ever made use of Polaroid in its automobile headlights. In fact, if the war had not come along, the Polaroid Corporation might well have gone under. As it was, the company prospered during the war, making a variety of sun goggles for the military and working on the design of heat-seeking missiles.

NONE of this had anything to do with photography. But in December 1943, Land had a second inspiration, now also a part of the Polaroid legend. On a rare vacation with his family in New Mexico, he spent some time with his daughter Jennifer, then three years old, walking around Santa Fe and taking pictures, with Jennifer directing the picture taking. When they got back to where they were staying, Jennifer asked her father about the pictures he had taken: "Why can't I see them now?"

Our knowledge of the circumstances of this question, and what happened next, comes from Land. Since Wensberg quotes from what appears to be Land's published account, one has the impression that he never was able to ask Land about it either. This is what Land wrote:

> As I walked around that charming town [Santa Fe] I undertook the task of solving the puzzle [Jennifer] had set me. Within the hour, the camera, the film, and the physical chemistry became so clear to me that with a great sense of excitement I hurried over to the place where Donald Brown [Land's patent attorney, who was conveniently in Santa Fe] . . . was staying, to describe to him in great detail a dry camera which would give a picture immediately after exposure.

To a *Time* interviewer, Land put things slightly differently. The *Time* story reads: "He now claims jokingly that by the time he and Jennifer returned from their walk, he had solved all the problems 'except for the ones that it has taken from 1943 to 1972 to solve.'"

In 1972, Land introduced the SX-70, the first color "instant" camera. The best simple explanation I know of how this camera works was given by Land in a talk he delivered in 1956 at the Franklin Institute; it has been reprinted in the *Journal of the Franklin Institute* under the somewhat ponderous title "From Imbibition to Exhibition." (At his best, Land was a graceful writer, but writing, one gathers, did not come easily to him, and much of his prose reads that way.) In essence, the idea of one-step photography is to make a sandwich in which a negative and a positive sheet of paper encase an extremely thin layer—0.003 inches in the example Land gave in his 1956 lecture—of a chemical reagent used in developing photographs. The reagent is contained in what Land called a "pod." When the pod is run through the camera, the pressure on it breaks one end, and the fluid runs out between the negative and the positive papers.

It is not difficult to imagine Land having thought up this part of the process. The rest of it took genius. In a conventional camera, the film is made up of silver halide, a compound of a halogen, a nonmetallic chemical element, and another element. When enough light falls on one of the grains of this material, a speck of silver is produced. If chemical developer is applied, silver ions are induced to migrate through the photographic emulsion, where they deposit themselves on the exposed silver speck. This dark silver represents the exposure to light on the negative. The unexposed grains are then washed away with a solvent ("hypo"), and the result is the photographic negative we have all seen. If this sheet is placed in contact with a light-sensitive sheet—the positive paper on which the photograph is printed—and exposed to light, the picture soon appears. This is the normal two-step process that leads from exposing a negative in a camera to producing a photograph.

Land's completely novel idea was to have the negative and the positive made at essentially the same instant. This can be done because the reagent in the pod can transport the unexposed silver ions from the negative across the very narrow gap to the positive. In practice, the positive is doped with a catalyst that has a chemical affinity for silver. Thus, instead of washing away the silver not attached to the negative— the usual procedure—this silver is attached to the positive, creating the positive image essentially simultaneously with the negative image. The dark spots on the negative correspond to the white spots on the positive, since the silver that has attached itself to the negative cannot migrate across to the positive. The silver that the negative cannot retain becomes the basis for the image on the positive. In the original versions of Land's camera, the exposed negative and positive had to be physically separated. In a famous *Life* magazine picture of Land, he is looking at a picture of himself which he is revealing by separating the two sheets.

How much of this process Land envisaged that night in 1943, I do not know, but Nobel prizes have been given for less. (To cite two examples: in 1912, Nils Gustaf Dalén was given the Nobel Prize in physics for a device that automatically regulates lights on lighthouses and buoys; and, more pertinently, in 1908, Gabriel Lippmann was given the Nobel prize in physics for his method of reproducing colors photographically.) In November 1948, the first Land camera went on sale for ninety-five dollars at Jordan Marsh in Boston. It weighed five pounds, took sepia-colored pictures, and was an immediate success. Two years later, Land introduced black-and-white film, and it was a disaster. The film, once removed from the camera, continued to develop itself until the sharp images simply disappeared. To combat this the positive had to be chemically fixed—by hand painting it—which removed any illusion of the process being "one step."

Land then made a decision of the kind that seemed characteristic of him. He decided to go for broke and develop an instant color process in which the resulting print would be fixed once and for all. (It remains unclear from Wensberg's book whether the black-and-white problem was ever really solved.) This effort culminated in 1972 with the introduction of the SX-70, perhaps the most sophisticated invention involving the interaction between camera and film ever achieved. One of the innumerable problems that had to be solved was the battery. Each film pack contains its own battery that runs the automatic focus and the flash lamp. These batteries kept expiring before the film could be used—and still cannot be stored for long without going flat. Polaroid had to develop special batteries.

All of this is clearly described in Wensberg's book, as is the marketing of the camera. (Sir Laurence Olivier, chosen to sell the SX-70 on television, was stymied by the pronunciation of "SX," until he decided it should be "Essex.") Wensberg is also good on Land's break with the Polaroid Corporation. He makes it clear that the same obsessiveness that was at work when he quit Harvard at the age of eighteen to go to

New York to make a polarizer, could be disastrous when his intuition turned out to be wrong.

Land insisted that the SX-70 have a complex viewfinder even though consumer surveys indicated that people didn't like it. His attitude was that they would have to be educated to like it. He apparently never spoke again to the man who reported the market research to him. Even worse was the disaster of Polavision, a soundless system for taking home movies which was introduced at the time home video was taking hold. By 1977, when the system was introduced, Polaroid had spent millions on it, most of which was lost. By 1982, all of Land's ties with the company were severed.

Land's interest in color vision, not discussed at all in Wensberg's book, goes back at least to the 1960s. Like many scientific ideas of great importance Land's theory starts from a phenomenon we all recognize but do not attach much importance to until someone like Land calls our attention to how remarkable it really is. This is what Land and his collaborators call "color constancy." It is a fact of common experience that colors retain something like the same appearance, regardless of how the colored object is illuminated. A blue object, for example, looks recognizably blue when viewed from sunrise to sunset. This ability of the brain to maintain the near constancy of colors, even as the illumination is varied, would give a species that had it an evolutionary advantage. An edible red berry, for example, would look like an edible red berry whether encountered at 8:00 A.M. or at 5:00 P.M.

Land devised an experiment to exhibit this remarkable fact quantitatively. (He showed a version of it to us in Minnesota in 1982.) It involved boards Land called "Mondrians" because they resemble the work of that artist. Paper rectangles of different sizes and different colors are pasted on each board. For the sake of illustration, we can imagine two adjacent rectangles, one red and one white. Each color is associated with a specific wavelength of light. When we say that the rectangle or any other object is red, we mean that it will absorb all the wavelengths of light except red ones and reflect back to our eyes only the red wavelength, and hence look red to us. A white object, on the other hand, reflects back all the wavelengths impinging on it, so no color is singled out, and thus looks white. At least, that is the naïve description. The situation, as Land shows, is much more complicated and involves an act of cerebral perception.

In Land's experiment, the rectangles are illuminated by three colored spotlights—say, red, green, and blue. When this is done, the white rectangle reflects all three colors from the spotlights about equally, while the red rectangle absorbs much of the blue and green light and reflects the red. This is what we would expect.

The surprise comes when one begins to change the intensity of the light coming from the different-colored spotlights. One can adjust the intensity of the spotlights so that the reflected light coming from the red rectangle has just the mixture of intensities that formerly were reflected from the white rectangle. Naïvely speaking, one could say the reflected light is now indistinguishable from white light. One might, therefore, be tempted to think that the red rectangle would now look white, just as one might be tempted to think that a red berry viewed at noon would have a different color from that of a red berry viewed at 9:00 A.M. But this is not what happens, either for the berries or, more dramatically, for the Mondrians, where the light intensities can be precisely adjusted. In both cases, the red object continues to look red.

This presents a difficult problem for any theory of color. We know that on the outer layer of the retina there are visual cells called "cones." (There are also "rods," which have a part in night vision.) Fundamentally there are three types of cone, each one sensitive to wavelengths appropriate to a given primary color. So, for example, approximately a third of the cones respond selectively to red light. (In reality, there is some overlap in the sensitivity of the different cones, or we could not see a color like orange; but that is a nuance that need not concern us here.) It would be tempting to say that we see red when our red cones are stimulated by red light; and that the more they are stimulated, the more red we see. But, then, how do we explain Land's experiment in which a red square still looks red even though it reflects, under suitable illumination, the same mixture of light intensities that made a white square look white? The clear implication is that there must be more to color vision than such a naïve processing of intensities.

That this is the case was made dramatically clear by the work of Oliver Sacks and Robert Wasserman. They studied a painter they call Jonathan I., who lost his sense of color vision when he was injured in a car accident. Elaborate tests showed that his cones were intact. He did not have colorblindness in the usual sense of having defective cones. He was able therefore to register the intensities of different colors when they were presented to him, but he couldn't see the colors. Still, the images he saw looked different to him when the intensities of the spotlights were changed, whereas a person with normal color vision would have noticed no change.

To see color, the brain must therefore be able to do some analysis of visual data beyond simply analyzing the intensities. Land, in collaboration with John J. McCann, suggested such a model, which they called the "retinex theory." Basically the idea is that, by scanning the entire visual area—not, say, one rectangle but the entire Mondrian—the data-processing system responsible for color vision produces three so-called lightnesses: one for short wavelengths, one for medium wavelengths, and one for long wavelengths. It is the combined effect of these lightnesses—a single point in color space, one could say—that determines what color we actually see. I am not enough of an expert on the theory of color vision to describe just how Land's model is to be compared with other models for color constancy, and none of this is to be found in Mr. Wensberg's book. Some day a truly serious biography of Land will be written. It is a pity Land did not do it himself.

CHAPTER 9

Einstein When Young

WHEN ALBERT EINSTEIN DIED, at the age of seventy-six, on 18 April 1955, the terms of his estate had been fixed by a will he had signed five years earlier—on 18 March 1950. The will read, in part, "I give and bequeath all of my manuscripts, copyrights, publication rights, royalties and royalty agreements, and all other literary property and rights, of any and every kind or nature whatsoever, to my Trustees hereinafter named." The two trustees he named were the late Otto Nathan, an economist at Princeton University, who had befriended him when he came to the United States, in the 1930s; and Helen Dukas, Einstein's secretary since 1928. Miss Dukas was really a part of the Einstein household: along with Einstein's stepdaughter, Margot Einstein, she shared his modest house at 112 Mercer Street, not far from the center of Princeton. But Einstein chose Dr. Nathan as the sole executor of the estate; he no doubt wanted the estate to provide an income—a living—for Miss Dukas and his stepdaughter, and felt that Dr. Nathan would be well suited to handling the practical management of his papers. Indeed, Dr. Nathan did, to his credit, proceed to sort out the complicated matters involving copyrights and the like. What Einstein did not anticipate was that Dr. Nathan would set himself up as a sort of arbiter of how the papers would be used by scholars and others. I turned up this side of the coin when, in 1973, I wrote a profile of Einstein for the *New Yorker*. Before giving me permission to use published material controlled by the estate, Dr. Nathan insisted on his right to read (and, presumably, approve) my manuscript—a request I was forced to accede to, since the profile would have suffered irreparably without Einstein's own voice. I felt at that time, and feel now, that this condition went far beyond anything Einstein might have intended, and, indeed, that it was an intolerable intrusion.

While this was going on, I learned that the Princeton University Press, which two years earlier had entered into an agreement with Dr. Nathan to publish a complete collection of the Einstein papers, was having its own troubles: Dr. Nathan had instigated legal proceedings against the press; they were eventually settled by arbitration in 1980, and the settlement effectively removed Dr. Nathan from a position in which he could block the publication of the Einstein papers. In the meantime, Dr. John Stachel, a professor of physics at Boston University, had been engaged as the editor of the papers and, in January of 1977, began readying them for publication. In view of the uncertainties, the project had difficulty raising money. It was saved from bankruptcy by a million-dollar endowment from Harold W. McGraw, Jr.; and the papers themselves, in accordance with Einstein's will, became the responsibility of the Hebrew University of Jerusalem in 1982, which then became the partner of the press in their publication. Finally, in 1987, thirty-two years after Einstein's death, the first volume of what will be at least a thirty-volume series appeared.

In truth, despite all the delays and the publicity surrounding the publication of the papers, it was not an event I anticipated with any special enthusiasm. The reason was that, as far as I knew, the first volume, entitled *The Early Years, 1879–1902,* was going to consist of material that, in one form or another, I had already seen. It is, of course, valuable to have together in one convenient place such items as Einstein's high-school report cards; the affectionate short biography written by his sister, Maja, in 1924; his rejection, in 1901, for combat service in the Swiss Army because of *"Pes planus"* (flat feet); the rather moving advertisement offering private lessons in physics and mathematics which he inserted in a Bern newspaper in 1902 (giving such lessons was almost his only means of support at the time). But it did not seem to me that there would be anything really new—anything that someone who, like me, had been reading the available Einstein literature for decades would find particularly exciting or revelatory. But a few months prior to the publication of the first volume, I was alerted by people close to the project that in fact something remarkable had happened. A cache of some five hundred letters—correspondence between Einstein and his first wife, Mileva Marić, together with letters written by Marić to friends—had been discovered. The letters belong to the Einstein Family Correspondence Trust, of which Dr. Thomas Einstein—the son of the late Hans Albert Einstein, one of the two sons Einstein had with Marić—is the chief trustee. Fifty-one of these letters have been included in *The Early Years* (the others will follow in chronological order), and as far as I am concerned they have transformed what had promised to be a relatively routine scholarly enterprise into a fascinating, almost hypnotic, and, above all, extremely moving human document. As I read these letters, I kept thinking that both for what they revealed and for what they kept just out of sight they were the equivalent of clues in a novel like Nabokov's *Pale Fire*, in which an entire world is hinted at but never quite revealed.

Albert Einstein entered the Eidgenössische Polytechnische Schule— the Swiss Federal Polytechnical School—in Zurich in October 1896, at the age of seventeen. He was slightly younger than his classmates, among whom was Mileva Marić, three years his senior. She was born in Titel, in an area of southern Hungary that is now part of Yugoslavia. Her parents were Greek Orthodox. None of the letters cast any light on how she made her way to the polytechnical school. That cannot have been a trivial accomplishment, because there was a stiff entrance examination; Einstein himself had failed the section on general knowledge a year earlier. Zurich was then a city in which liberal tendencies flourished, and the school was one of the few places in continental Europe where a woman could be educated in science. The first of the letters is from Marić. It is written from Heidelberg the following fall (1897), after she had temporarily withdrawn from the school and was auditing courses at the University of Heidelberg. It is clear from this letter that she and Einstein had already begun their friendship. (In quoting from it and the other letters, I will use a translation from the German—all the letters are printed in the original language—provided by the Princeton University Press. The translations, which seem adequate, were done by Anna Beck and Peter Havas, and are available as a paperback supplement to purchasers of the book. Many of the letters are written in a kind of slang, and the translators have tried to preserve that flavor; when puns and the like seem untranslatable, they say so.) In this letter, Marić writes:

My father gave me some tobacco to take with me and I was supposed to hand it to you, he wanted so much to whet your appetite for our little country of brigands. I talked with him about you, you absolutely must come with me someday. The marvelous conversations you would have here! But I will take over the role of interpreter. But I cannot send it [presumably, the tobacco] to you, you would have to pay duty on it, and then you would curse me along with my present.

Despite the familiar tone of the letter, it is written employing the formal *Sie*. At the end of it, there is a brief mention of physics; and, indeed, this became a characteristic of their correspondence—a continual mixing of physics and the personal. This has led several of the commentators on these letters to remark that Einstein and Marić had a kind of collaboration in physics, and some of what Einstein later writes to her seems to bear this out.

In the next letter, written by Einstein from Zurich the following February, also using the formal *Sie*, and beginning *"Geehrtes Fräulein!"*—"Esteemed Miss"—he congratulates her on having decided to return to her studies at the school, which she does the following April. By August 1899, the letters—written by Einstein to Marić when he is on vacation with his mother and sister—have taken on a more intimate tone. He addresses her as "L.D.," for *Liebes Dockerl*—"Dear Little Doll." There are tantalizing glimpses of what is obviously a developing personal relationship. For example, he writes, "To be sure, in our place in Zurich you are the mistress of the house, which is not bad either, and of what a marvelous household at that!" They are certainly not yet living together, so it is not clear what this refers to. In these letters, Einstein sends the affectionate greetings of his mother and sister; there is not a hint of the storm of animosity that was about to descend. The situation appears to be relatively innocent—two young students happy in each other's company. But by the year 1900—Einstein's final year at the polytechnical school—their relationship had blossomed into a love affair. Marić writes, "Since I like you so much and you are so far away that I cannot give you a kiss, I am writing this little letter and am asking you whether you like me as much as I do you? Answer me *immediately*. Thousand kisses from your D."

By this time, both Einstein's mother and his sister have become seriously alarmed. It is not entirely clear what they have against Marić. The fact that she is older than Einstein is brought up, and so is the fact that she has not been able to obtain her diploma. She has taken the final examination twice, and both times she has failed it. Perhaps their objections are based on the difference in religion or cultural background, or perhaps on some feeling so deep and instinctive that they are unable to fully articulate it. As is widely recognized, Einstein had a stubborn side to his character—the tenacity of a mule, as he sometimes put it. In the matter of his relationship with Marić, he simply dug in his heels and decided to go his own way. There is a remarkable description in a letter he writes to her in July of 1900:

We come home, I into Mama's room (just the two of us). First I have to tell her about the examination [the first one that Marić failed], then she asks me quite innocently: "So, what will become of Dockerl?" "My wife," say I, equally innocently, but prepared for a real "scene." This then ensued immediately. Mama threw herself on the bed, buried her head in the pillow, and cried like a child. After she had recovered from the initial shock, she immediately switched to a desperate offensive: "You are ruining your future and blocking your path through life." "That woman cannot gain entrance to a decent family." "If she gets a child, you'll be in a pretty mess." At this last outburst, which had been preceded by several others, my patience finally gave out. I rejected the suspicion [that] we had been living in sin with all my might, scolded properly and was just ready to leave the room when Mama's friend Mrs. Bär entered the room, a small, lively little woman full of life, such a sort of hen of the nicest kind. Thereupon we immediately started to talk with the greatest eagerness about the weather, new spa guests, ill-behaved children, etc. Then we went to eat, after that we played some music. When we said "good night" to each other in private, the same story started again, but "più piano." Next day things were already better, and this, as she herself said, for the following reason: "If they have not yet had intimate relations (so much dreaded by her) and will wait so long, then ways and means will surely be found." Only what is most terrible for her is that we want to stay together always. Her attempts at converting me were based on speeches like: "She is a book like you—but you ought to have a wife." "When you'll be 30, she'll be an old hag," etc. But as she sees that in the meanwhile she is accomplishing nothing except to make me angry, she has given up the "treatment" for the time being.

By the spring of 1901, Marić and Einstein were going off on short vacation trips together, and it must have been then that Marić became pregnant. There is a casual reference in one of Einstein's letters to her to the "child and the [child] mood." It is clear that Einstein wanted to marry her—he did so in 1903—but had no way to support her. From the time of his graduation from the polytechnical school, in the spring of 1900, until June 1902, when he was appointed a technical expert third class at the patent office in Bern, he was unable to find a proper job. In a letter Marić wrote to her friend Helene Savić in the fall of 1901, she explains the reasons for this as lucidly and succinctly as they have ever been explained: "It is not likely that he will soon get a secure position; you know that my sweetheart has a very wicked tongue and is a Jew into the bargain." (The German reads: *"Du weisst mein Schatz hat ein sehr böses Maul und ist obendrein ein Jude."* *Maul* is the equivalent of "maw"—an animal's mouth—and *böses* can be translated as "nasty.") The fact that Einstein's manner at this time was irritating to many people, including his teachers, has been well known, but we have it here from the woman who loved him.

At the end of that year, Marić went back to Hungary to have her baby. Einstein did not accompany her—something that I find odd. He certainly loved her, at least then. ("I always find that I am in the best company when I am alone, except when I am with you.") Yet, for whatever reasons, he let her return to her home by herself—which must have been very painful for her—to await the birth of their child. In January 1902, a girl, whom they called Lieserl (a diminutive of Liese), was born. Perhaps the most remarkable letter in the collection is the one Einstein wrote to Marić after he received a letter from her father announcing the birth. It had been, apparently, a difficult labor:

> Poor, dear sweetheart, you must suffer enormously if you cannot even write to me yourself! And our dear Lieserl too must get to know the world from this aspect right from the beginning! I hope that you will be up and around again by the time my letter arrives. I was scared out of my wits when I got your father's letter, because I had already suspected some trouble. . . . But you see, it has really turned out to be a Lieserl, as you wished. Is she healthy and does she already cry properly? What kind of little eyes does she have? Whom of us two does she resemble more? Who is giving her milk? Is she hungry? And so is she completely bald? I love her so much & I don't even know her yet! Couldn't she be photographed once you are totally healthy again? Will she soon be able to turn her eyes toward something? Now you can make observations. I would like once to produce a Lieserl myself, it must be so interesting! She certainly can cry already, but to laugh she'll learn much later. Therein lies a profound truth.

To this letter Einstein appended a sort of schematic drawing of his room in Bern. It resembles the kind of drawing he often made later when he was describing his *Gedanken* experiments—the "thought" experiments in which he envisioned how physics might look in various situations. In this diagram, he labels the parts of his room with letters, as in "B = Betterl" ("little bed"), and "b = Bilderl" ("little picture"). The thought experiment here seems to involve how Marić and Lieserl can be made to fit into this room. He never actually asks Marić to come and live with him; and by the time they do get married, a year later, Lieserl has disappeared. Dr. Stachel tells us in an introduction that no one involved with the Einstein papers has been able to trace what happened to her or to discover whether Einstein ever saw her. Without the evidence of a handful of letters, she might never have existed.

What, then, is one to make of all this? At the age of sixty-seven, Einstein undertook to write something like an autobiography, and there is no mention in it of either Marić or any of his children; indeed, in it he talks about his lifelong attempt to free himself from the "chains of the 'merely personal.' " On their face, these letters appear to show Einstein in the toils of the "merely-personal." I say "on their face" because in almost all his letters physics is not far away. The letters are full of casual comments on his developing ideas in physics—comments that will keep historians of science busy for years. The letters in this volume and those to come will also keep biographers of Einstein busy for years. For example, the notion given in *Einstein: The Life and Times,* by Ronald W. Clark, that Einstein "tumbled into marriage, almost by accident, possibly while thinking of more important things" seems now disputable. As these often anguished letters show, there was a time when his relation to Marić was—his physics apart—the most important thing in his life. Eventually, it went sour. They were divorced in 1919, and had been separated for several years before that. In *Einstein: His Life and Times,* Philipp Frank, who knew them a few years after they were married, wrote, "For Einstein life with her was not always a source of peace and happiness. When he wanted to discuss with her his ideas, which came to him in great abundance, her response was so slight that he was often unable to decide whether or not she was interested." By this time, Marić had borne two sons, and may well have had little or no time to be interested in physics. However, the letters collected in this volume suggest that in the early days Einstein thought of Marić almost as a collaborator in physics. He keeps referring to "our theory" and to how the two of them will test it. But as far as I know, he never made any mention, in any paper he wrote, of a collaboration with her. The letters show that as early as 1899 he was corresponding with Marić about the electrodynamics of moving bodies—the eventual title of his 1905 relativity paper. Yet in that paper he thanks, for "loyal assistance," his "friend and colleague" the engineer Michele Besso, to whom he is "indebted . . . for several valuable suggestions." Discrepancies of this sort are the reason I find these early letters so compelling. Through them we get as close to the young Einstein as we are ever going to. Still, he remains—at least to me—as much of an enigma as before.

CHAPTER 10

The Merely Personal

In 1968, James Watson published his widely acclaimed autobiographical account of the discovery of the structure of DNA—*The Double Helix*. "Widely acclaimed" probably does not do justice to its impact. Many people were outright scandalized. One of the things that appeared to exercise them was the not overly surprising fact that Watson seemed to have a sizable interest in persons of the other gender—women—and was prepared to write about it, in an ostensibly *scientific* autobiography, with what people at the time regarded as too much candor. Here are a couple of the kind of *osé* passages that upset many of Watson's readers.

There was no restraint in Francis' enthusiasms about young women [Francis is Francis Crick, Watson's collaborator]—that is, as long as they showed some vitality and were distinctive in any way that permitted gossip and amusement. When young he saw little of women and was only now discovering the sparkle they added to life. Odile [Crick's wife] did not mind this predilection, seeing that it went along with, and probably helped, his emancipation from the dullness of his Northampton upbringing. They would talk at length about the somewhat artsy-craftsy world in which Odile moved and into which they were frequently invited. No choice event was kept out of our conversation and he would show equal gusto in telling of his occasional mistakes. One occurred when there was a costume party and he went looking like a young G. B. Shaw in a full red beard. As soon as he entered he realized that it was a ghastly error, since not one of the young women enjoyed being tickled by the wet scraggly hairs when he came within kissing distance.

Here is another, even more risqué, fragment:

> Our conversation instead centered upon a young art student then about to marry Odile's friend Harmut Weil. This capture was mildly displeasing to Francis. It was about to remove the prettiest girl from their party circle. Moreover, there was more than one thing cloudy about Harmut. He had come out of a German university tradition that believed in dueling. There was also his undeniable skill in persuading numerous Cambridge women to pose for his camera.

Watson's book—as timorous as it seems in retrospect—opened a kind of floodgate of scientific confessions. At the present time—and this is the main subject of these remarks—we are all but drowning in biographies and autobiographies of scientists who seem almost desperately eager to tell us a lot more about themselves than we really want to, or probably should, know. Before I turn to this, let me point out that both Watson's confession, and its antithesis—the scientific autobiography that tells us next to nothing about the personal life of the scientist—have distinguished precedents.

The great sixteenth-century astronomer Johannes Kepler maintained a kind of horoscopic diary. In later life, incidentally, Kepler made his living to some extent—a little like consulting—by drawing horoscopes. To what extent he believed in them is not clear. In any event, here are a few entries from Kepler's horoscope:

> On the birth of Johann Kepler. I have investigated the matter of my conception, which took place in the year 1571, May 16, at 4:37 A.M. . . . . My weakness at birth removes the suspicion that my mother was already pregnant at the marriage, which was the 15th of May. . . . Thus I was born premature, at thirty-two weeks, after 224 days, ten hours. . . .
>
> 1575 [age four] I almost died of small pox, was in very ill health, and my hands were badly crippled. . . .
>
> 1585–86 [age fourteen–fifteen] During these two years, I suffered continually from skin ailments, often severe sores, often from the scabs of putrid wounds in my feet which healed badly and kept breaking out again. On the middle finger of my right hand I had a worm, on the left a huge sore. . . .

1592 [age twenty-one] I went down to Weil and lost a quarter florin at gambling.... At Cupinga's I was offered union with a virgin; on New Year's Eve I achieved this with the greatest possible difficulty, experiencing the most acute pains of the bladder.

That is autobiography! Or what about this bit of self-analysis:

That man [this is Kepler referring to himself] has in every way a dog-like nature. His appearance is that of a little lap-dog. His body is agile, wiry and well-proportioned. Even his appetites were alike: he liked gnawing bones and dry crusts of bread, and was so greedy that whatever his eyes chanced on he grabbed; yet, like a dog, he drinks little and is content with the simplest food. His habits were similar. He continually sought the goodwill of others, was dependent on others for everything, ministered to their wishes, never got angry when they reproved him and was anxious to get back into their favour. He was constantly on the move, ferreting among the sciences, politics and private affairs, including the lowest kind; always following someone else, and imitating his thoughts and actions. He is bored with conversation, but greets his visitors just like a little dog; yet when the last thing is snatched away from him, he flares up and growls. He tenaciously persecutes wrong-doers—that is he barks at them. He is malicious and bites people with his sarcasms. He hates many people exceedingly and they avoid him, but his masters are fond of him. He has a dog-like horror of baths, tinctures and lotions. His recklessness knows no limits, which is surely due to Mars in quadrature with Mercury, and in trine with the moon.

If this is the "anode" of scientific autobiography, then the "cathode" must surely be Einstein's *Autobiographical Notes*, written when he was sixty-seven. Indeed, by its fourth paragraph Einstein makes it clear that the whole point of his having chosen science as his life's work was to free himself from what he calls the "merely personal"—autobiography. The conjunction of the words *merely* and *personal* is enough to set off rockets:

It is quite clear to me that the religious paradise of youth . . . was a first attempt to free myself from the chains of the "merely personal," from an existence which is dominated by wishes, hopes and primitive feelings. Out yonder there was this huge world, which exists independently of us as human beings and which stands before us like a great eternal riddle, at least partially accessible to our inspection and thinking. The contemplation of this world beckoned like a liberation, and I soon noticed that many a man whom I had learned to esteem and to admire had found inner freedom and security in devoted occupation with it. . . . The road to this paradise was not as comfortable and alluring as the road to the religious paradise, but it has proved itself as trustworthy, and I have never regretted having chosen it.

Given Einstein's apparent disdain—even contempt—for the "merely personal," one is not surprised to find that his autobiography has very little to do with the details of his actual life. For example, there is no mention at all of either of his two wives or his two sons, to say nothing of his illegitimate daughter. What the autobiography does contain is a wonderful account of how he came upon various of his great ideas in physics—his discovery of the relativity theory, for example. Indeed, when one finishes reading it, one asks oneself if there is anything more that needs to be said. This question is particularly acute if one happens to be embarked on the project of writing a biography of Einstein, which was my situation some years ago. I decided that there was more to be said. (In any case, I said more, since I wrote the biography.) In the first place, Einstein's *Autobiographical Notes* is extremely technical. I doubt that it is fully accessible to anyone who is not a professional physicist. For this reason alone, I think one has, if one is able, an obligation to make this intellectual history available to a wider audience. Einstein was one of the great treasures of our century, and anyone who is interested should have the opportunity to understand some of his ideas and achievements. In the second place, Einstein was not able to detach himself fully from the "merely personal" either. He did, after all, marry twice. But his life *was* a wonderful moral example. We all need heroes, and if one takes Einstein as one's hero one will not do too badly. In fact, to write a biography of Einstein that tries to "humanize" him by showing his faults—his "humanness" in some trivial sense—misses the point. There are a few people who are simply better than most people—"the inconvenient saints," in T. S. Eliot's phrase; and to try to make them less than they were, less different than they were, distorts what they were. This is what so many historians of science found so offensive about Roland Clark's biography, *Einstein: The Life and Times*. The title, incidentally, bears an uncanny relation to the title of Philipp Frank's wonderful biography, *Einstein: His Life and Times*. The last paragraph of Clark's book is a perfect précis of what is wrong with it:

Perhaps he [Einstein] should not have been so bearish about people? Perhaps he should never have gone to Berlin, made the way so much easier for the aggressors with his pacifism, or hated the Germans so much that he encouraged Roosevelt into the nuclear age? Perhaps he should not always have put science first? [Maybe he should have taken up ballroom dancing?] But on this there was, of course, no room for doubt, no cause for regret. As he took two deep breaths and died, it is unlikely that Einstein regretted much. [It is also unlikely that Clark was there to observe this bathetic scene.] But Mrs. Rozel [the night nurse in the hospital] did not understand his German. And anyway, as Elsa [Einstein's second wife, with whom Clark is now on a first-name basis] had felt nearly twenty years before, dear God, it was too late now. [Dear God! is right.]

As I mentioned earlier, my real concern here is to discuss the flood of confessional scientific biographies and autobiographies that Watson's *Double Helix* appears to have turned loose. In the following paragraphs are quotations from two recent examples. I will simply give the quotations after identifying the books and describing very briefly their subjects and save most of the commentary for later.

Salvador Luria, who won the Nobel Prize for medicine in 1969, was Watson's principal scientific mentor when Watson was a student at the University of Indiana. In the introduction to his autobiography, *A Slot Machine, A Broken Test Tube,* Luria makes it quite clear that he regards *The Double Helix* as a model of what a scientific autobiography should be: "If an autobiography is to be more than a superficial record of events, it must be something of a confession." But a confession of what? Here are two paragraphs taken from near the end of the book.

The story of my depressions, which caused much suffering to me and to my family, ought to be told in some detail, if only for the purposes of medical history. Depressive episodes of various intensities and durations came at intervals of several months for three decades, demanding of me a staggering effort, while they lasted, to keep functioning at a more or less normal pace. Over twenty years, at different times and in different cities, by psychiatrists and psychologists, I was subjected to psychotherapy of various ilks, from Freudian psychoanalysis to less doctrinaire treatments. I was exposed over those years to what I saw then and see now as a series of intellectually vacuous interactions claiming to have therapeutic validity. Only my suffering and a sense of duty to seek treatment justified my willingness to persist. What seems to me unforgivable is that even when, in the 1960's, antidepressive medication became available it was either not prescribed for me or prescribed in preposterously small doses, fifty times smaller than was used by competent practitioners, as I later found out.

I might still be suffering under pointless treatment by some psychotherapist if a major depressive attack had not brought me into the hands of a competent psychiatrist. Three months of adequate doses of antidepressant drugs followed by long-term lithium treatment have freed me of all symptoms of depression for the past ten years, adding a new dimension to my enjoyment of life and making my family life serene, relieved from fear of impending depressions.

I pass from these paragraphs to the other example, withholding, for the moment, any comment.

This example I take from Richard P. Feynman's book called *"Surely You're Joking, Mr. Feynman!"* Feynman was, perhaps, the most original genius produced in theoretical physics since the war. He won the Nobel Prize for physics in 1965. He is, as this book makes abundantly clear, an incredible character. The book appears to be the transcription of a number of tape-recorded conversations that Feynman had with a friend of his named Richard Leighton. Each conversation has its own chapter; and put together, they make a kind of mosaic of Feynman's life and times. This quotation is taken from a chapter called "You Just *Ask* Them?":

When I was back at Cornell in the fall, I was dancing with the sister of a grad student, who was visiting from Virginia. She was very nice, and suddenly I got this idea: "Let's go to a bar and have a drink," I said.

On the way to the bar I was working up the nerve to try the master's lesson on an *ordinary* girl. [The "master" was the master of ceremonies in a small nightclub in New Mexico Feynman had once encountered.] After all you don't feel so bad disrespecting a bar girl who's trying to get you to buy her drinks—but a nice, ordinary, Southern girl?

We went into the bar, and before I sat down, I said, "Listen, before I buy you a drink, I want to know one thing: Will you sleep with me tonight?"

"Yes."

So it worked even with an ordinary girl! But no matter how effective the lesson was, I never really used it after that. I didn't enjoy doing it that way. But it was interesting to know that things worked much differently from how I was brought up.

What these examples have in common is that they are taken out of context. But they are out of context in the same sense that a sore thumb is out of context, and to the same effect. One can't, in a manner of speaking, stop staring at them. Good writers have, as a rule, some sort of internal gyroscope that tells them at what point the material is about to tip over and bring the entire enterprise crashing down. The authors here are both professional scientists and do not seem to possess this faculty. Do we, referring to Luria's book, really need to know that he has been taking lithium for the last ten years for his depressions? Luria's book is one in the series sponsored by the Alfred P. Sloan Foundation in aid of, as the preface says, the "public understanding of science." This charter, one might have thought, would provide some useful guidance to the book's contents. And Feynman. In much of his book, Feynman takes enormous pleasure in describing his avocations—*hobbies* is much too light a word—such as drawing and music, where he has made real achievements. Since he wanted his drawings to be judged for what they were and not because he was Feynman, he took to signing them "Ofey." He writes: "I didn't want people to buy my drawings because the professor of physics isn't supposed to be able to draw, isn't that wonderful." But isn't Feynman's anecdote about the Southern girl a perfect example of "the professor of physics" doing something he is not supposed to know how to do? If that anecdote had been told to one by a taxi driver, would one have given a damn, let alone put it in a book? I, at least, find the Swiftian tones of Kepler's "That man has in every way a dog-like nature" much more palatable—indeed, even high art. But then Kepler was, in addition to being a great astronomer, a truly marvelous writer. In fact, his *Somnium: Sive Astronomia Lunaris*— usually translated simply as *Dream*—was the first great science fantasy. Perhaps scientists writing about themselves, and other scientists, should keep in mind that more not only can be less, but also can be disastrous.

All of this having been said, I think there are some examples from the recent literature where both the Scylla of the "merely personal" and the Charybdis of the totally impersonal have been avoided; the result is some first-class writing about scientists and their lives. Let me close by discussing two such works: *Hackers* by Steven Levy and *The Periodic Table* by Primo Levi. (I have no reason to suppose that the two authors are related.) The books have in common that they were both written by people one might describe as professional—or, at the very least, seri-ous—writers, although for many years, Primo Levi earned his living as a chemist. Steven Levy writes for *Rolling Stone*.

The use of the terms *hack, hacking,* and *hacker* in the sense of Levy's book seems to have developed at MIT in the 1950s. It is difficult to give an entirely precise definition of what a *hack* is. It is more than a "trick." It is a very elegant way of doing something—solving something—that a priori might seem undoable or unsolvable or even uncreatable. The German word *witz* conveys the same idea, if one happens to know German. A person who is able to hack consistently comes to be regarded as a hacker. I see it as a designation with broad applications. Glenn Gould and Duke Ellington were hackers, as was Mozart. Beethoven wasn't. Nabokov and Thomas Pynchon were and are hackers. Socrates was and Aristotle wasn't. Kant certainly wasn't. As my friend Marvin Minsky, who was regarded by a whole generation of MIT students as the king of the computer hackers, once noted, "If you do enough hacking you often get something profound." This was certainly true of Mozart.

Levy's book deals with what might be called the rise and fall of computer hacking in this country. The book begins and ends at MIT, as is only fitting. In the early 1960s, almost no one imagined that computers would ever be a part of the household furniture; they were humongous machines presided over by acolytes. A few visionaries— originally people like Alan Turing and von Neumann, and later, younger people like Minsky—had the idea that these machines might, if iterated, become models of ourselves, our thinking, problem-solving selves. Turing even invented a fanciful test to help decide whether, and when, that had happened; the criterion was that if an entity, which is generally agreed to be human, cannot decide from the output whether a second entity is a human or a machine, then the second entity has passed its "Turing test." For better or worse, no machine has yet passed.

The following paragraph from Levy's book is both an illustration of its style and an explanation of why hacking took hold at MIT. To set the scene: a sixteen-year-old freshman named Jerry Sussman arrived there in the middle 1960s. Like most of the future hackers, he had spent his high-school years being what Levy calls an "electronic junkie." One of the first things he did was to seek out the large computer. There was a man working on it who seemed to belong there, so Sussman asked if he, too, could fool around with the computer. He was told to go ahead and try. Here is what happened:

Sussman began working on a program. Not long after, this odd-looking bald guy comes over. Sussman figured the guy was going to boot him out, but instead the man sat down, asking, "Hey, what are you doing?" Sussman talked over his program with the man, Marvin Minsky. At one point in the discussion, Sussman told Minsky that he was using a certain randomizing technique in his program because he didn't want the machine to have any preconceived notions. Minsky said, "Well it has them, it's just that you don't know what they are." It was the most profound thing Jerry Sussman had ever heard. And Minsky continued, telling him that the world is built a certain way, and the most important thing we can do with the world is avoid randomness, and figure out ways things can be planned. Wisdom like this had its effect on sixteen-year-old freshmen, and from then on Sussman was hooked.

Over the next few years Minsky built his laboratory into one of the most powerful computer centers in the world. It was also a very open place. *Proprietary* was an obscene word. Part of the hacker ethic was that everyone had a right to know what everyone else was doing. This is one reason hackers spent so much time and energy breaking into secret computer programs. The other reason was that it was a lot of fun. It is no longer regarded as fun, and one can go to jail for it.

This Eden could not last. Ironically, its downfall was caused by the hackers themselves, especially the California hackers in the person of Steve Wozniak and the Homebrew computer club that met in the mid-1970s in various places in what became known, not long after, as Silicon Valley—not far from San Francisco. By the time Wozniak— known in the trade as "Woz"—had finished high school, he was already *designing* computers. After a couple of desultory years at Berkeley where, among other things, he designed, and attempted to sell, "blue boxes"— electronic devices that could be used to make long-distance phone calls for free (Wozniak used *his* to attempt to call the Pope), Wozniak went to work for Hewlett-Packard. In his spare time, he designed computer games for Atari, where his high-school friend Steven Jobs was then employed. That Wozniak is a hacker is beyond any doubt. The case of Jobs is harder to call. After reading Levy's book and a related one called *The Little Kingdom* by Michael Moritz—which also deals, in more detail, with Wozniak and Jobs—I have decided that Jobs was, and is, one of the greatest salesmen who has ever lived. He persuaded Wozniak to put together the computer he had designed, and then began to sell them. Needless to say, the computer was what is now known as the Apple II, and the rest, as they say, is history.

Once the personal computer was launched, and this certainly was a consequence of the incredible success of the Apple, there had to be a reason for people to use them. Enter the computer game. This, too, had its origins with the hackers. In the 1960s, a game called Spacewar was created at MIT. It was designed to run on a large mainframe computer. Before the hackers got tired of it, they had added every conceivable wrinkle, including an extra "sun" that provided a hazardous gravitational field. The tapes were given away to anyone who wanted a copy and also had a mainframe computer to run them on. But after the success of the Apple, it became clear that *everyone* could have a facility on which to play games. The problem was to create them. Here the motivation was pure profit. The first of the great computer game entrepreneurs, Ken Williams, is quoted by Mr. Levy as saying, "I guess greed would summarize me better than anything. I always want more." Williams's wife, Roberta, created the first commercially successful computer game, Mystery House, and then followed it with an even more successful one called The Wizard and the Princess. It sold over sixty thousand copies at $32.95 a copy. Levy notes that the Williamses used to sit in their newly installed hot tub in California and "shake their heads, saying, 'Do you believe this?' " It was, in some sense, the end of the era of the hackers. There appears, however, to be at least one survivor; and Levy ends his book with a tale about him, one Richard Stallman. He came to MIT in 1971 and, by the 1980s, had decided that the whole hacker ethic was dead or dying. He spent his last years at MIT re-creating commercial programs in order to give them away. As one of the MIT establishment noted with awe, "In a fairly real sense he's been outhacking the whole bunch of them." This is a fine, strange, funny book and, I think, demonstrates that Levy is himself a hacker.

Primo Levi's book is something else again. I have long thought that there are two "limiting cases"—as the mathematicians would say—of autobiographies. One could imagine an individual who was a meticulous observer of almost nothing at all, someone who had led a perfectly ordinary life, but who had observed it so closely and deeply that he or she could make it fascinating. On the other hand, one could imagine someone who had a fantastically interesting life but whose perceptions of it were essentially trivial; some mountain climbers fall into this class. Nonetheless, the autobiography of such a person could be, and sometimes is, fascinating simply because of the events themselves. Primo Levi falls into a third class—the best and rarest of classes—

someone who has led a profound and deep life and whose perceptions of it are equally profound and deep.

When one reads him, one has the sense of being in the hands of a real writer for whom the "merely personal" becomes something else—something that in the hands of the nonwriter turns to dross (see chapter 11).

When, for example, Primo Levi writes, "I was in a laboratory with two other skilled prisoners, similar to those educated slaves that the rich Romans imported from Greece," one knows one is in the hands of a master.

The lesson for the scientist who wants to write about himself or other scientists is, in my view, summarized by one of the few aphorisms of Wittgenstein I really understand: "Whereof one cannot speak, thereof one must be silent [Wovon man nicht sprechen kann, daruber muss man schweigen]."

CHAPTER 11

The Chemistry of
Primo Levi

SOMETIME IN 1984 I was sent the *The Periodic Table*, by Primo Levi, for review. (The Italian original, *Il Sistema Periodico* had been published by Einaudi some nine years earlier.) I had never heard of Primo Levi and assumed that any book entitled *The Periodic Table* was likely to be about the Russian chemist Dimitry Mendeleev who, in 1869, made the discovery that if the chemical elements are arranged in a table in order of increasing atomic weight, then there are periodicities in their observed chemical properties. For example, the so-called noble gases such as helium, neon, and argon, occur in the second, the tenth, and the eighteenth places, respectively. That as an American, an American Jew, I had not heard of Primo Levi at that time was not, I believe, unusual. Indeed, when I tried to obtain Levi's two books that preceded *The Periodic Table*—*Survival in Auschwitz* and *The Reawakening*—I discovered that they were unavailable here, and had to order them from England. The American publisher of *The Periodic Table,* Schocken Books, must also have had difficulty in locating American authors who had heard of Primo Levi, since all the quotations on the back of the book jacket are by Italians: Umberto Eco, Italo Calvino, and Natalia Ginzburg. The use of a quotation from Natalia Ginzburg is somewhat ironic since she had, as a reader for Einaudi, turned down—for reasons she herself does not now understand—*Survival in Auschwitz* when it was first submitted in 1946. She was not alone. Several other Italian publishers also turned it down. In 1947, the small publishing house of De Silva brought it out in an edition of twenty-five hundred copies and then went out of business. The book was saved from oblivion by a reissue in 1958 by Einuadi; and its success—it has by now sold well over five hundred thousand copies in Italy alone—encouraged Levi to write its successor *The Reawakening,* which was published by Einaudi in 1963. Of the myriads of books written about the Holocaust, Primo Levi's memoirs and, above all *Survival in Auschwitz,* are surely among the greatest.

As I have mentioned, when I opened *The Periodic Table* I expected to find a book about chemistry. What I did find, and this is really the subject matter of this essay, is a book that could have been written only by a chemist. Indeed, as I will point out, it was Primo Levi's chemistry that both saved his life in Auschwitz and made him the particular kind of writer he was. Primo Levi died in 1987 under circumstances I will discuss later. As readers of *The Periodic Table* know, it is a book that is organized around twenty-one chemical elements ranging from argon to zinc. (The order in which these evocations are arranged in the book by element does not follow any plan discernible to me.) Like Proust's *madeleine* cake dipped in tea, each of these elements brings forth a set of memories. What is striking about these associations, at least to me, is the intimacy of Levi's feelings about each of the elements. It is a feeling that is the special province of chemists whose job it is to identify and rearrange these often very rare entities; who know them by sight, by feel, by smell, and often by taste. It is a very different feeling from that a physicist would have toward an element: to him, it is a more or less abstract collection of neutrons, protons, and electrons circulating in their quantum-mechanical orbits. I can imagine a physicist writing as Levi does of someone in *The Reawakening:* "He was a wonderfully equipped person. Intelligence and cunning radiated from him like energy from radium, with the same silent and penetrating continuity, without a pause, without a sign of exhaustion, in all directions at once." But only a chemist could write as Levi does in *The Periodic Table* under the entry "Nickel":

> I fell in love with my work [in a mine where an attempt was being made to extract nickel] from the very first day, although it entailed nothing more at that stage than quantitative analysis of rock samples: attack with hydrofluoric acid, down comes iron with ammonia, down comes nickel (how little! a pinch of red sediment) with dimethylglyoxime, down comes magnesium with phosphate—always the same, every blessed day—in itself, it was not

very stimulating. But stimulating and new was another sensation: the sample to be analyzed was no longer an anonymous, manufactured powder, a materialized quiz: it was a piece of rock, the earth's entrail, torn from the earth by the explosive's force; and on the basis of the daily data of the analysis little by little was born a map, the portrait of the subterranean veins. For the first time after seventeen years of schoolwork, of Greek verbs and the history of the Peloponnesian War, the things I had learned were beginning to be useful to me. Quantitative analysis, so devoid of emotion, heavy as granite, came alive, true, useful, when part of serious and concrete work. It was useful: it was part of a plan, a tessera in a mosaic.

Most of Primo Levi's writing is autobiographical, but surprisingly little of it contains biography. Nowhere, so far as I know, does one learn the name of his wife, the circumstances of their marriage, even whether he had any children. Nowhere does one learn the name of the chemical factory in Turin which he managed until he retired in 1977, at the age of fifty-eight, in order to write full time. Most of his fellow prisoners in Auschwitz are identified by only their first names. It is a surprise when suddenly a last name appears—such as that of Leonardo de Benedetti, a fellow Jew from Turin, a doctor, who somehow survived a year of manual labor in Auschwitz, and returned to practice in Turin. He appears as Leonardo in *The Reawakening* and is only completely identified in the "Afterword" to the 1986 edition of the book. It is by paying careful attention—by reading back and forth among his works—that one glimpses "the subterranean veins" of Primo Levi's life. I am not sure why he adopted this style of writing, but it may be the reticence of someone whose principle profession was not writing. I can fully empathize with this, having myself found my way into writing by way of a career in physics. Indeed, one of the reasons that Primo Levi's writing means so much to me is that I can see so much of myself in him. We got our respective Ph.D.'s at about the same age; had about the same inexperience with women; felt about the same indifference to our religious heritage; even discovered mountain climbing at about the same age. (Primo Levi describes this experience in a chapter called "Iron" in *The Periodic Table*. He learned to climb with a fellow student Sandro Delmastro—one of the few people given a last name—who became one of the first partisans to be killed in the Italian resistance.) We also shared the same revulsion and ineptness in the face of violence. Suppose our lives had been interchanged, and I, at the age of twenty-five, had suddenly found myself in Auschwitz—could I have survived?

As I have mentioned, apart from a rude mountaineer's physique, that Primo Levi survived Auschwitz can be traced back, in a whole variety of ways, to chemistry. He was captured by the Fascist militia on 13 December 1943. His small group of partisans had been betrayed by an informer. During the subsequent interrogations, he admitted to being an "Italian citizen, of Jewish race." As such, he was sent to a detention center, Fossoli, near Modena and, along with some six hundred fellow Italian Jews, turned over to the German SS for deportation to Auschwitz. On 22 February 1944, his group, packed into sealed box cars, with "only" some fifty to a car (in many of the deportations there were a hundred and fifty, or more, to a car), began the many-day trip to Auschwitz. It was the first such convoy of Jews to leave from Fossoli. Knowing nothing of what lay in store, the deportees brought food, but no water and no latrine facilities. In one of the magnificent essays in his wonderful collection entitled *The Drowned and the Saved* (the collection, published in Italy in 1986, contains some of the greatest of Primo Levi's writing), an essay entitled "Useless Violence," he writes:

> It was our paradoxical luck (although I hesitate to write this word in this context) that in our car were also two young mothers with their infants of a few months and one of them had brought along a chamber pot: one only, and it had to serve about fifty people. Two days into the journey we found some nails stuck into the wooden sides, pushed two of them into a corner, and with a piece of string and a blanket improvised a screen, which was substantially symbolic: we are not yet animals, we will not be animals as long as we try to resist.

Of the fifty or so people in Primo Levi's carriage, only four returned—and this, he points out, was a *high* number. Over 98 percent of the people who entered Auschwitz did not return alive.

Primo Levi tells us that he, unlike many of his fellow passengers, had a pretty clear idea of what the deportation meant. The others thought that they were being sent to a labor camp. In a sense, this was true—for the relatively few. What Primo Levi did not know, and could not know, was that at the end of 1943, the time of his capture, the Germans were faced with a shortage of manpower—loss on the eastern front played a role—and decided that all the concentration camp inmates—even Jews—who had not been gassed upon their arrival—as had essentially all the women and children in Levi's group—would be pressed into slave labor. They were to be kept alive for more than the nominal three months the Germans had calculated that a typical *lager* inmate would live. Prior to this decision, much of the work people were given to do in the camps was kept deliberately meaningless. Primo Levi tells of the women of Ravensbrück who were kept working for days under the hot July sun: they were lined up in a circle, and each deportee had to move a pile of sand to her neighbor in an endless, useless round. Later on, the women were incorporated into factory work squads. Many German industries made huge profits on the economics of this slave labor, and among them was the chemical giant IG-Farben. In fact, IG-Farben maintained an essentially private concentration camp—Monowitz-Buna—in Auschwitz for the manufacture of synthetic rubber. I will return to the circumstances—almost beyond belief—of how Primo Levi ended up working at Buna, but here I want to point out that Auschwitz was not a single camp. There were thirty-nine *lagers* forming an entire malignant universe with the main camp at Auschwitz as its administrative center. It was in this camp that there was a special children's block in which children were subjected to medical experiments. In addition, there was the extermination camp at Birkenau with its crematoria manufactured by Topf of Wiesbaden. (In his preface to *The Drowned and the Saved*, Levi informs us that this company was still making crematoria for civilian use under this name as late as 1975.) On one record day in August 1944, some twenty-four thousand people were put to death in Birkenau. Then there were small camps near mines—punishment camps—where inmates were worked to death in the mines in a few weeks. In Monowitz-Buna where Levi was interred, there were some ten thousand inmates at any given time.

The fact that, before Levi arrived, the Germans had decided, for economic reasons, to extend the life of the slave laborers who would work in Buna, was a piece of good fortune—related indirectly to chemistry—over which he had no control. The first place where his education as a chemist played a direct role in saving him was in the matter of language. The language of the SS was a kind of gutter German. In an essay entitled "Communicating" in *The Drowned and the Saved*, Levi explains:

> We immediately realized, from our very first contacts with the contemptuous men with the black patches, that knowing or not knowing German was

a watershed. Those who understood them and answered in an articulate manner could establish the semblance of a human relationship. To those who did not understand them the black men reacted in a manner that astonished and frightened us: an order that had been pronounced in the calm voice of a man who knows he will be obeyed was repeated word for word in a loud, angry voice, then screamed at the top of his lungs as if he were addressing a deaf person or indeed a domestic animal, more responsive to the tone than the content of the message.

Then came the blows, often with rubber truncheons—the *lingua franca* of Auschwitz: "This was a signal. For those people we were no longer men. With us, as with cows or mules, there was no substantial difference between a scream and a punch."

Ironically, Levi had had to learn some German to obtain his Ph.D. Many of the basic texts were written only in German. (This was still true a decade later when I took my Ph.D. in physics.) However, he soon realized that the German he knew was not enough:

> Flung into Auschwitz, despite my initial bewilderment (actually, perhaps indeed thanks to it) I soon understood that my extremely meager *Wortschatz* had become an essential factor of survival. *Wortschatz* means "lexical patrimony," but, literally, "treasure of words"; never was a term more appropriate. Knowing German meant life: I had only to look around me. My Italian companions did not understand it, that is almost all . . . were drowning one by one in a stormy sea of not-understanding: they did not know what the orders meant, they received slaps and kicks without comprehending why. . . . They looked around them with bewildered eyes, like trapped animals, and that is what they had in fact become.

Levi found an Alsatian prisoner to give him private German lessons,

> spread over brief whispers, between the moment of curfew and the moment when we gave way to sleep, lessons to be recompensed with bread, since there was no other currency. He accepted, and I believe that never was bread better spent. He explained to me what the roars of the *Kapos* and the SS meant, the foolish or ironic mottoes written in Gothic letters on the hut's roof trusses, the meaning of the colors of the triangles we wore on our chests above the registration number. So I realized that the German of the Lager—skeletal, howled, studded with obscenities and imprecations—was only vaguely related to the austere language of my chemistry books, or to

the melodious, refined German of Heine's poetry that Clara, a classmate of mine, used to recite to me.

Levi chose, after his release from Auschwitz, to retain his number, 174517, tattooed on his left arm. He could have had the tattoo removed. He could also have learned to speak a more refined German—his chemical factory had many business dealings with Germans—but he chose not to do that either. He writes:

In Auschwitz "to eat" was rendered *fressen,* a verb which in good German is applied only to animals. For "go away" the expression *hau'ab* was used, the imperative mode of the verb *abhauen;* in proper German this means "to cut, chop off," but in Lager jargon it was equivalent to "go to hell, get out of the way." I once happened to use this expression *(Jetzt hauen wir ab)* in good faith shortly after the end of the war to take leave of certain well-mannered functionaries of the Bayer Company after a business meeting. It was as if I had said, "Now let's get the hell out of here." They looked at me with astonishment: the term belonged to a linguistic register different from that in which our preceding conversation had been conducted and is certainly not taught in "foreign language" courses. I explained to them that I had not learned German in school but rather in a Lager called Auschwitz; this gave rise to a certain embarrassment, but since I was in the role of a buyer they continued to treat me with courtesy. I later on realized also that my pronunciation is coarse, but I deliberately have not tried to make it more genteel; for the same reason, I have never had the tattoo removed from my left arm.

A good deal of fiction has by now been written about the Holocaust. I find most of it unsatisfactory—an exception being *The Last of the Just* by André Schwarz-Bart, in which the Holocaust is used almost allegorically. Still less do I like the TV docudramas with their well-paid and well-fed actors made up to look like *Häftlinge*—prisoners—in the Lagers. None of this fiction is as inventive as reality. I doubt that any fiction writer could think up a scene like the one Primo Levi describes in the chapter called "Chemical Examination" in *Survival in Auschwitz.* It did not take long—usually only a few days—to dehumanize someone in Auschwitz. The prisoners were at once deprived of all their possessions—even their hair. Their shoes were replaced by ill-fitting and ill-matched wooden shoes, and the prisoners were rapidly forced-marched wherever they went. This meant that they all had sores on

their feet, and elsewhere, from the heavy construction work, which
never healed. They were also kept half starved. In addition, there was
the smell: "It is not the smell of the badly washed, but the smell of the
Häftling, faint and sweetish, which greeted us at our arrival in the Lager
and which tenaciously pervades the dormitories, kitchens, washrooms
and closets of the Lager. One acquires it at once and one never loses
it: 'So young and already stinking!' is our way of greeting new arrivals."
Some three months after his arrival in Auschwitz in February of 1944,
Levi was summoned to Buna to take an examination in chemistry. By
this time, the synthetic rubber factory had been nearly constructed—in
the event, it never produced a single pound of rubber—and with typical
cynical efficiency, the IG-Farben chemists who ran it decided to make
a search among the prisoners to see whether any of them had a background in chemistry. An examination was to be given:

> And obviously it will be in German and we will have to go in front of some
> blond Aryan doctor hoping that we do not have to blow our noses, because
> perhaps he will not know that we do not have handkerchiefs, and it will
> certainly not be possible to explain it to him. And we will have our old
> comrade hunger with us, and we will hardly be able to stand on our feet,
> and he will certainly smell our odour, to which we are by now accustomed,
> but which persecuted us during the first days, the odour of turnips and
> cabbages, raw, cooked and digested.

The examiner is one Dr. Pannwitz. The Kapo—a *Häftling* who had
been put in charge of a squad of fellow prisoners and often treated them
brutally—points out to Pannwitz that Levi has been in the Lager for
only three months and is already half dead—implying that it will be a
waste of time to give him an examination in chemistry. Pannwitz asks
Levi where he took his degree. Levi replies, "I took my degree in Turin
in 1941, *summa cum laude:*

> While I say it I have the definite sensation of not being believed, of not even
> believing it myself; it is enough to look at my dirty hands covered with sores,
> my convict's trousers encrusted with mud. Yet I am he, the B.Sc. of Turin,
> in fact at this particular moment it is impossible to doubt my identity with
> him, as my reservoir of knowledge of organic chemistry, even after so long
> an inertia, responds at request with unexpected docility. And even more,
> this sense of lucid elation, this excitement which I feel warm in my veins, I
> recognize it, it is the fever of examinations, *my* fever of *my* examinations, that

spontaneous mobilization of all my logical faculties, and all my knowledge, which my friends at university so envied me.

After the examination, Levi is forced-marched back to his barracks by his Kapo, Alex. They need to climb over a cable, thick with grease, to steady himself, Alex takes hold of the cable and finds that his hand is black with grease. Levi writes, "In the meanwhile I have joined him. Without hatred and without sneering, Alex wipes his hand on my shoulder, both the palm and the back of the hand to clean it."

By November 1944, only twenty-one of the ninety-six Italians who arrived with Levi have survived. He has "passed" his examination which has entitled him and the other "chemists" to move sacks of phenylbeta—a chemical essential in the manufacturing of rubber—back and forth between a warehouse and a storage cellar—filthy, dangerous work since the chemical burns patches of their skin. The reason for this apparently senseless activity was the almost daily air raids on the Buna facility. As Levi describes them, these air raids were highly specialized. A single bomb would be dropped, which was enough to cripple the production facility, but not enough to destroy it. Levi does not think that this was accidental. Indeed, when in 1982, he made the second of two postwar visits to Auschwitz, he observed that the part of the camp in which he had actually lived no longer existed, having been subsumed in what is now a working Polish rubber factory. What is more puzzling is that although the death camp at Birkenau was only a few miles away, no bomb was ever dropped on it. The only time its activities were temporarily halted, prior to the liberation, was when, in the fall of 1944, one of the crematoria in Birkenau was blown up in a desperate act of sabotage by the inmates who operated it. They were killed to a man.

By the beginning of winter, three *Häftlinge*, including Levi, were chosen to actually begin working inside the Buna facility. This was very fortunate for them, since few inmates ever survived two *winters* in Auschwitz. Apart from the warmth of a heated building, and the fact that the work was less physically demanding—the food ration for the three chemists was not increased—this transfer gave Levi a license to steal. He has often remarked that while he was in Auschwitz he stole everything except another man's bread. The Buna stealing ethos was also rather particular. Since it was a sort of private Lager run by the IG-Farben Company, the SS did not apply its rigid rules about stealing to it. An inmate caught stealing Lager property in the rest of the camp was summarily hanged. Hence in Buna, Levi stole everything he could get his hands on: soap; petrol; alcohol; a broom which he had to saw into two parts to carry under his coat; and, above all, twenty "grey, hard, colorless, tasteless little rods." (This description is from *The Periodic Table* under the element "Cerium.") The curious thing about the jar containing these rods is that it had no label:

> This was very strange because it was a German laboratory. Yes, of course, the Russians were a few kilometers away, catastrophe was in the air, almost visible; there were bombings every day; everybody knew the war was about to end: but finally some constants must still subsist, and among these were our hunger, that the laboratory was German, and that Germans never forgot labels. In fact, all the other jars and bottles in the lab had neat labels, written on the typewriter or by hand in beautiful Gothic characters—only that jar lacked a label.

He took the rods back to the Lager and to his friend Alberto. (Alberto, whose last name is not given, died on a forced march from Auschwitz just prior to its liberation by the Russians. In a desperate effort to conceal what had gone on there, the Germans evacuated the camp, and something like twenty thousand survivors died in that march. Levi was spared because, at the time, he was too ill to move; and it was, no doubt, assumed that he would die anyway.) When they scratched a rod with a penknife, it emitted yellow sparks. Levi knew at once that it must be iron-cerium, the metal used for flints for cigarette lighters. The two men spent three nights trimming the rods down to a size suitable for the lighters then being illegally made in the Lager. The flints were traded for bread—the precious bread needed to survive.

Levi has written in *The Drowned and the Saved* that he, like many other educated survivors of the Lagers, regarded them as their "universities." By this, Levi meant that the people he encountered there became the food for intense intellectual activity. The particular form this took in Levi's case he credited again to his training in chemistry:

> [F]rom my trade I contracted a habit that can be variously judged and defined at will as human or inhuman—the habit of never remaining indifferent to the individuals that chance brings before me. They are human beings but also "samples"; specimens in a sealed envelope to be identified, and weighed . . . food for my curiosity, which some people then and later,

have judged to be detached. A food that certainly contributed to keeping part of me alive and that subsequently supplied me with the material for thinking and making books.

Of special interest to Levi in the Lager, was his encounter with almost ordinary Germans—ordinary in the sense that they were not part of the SS—who worked there, especially in the chemical plant. Among them were three perfectly ordinary German girls who chattered happily about the coming Christmas holidays, filed their nails, and ate bread and jam a few feet from what they referred to openly as the *"Stink-jude"*—the stinking Jews—in their prison stripes. Levi never did find out how they had come to Auschwitz. Nor did he learn much about Dr. Pannwitz, the chemist who had examined him. But he did learn something about one Dr. Lothar Müller.

This episode, for me one of the high points of *The Periodic Table,* is recounted there under the element "Vanadium." It, too, as far as I am concerned, surpasses fiction. After the war, the Allies broke up the IG-Farben Company into smaller independent subcompanies, one of which Levi identifies only as W. The chemical firm Levi had worked for in Turin sold varnishes, and had purchased from W. a special kind of resin which, as it turned out, turned the varnish mixed with lamp-black—black paint—into a sticky useless mass. As the manager, it was Levi's duty to write to W. with the complaint. He received from W. a long, pompous, and essentially superfluous letter instructing him to use various procedures which, in fact, he was already employing. Since W. was the only available supplier of this resin, Levi was forced to make a second order, at the same time asking W. to take special precautions about the interaction of the resin with lampblack. Along with the confirmation of this order, he received a long letter from one Dr. L. Müller telling him that the problem could be cured by adding to the resin a small amount of vanadium naphthenate, an additive that Levi notes had until then "never been heard of in the world of varnishes." The name Müller had some sort of resonance for Levi, but since there are at least two hundred thousand Müllers in Germany, he would have dismissed any further thoughts on the matter except for an odd spelling mistake. This Müller spelled, and repeated it twice, "naphthenate" as "naptenate." "Now I conserve pathologically precise memories of my encounters in that by now remote world: well, that other Müller too, in an unforgotten lab full of freezing cold, hope and fear, used to say 'beta-Naptylamin' instead of "beta-Naphthylamin." ' The other Müller used to come into the laboratory from time to time to make sure instructions were being followed. With his "pathologically precise" memory, Levi remembered that there were precisely three times when this Müller had actually spoken to him. The first time was to ask what dosage of "Naptylamin" was being used. The second time was to ask why Levi's beard was so long. To this, Levi replied that the *Häftlinge* were not allowed any razors, and that their beards were shaved only on Mondays. On the third occasion, Müller gave Levi a note that allowed his beard to be shaved on Thursdays as well, along with a note allowing him a pair of leather shoes. He then asked, employing the German formal *"Sie,"* "Why do you look so perturbed?" Levi recalls thinking to himself in German, "This man does not have a clue. [*Der Mann hat keine Ahnung*]." Could the two Müllers be one and the same?

Levi reports that he contacted W.'s local representatives, whom he knew quite well. They discovered that W.'s Müller had indeed worked at Buna. Levi found out his private address and sent him a copy of the German edition of *Survival in Auschwitz,* with a letter asking whether he was, indeed, the Müller of Buna. Levi writes:

> I began to wait for the reply, while on the company level there continued, like the oscillation of an enormous, very slow pendulum, the exchange of chemico-bureaucratic letters concerning the Italian vanadium that did not work as well as the German. Would you please in the meantime be so kind as to send us urgently the specifications of the product and ship to us by air freight 50 kilograms, whose cost you will deduct, etc.? . . . Meanwhile, as is the custom, we threatened each other with legal action, *'gerichtlich vorzugehen.'*

The private silence continued for two months. Finally on 2 March 1967, on elegant paper, with what Levi recalls as "vaguely Gothic characters," he got a reply. Indeed, Müller had been at Buna and had a clear recollection of Levi. He proposed a meeting for the purpose of "overcoming that terrible past." At this point, Levi was in a quandary. What did the man want? Some sort of absolution? Levi does not really confront the question of what exactly *he* wanted when he wrote to Müller in the first instance. Levi decided to reply—in Italian, he wanted the security of his own language—by asking a certain number of specific questions. Did Müller know under what circumstances IG-Farben had taken on the slave labor force? Was he aware of the "installations"—the crematoria a few miles away? Did he accept the judgments of Levi's book? Of Müller's proposed meeting, Levi said nothing. Levi thought that, if he got a reply, it would be either glacial and unrepentant or the warm Christian outpouring of the self-redeemed. The reply, when it came, was neither. It was an eight-page letter and contained a photograph of an aging Müller, whom Levi immediately recognized as the same man who had asked him, "Why do you look so perturbed?" Of the letter in general, Levi writes that "it was visibly the work of an inept writer: rhetorical, sincere only by half, full of digressions and farfetched praise, moving, pedantic, and clumsy; it defied any summary, all-encompassing judgment."

Müller's history was typical of many—too many—young Germans of the 1930s. He had been swept up—"dragged along"—by the general enthusiasm for Hitler. He had joined a nationalistic student league which then became incorporated in the *Sturmabteilungen*—the storm troopers. When this happened, Müller said he had gotten himself discharged. "This too was therefore possible," he noted. When the war came, he had been mobilized into the antiaircraft corps. Confronted, he said, by the ruins of the cities, he experienced what he described as "shame and indignation." In May of 1944, he had gotten his status as a chemist recognized and been assigned to the synthetic rubber plant run by the IG-Farben company in Schkopau—a model for the larger plant being built at Buna. There he trained a group of Ukrainian girls and with them was assigned to Auschwitz in November of 1944. At the time, he recalled, the name Auschwitz meant nothing to him. Upon his arrival, he was told by the technical director at the laboratory that "the Jews in Buna must be assigned only the most menial tasks, and compassion was not tolerated." His immediate superior, of whom he had a low opinion, was Dr. Pannwitz who, he said, had died of a brain tumor in 1946.

At this point, Müller's letter took on a different tone—one also only too familiar to people (my father was one of them) who dealt with Germans during the occupation not long after the war. It was he, Müller, he explained, who had actually chosen the three prisoner-specialists, and Levi in particular, knowing nothing about Pannwitz's examination. In consequence, Müller recalled that, and I quote Levi, "he [Müller] had had a relationship with me almost of friendship between equals; that he had conversed with me about scientific problems and had meditated, on this occasion, on [according to Müller] what 'precious human values are destroyed by other men out of pure brutality.' " Levi remarks:

> Not only did I not remember any such conversations (and my memory of that period, as I have said, is excellent), but against the background of disintegration, mutual distrust, and mortal weariness, the mere supposition of them was totally outside reality, and could only be explained by a very naive ex post facto wishful thinking; perhaps it was an incident he told a lot of people and did not realize I was the one person in the world who could not believe it.

Müller had no specific recollection of the leather shoes or the beard, but said that he remembered other such incidents which, considering his own experience, Levi considered plausible. Then came the matter of the IG-Farben Company, the slave labor, and the crematoria. Levi writes:

> To my question about IG-Farben he answered curtly that, yes, it had employed prisoners, but only to protect them: actually, he put forward the (insane!) opinion that the entire Buna-Monowitz plant, eight square kilometers of giant buildings, had been constructed with the intention of "protecting the Jews and contributing to their survival," and that the order not to have compassion for them was *"eine Tarnung"* ("camouflage"). *Nihil de principe*, no accusation against IG-Farben: my man was still an employee of W., which was its heir, and you do not spit into your own dish. During his brief sojourn at Auschwitz he 'had never gained knowledge of any proviso that seemed aimed at the killing of Jews.' "

Levi comments, "Paradoxical, offensive, but not to be excluded: at that time, among the German silent majority, the common technique was to try to know as little as possible, and therefore not to ask questions. He too, obviously, had not demanded explanations from anyone, not even from himself, although on clear days the flames of the crematorium were visible from the Buna factory."

Müller had been captured by the Americans and detained under conditions he described to Levi as being "primitively equipped." Then, in June 1945, he had returned to his family and to W. Now, he wanted a meeting with Levi to "overcome" the past. After much soul searching, Levi decided to answer the letter to explain to Müller that in his view every German, every *man,* was responsible for Auschwitz, and each individual would have to deal with his own conscience. He had decided not to meet with Müller. But that very evening, Müller called from Germany and implored Levi to meet with him. Caught unawares, Levi agreed and put aside the draft of his letter. Eight days later, he received a letter from Mrs. Müller announcing the unexpected death of her husband at the age of sixty.

Recently three new books involving Primo Levi have appeared. I use the word "involving" because two of them—*Dialogo* and *Conversations with Primo Levi*—are what their titles would indicate: a dialogue, in the first instance, with the Italian physicist Tullio Regge; and conversations, with the journalist Ferdinando Camon. I will return to these two fascinating books shortly after discussing the third, *The Mirror Maker,* which is a collection of Primo Levi's most recent, and presumably the last that remain, stories and essays. I have a theory about this collection—a collection that I think is relatively weak—based to some extent on my own experience as a physicist-writer. As I have mentioned, until 1977, Primo Levi worked full time as an industrial chemist. The writing that he did was done on Sundays and in the evenings. He was, in short, a *chemist* who wrote. Then, in 1977, he decided to write full time and he stopped being a chemist. In the *Dialogo,* he explains what a release this was—at first:

> No more office hours, no more crossing town during the rush hours; and every blessed day, no night calls because a valve has broken or a rainstorm has flooded the cable beds. I felt I had avalanches of free time at my disposal: if before I had written three or four books, working in the evening and on Sunday, now I would write another twenty or thirty.

The fact that this did not happen Levi attributes to having too much time. He quotes a friend who said that in order to do things, "one mustn't have time." I think that this is only part of the problem for someone like Levi. Once one becomes a *writer* who was a chemist—or a physicist, for that matter—one loses all kinds of defenses. One is now *expected* to write; indeed, *obliged* to write, no matter what. The situation is compounded when one is someone of Levi's stature. Almost anything he was willing to write was snatched away by a host of eager hands. Levi became a regular contributor to the Turin daily *La Stampa.* A number of the pieces in this collection were first published in *La Stampa.* There is nothing wrong with them especially, but they seem to have been *written* rather than torn from the earth as, say, *Survival in Auschwitz* was. We really do not need Primo Levi to describe New York skyscrapers or Buck, Jack London's fictional dog; nor do we need his ventures into science fiction—all subjects of this book. I don't know what Primo Levi would have written if he had maintained his connection with chemistry, but I very much doubt that it would have been this book.

I never had the good fortune to meet Primo Levi, but I have known his co-dialoguee, Tullio Regge, in the *Dialogo,* for some thirty years. To fully appreciate the *Dialogo,* it helps to have in mind a picture of Regge. Regge is an outsized, extremely likable, and extremely voluble, brilliant, Italian physicist. He has a clown's mop of red hair and is given to wearing elegant, often vividly colored, hand-tailored suits which, when I admired them, he told me were made specially for him by a tailor in Milan who, subsequently, became quite famous. In recent years, Regge has used two canes to aid in his walking, which only add to his general *figura.* Until I read the *Dialogo,* I had always assumed that Regge was an example of the occasional sport that arises in European families of nobility who become, against all odds, scientists. (The Prince Louis de Broglie, one of the creators of the quantum theory, was a notable example.) But not at all. In the *Dialogo,* Regge informs us that his father was born a very poor peasant who started life by working the fields in the plains at Vercelli. By "working like an animal," he managed to save sixty lire, which he used to buy a surveyor's diploma and to move to Turin, where Regge, who, like myself, is several years younger than Primo Levi, grew up. It is difficult for me to imagine two more contrasting types then the ebullient, large-sized, Catholic Regge and his compact, reserved, precise, Jewish counterpart—Levi. Although I have occasionally talked to Regge about his new career, as a successful popular interpreter of science in Italy—he, like Levi, writes for *La Stampa*—it never would have occurred to me to ask him whether he knew Primo Levi. (Regge, incidentally, *has* remained a working physicist and is professor of physics at the University of Turin.)

In a lengthy preface, Regge describes how the *Dialogo* came about. He first met Primo Levi, he recalls, some years ago when Levi was brought to his house by a mutual friend for dinner. They hit it off at once and met often after that. While they discussed many things, the one thing they barely discussed was the Holocaust. Regge found the subject too intimidating. He recalls that, once when he was talking to Levi, the latter's sleeve happened to slide back revealing the concentration camp tattoo. In his nervousness, Regge remembers saying, "I take it to be the original." To which Levi replied, "What else? Nobody goes around buying fake Nazi tattoos." Sometime after he began writing for *La Stampa*, Regge was approached by a publisher about writing a book. The publisher, who knew Regge, knew—and Regge freely acknowledges this—that he was much too lazy to actually *write* a book. But, the publisher proposed a series of interviews with Regge at the hands of some suitable journalist—if any could be found. Then all Regge would have to do, would be to make a few corrections, and the project might actually come to pass. None of the journalists proposed, suited Regge, however, until he had the inspired idea of inviting Primo Levi to join him in a kind of *mutual* interview—a dialogue. The result is this book.

As much as I am used to the unexpected in conversations with Regge, I was nonetheless taken entirely by surprise by the opening subject of the *Dialogo:* namely, ancient Hebrew. I had always assumed, from talking to him, that Regge was a complete agnostic, with little or no interest in religion. Judging from his response in the *Dialogo*, Levi was equally surprised. Indeed, Levi remarks that he himself had not studied Hebrew since the age of thirteen—his bar mitzvah—and had forgotten it all by the time he was eighteen. It appears that Regge's interest had been aroused by the notion that the Italian text of the Old Testament had been "tampered" with. He reports to Levi that he has now learned enough Hebrew to ascertain that, in the Italian text, the woman who ensnared Joshua's two spies in Jericho is not correctly described as being a prostitute. That subject having been disposed of, the two men begin to reminisce about their fathers. Regge's, as I have mentioned, was a peasant farmer who, by self-study, turned himself into a surveyor. Both fathers were ferocious autodidacts. Indeed, it was Regge's father who had aroused his son's interest in Hebrew, after he had purchased several religious books, including the Talmud, in order to study them. Levi's father, he explains, was a successful engineer from a well-to-do Italian family. He, too, was a constant buyer and reader of books. Both fathers, it turns out, had a common dislike of "nature"—the countryside. Levi comments:

> My father hated nature. He had a savage hatred of the countryside, which to him meant staying locked up in the house without ever sticking out his nose, because there were ants, dust, because it was hot. The few times we managed to get him to take a walk, he brought along two books stuffed into

his pockets and as soon as he arrived at the destination, instead of looking at the panorama, the mountains or the sea, he sat on the ground, on a newspaper so as not to dirty his suit, and pulled out his books.

When Levi took up mountain climbing and skiing, his father suggested that he take up drinking, smoking, and girls instead. Both boys, Regge and Levi, found their way into science in their early teens.

Much of the *Dialogo* is taken up with several lengthy explanations by Regge of some of the more outré aspects of modern physics. Since this is, more or less, how I earn my living, this part of the book was of somewhat less interest to me than it might be to a layperson. What was of great interest to me was a section near the end of the book where Levi discusses the role of chemistry in his actual writing style. Before turning to this, I want to discuss the question often asked Levi: namely, if he had not had the experience of the camps, would he have written at all, at least professionally? In the "Nickel" section of *The Periodic Table*, Levi tells us that his first writing was done while he was living alone in the nickel mine, the job he took after getting his degree. He wrote two short stories which, as far as I know, were never published. Then came the Lager. In an afterword to the latest edition of *The Reawakening*, in which Levi discusses his writing, he seems to have forgotten about these early stories:

> [I]f I had not lived the Auschwitz experience, I probably would never have written anything. I would not have had the motivation, the incentive, to write. I had been a mediocre student in Italian and had had bad grades in history. Physics and chemistry interested me most, and I had chosen a profession, that of chemist, which had nothing in common with the world of the written word. It was the experience of the Camp and the long journey home that forced me to write. I did not have to struggle with laziness, problems of style seemed ridiculous to me, and miraculously I found time to write without taking even one hour away from my daily professional work. It seemed as if these books were all there, ready in my head, and I had only to let them come out and pour onto paper.

In the *Dialogo*, however, Levi makes it quite clear that it was precisely his profession as a chemist that gives his writing the particular style that it has. Many people have commented on the style, but I think no one has grasped it as clearly as Levi does himself. This is what he told Regge:

As far as my experience goes, I must say that my chemistry, which was actually a "low" chemistry, almost culinary, first of all supplied me with a vast assortment of metaphors. I find myself richer than other writers because for me words like "bright," "dark," "heavy," "light" and "blue" have a more extensive and more concrete gamut of meanings. For me "blue" is not only the blue of the sky. I have five or six blues at my disposal. . . . I mean to say that I have had in my hands materials that are not of current use, with properties outside the ordinary, that have served to amplify my language precisely in a technical sense. Thus I have at my disposal an inventory of raw materials, of tesserae for writing, somewhat larger than that possessed by someone who does not have a technical background. Moreover, I've developed the habit of writing compactly, avoiding the superfluous. Precision and concision, which, so I'm told, are my way of writing, have come to me from my trade as a chemist. And so has the habit of objectivity, of not letting myself be easily deceived by appearances. . . . I've written that my model of a writing style was the short end-of-week report, and to a certain extent this is true. I was struck by a sentence attributed to Fermi, who also found it boring to write compositions in *liceo*. The only composition he would have written gladly would have been: describe a two-lira coin. Something like that happens to me: when I have to describe a two-lira coin. I'm quite successful. If I must describe something indefinite, for example a human personality, I'm less successful.

On 11 April 1987, Primo Levi was found dead at the base of the central stairwell in his home in Turin—the house in which he had been born. The general assumption has been made that this was a death by suicide. This, in turn, provoked an outpouring of speculation and commentary which included the notion—absurd to me—that Primo Levi's life was somehow a "failure." Both of the recently published interviews—Regge's and Camon's—which were done not long before Levi's death and published in Italy not long afterward, reopen the question of whether Primo Levi committed suicide at all. Before turning to this, I would like to take up a point raised by Cynthia Ozick, a writer whom I admire greatly. She has stated that she detected a sharp change of tone in the last book published before Levi's death, *The Drowned and the Saved*. She finds that Levi's pent-up rage suddenly erupts in this book, sweeping everything—every one of life's joys—before it. I have recently reread all of Levi's nonfiction, partly to see if I can also find such clues. I cannot. Rage is such a rare emotion in Levi's writing that, in the few places where it erupts, it hits you across the face like the crack of a whip.

Nowhere in all of Levi's writing does this have more of an effect than in the final paragraph of the chapter called "October 1944" in Levi's first book, *Survival in Auschwitz*. This chapter, which has to do with the "selections"—the *triage*—that the Germans used to select out and exterminate slave laborers they felt were no longer fit to work, is, to me, so devastating that I can hardly get through it. In the preface to the *Dialogo*, Regge confesses that *Survival in Auschwitz* had such an affect on him that he could not finish reading it. This chapter is surely one of the reasons.

It is October, and the winter of Silesia—the Silesia of Auschwitz—has already begun. Primo Levi says that all the veterans of the previous winter know what this means—seven out of ten of the prisoners will die before April—and to avoid dying will involve an almost impossible struggle. He writes:

> We will have to spend bread to acquire gloves, and lose hours of sleep to repair them when they become unstitched. As it will no longer be possible to eat in the open, we will have to eat our meals in the hut, on our feet, everyone will be assigned to an area of floor as large as a hand, as it is forbidden to rest against the bunks. Wounds will open on everyone's hands, and to be given a bandage will mean waiting every evening for hours on one's feet in the snow and wind.

During the summer, the Germans had constructed two large tents to hold over a thousand prisoners. With the arrival of winter, these tents were taken down, and Levi realizes that this means that space will have to be made for a thousand men; that there would inevitably be a "selection." A few try to prepare by bribing some official with bread or tobacco. Even after one has been selected, the numbers can still be switched or erased. Those who have nothing material to give, seek to reassure each other. They show each other their bodies, looking for reassurance. *"Du bist kein Musselmann. . . ."* Somehow the word *Musselmann* had come to be used in the argot of Auschwitz for someone who was weak or inept and probably headed for selection. "You are no *Musselmann*."

> Nobody refuses this charity to another: nobody is so sure of his own lot to be able to condemn others. I brazenly lied to old Werthheimer; I told him if they questioned him, he should reply that he was forty-five, and he should not forget to have shaved the evening before even if it cost him a quarter-

ration of bread. . . . It is absurd of Werthheimer to hope; he looks sixty, he
has enormous varicose veins, he hardly even notices the hunger anymore.

The selection comes on the afternoon of a "working" Sunday—a
Sunday where the prisoners are required to work:

> At Birkenau, the crematorium chimney has been smoking for days. Room
> has to be made for an enormous convoy arriving from the Poznan ghetto.
> The young tell the young that all the old ones will be chosen. The healthy
> tell the healthy that only the ill will be chosen. Specialists will be excluded.
> German Jews will be excluded. Low numbers will be excluded. You will be
> chosen, I will be excluded.

In midafternoon a bell sounds. This means *"Blocksperre":* everyone is to
be enclosed in their huts. This happens, Levi tells us, whenever there
is a selection, to keep people from running away; and it also happens
when people are taken to the gas chambers, to prevent others from
seeing them leave.

> Our *Blockältester* [the man responsible for running the hut] knows his busi-
> ness. He has made sure that we have all entered, he has had the door locked,
> he has given everyone his card with his number, name, profession, age and
> nationality and he has ordered everyone to undress completely, except for
> shoes. We wait like this, naked, with our card in our hands, for the commis-
> sion to reach our hut.

When it does, the *Blockältester* and his aides drive the frightened naked
men into the "day room"—two hundred men in a room seven yards by
four. There are two doors that lead to the outside. At the end of them
stands the SS subaltern, who will decide who will live and who will die.
The men are required to run a few steps between the doors and into the
cold October air and give the card to the SS man. He hands it either
to the man to his left or to the one to his right. One side is for life, and
the other for death. Each man's fate is decided in a few seconds; the
whole hut in three or four minutes; the whole camp of twelve thousand
men was "done" in the course of an afternoon.

The men are allowed to dress. There is speculation as to which was
the "bad side"—the right or the left. Levi and his friend Alberto decide
that the bad side must have been the left, and that they are spared—at

least for this selection. There seem to be some anomalies. Sattler, a huge
Transylvanian peasant, just arrived in the camp, has apparently been
selected. "Sattler," Levi writes, "does not understand German, he has
understood nothing of what has taken place, and stands in a corner
mending his shirt. Must I go and tell him that his shirt will be of no more
use?" Sometimes two or three days, or even longer, intervene before the
men selected are taken away to be gassed. The selected ones know who
they are. For reasons beyond Levi's fathoming—beyond anyone's fathoming—the selected ones are served double rations of soup. Ziegler has
been served only a single ration. But his card was put on the left. He
complains to the *Blockältester*, who checks his records; Ziegler gets his
second bowl. Here are the final paragraphs of the chapter:

> Now everyone is busy scraping the bottom of his bowl with his spoon so as
> not to waste the last drops of the soup; a confused, metallic clatter, signifying
> the end of the day. Silence slowly prevails and then from my bunk on the
> top row, I see and hear old Kuhn praying aloud, with his beret on his head,
> swaying backwards and forwards violently. Kuhn is thanking God because
> he has not been chosen.
>
> Kuhn is out of his senses. Does he not see Beppo the Greek in the bunk
> next to him, Beppo who is twenty years old and is going to the gas chamber
> the day after tomorrow and knows it and lies there looking fixedly at the
> light without saying anything and without even thinking any more? Can
> Kuhn fail to realize that next time it will be his turn? Does Kuhn not
> understand that what has happened today is an abomination, which no
> propitiatory prayer, no pardon, no explanation by the guilty, which nothing
> at all in the power of man can ever clean again?
>
> If I was God, I would spit at Kuhn's prayer.

As I mentioned, both Regge and Camon raise doubt, at least in my
mind, whether Primo Levi really did commit suicide. Prior to his death,
Levi had had a debilitating, but not critical operation on his feet from
which he was slow to recover. Regge gives the opinion of the Nobel
Prize-winning chemist Rita Levi-Montalcini, who was born in Turin
and knew Primo Levi well—the epilogue of her autobiography, *In Praise
of Imperfection,* is dedicated to describing the meaning of Primo Levi's life
and work. She is convinced that Levi's fall was an accident, a temporary
loss of control as an aftermath of the medical treatments he was taking.
Camon, in his interviews with Levi, discussed the matter of depression
with him. Camon said to Levi, "You have an ironical and tolerant

attitude, and you often smile. I have the feeling that by nature you're someone who loves life, who loved it before, and who loves it afterwards. Between the before and the after there's been a violent and total trauma. But it's over."

To this Levi replies:

> In general you are right. Since the concentration camp, however, I've had a few attacks of depression. I'm not sure if they go back to that experience, because they come with different labels, from one to the next. It may seem strange to you, but I went through one just recently, a stupid fit of depression, for very little reason: I had a small operation on my foot, and this made me think that I'd suddenly got old. It took two months for the wound to heal.

Nonetheless, Camon is convinced that Levi did not commit suicide. In fact, he received a letter from Levi two days *after* his death, written two days before it. The letter is full, Camon tells us, of wishes and plans for the future. "It is not," Camon writes, "a letter by someone thinking of suicide, but rather of someone who hasn't the slightest intention of ceasing to live and to struggle. This is why his death . . . seems to me an accident, not a voluntary act."

It is clear that the experience of the Holocaust is fading. Both the prisoners and their jailers are disappearing from the scene. Human beings, and this is probably fortunate, have a limited capacity to dwell on the tragedies of the past. But have the lessons been learned? There is now a rising trend of anti-Semitism in Germany—in *Germany!* There is even a school of "historians" who deny that there was a Holocaust at all, and others who argue about the exact number of Jews killed in Auschwitz—as if this is what mattered. Primo Levi was, of course, very aware of all of this. Some sense of his feelings about it can be found in the essays in *The Drowned and the Saved.* I was particularly struck by an anecdote he tells in an essay he calls "Stereotypes." It is about an experience that he says he remembers "with a smile." He had been invited to talk to a fifth-grade class about his book and to answer questions. One very bright youngster, who seemed to be the class leader, asked Levi the question he was often asked: namely, why didn't he, and the other Jews, simply run away—escape from Auschwitz? Levi tried to explain. He explained the conditions under which the prisoners were held; their general debilitation; the fact that an escape attempt by any prisoner could bring death and torture to anyone connected with him; the fact that the prisoners were easily identifiable by what they wore; the fact that they had no proper shoes. And, besides, where would they have escaped *to?* After he was finished, the boy was still not satisfied. He asked Levi to make a drawing of the camp, showing the barbed wire, the watch tower, the power station, and the rest. Levi writes:

> My interlocutor studied the drawing for a few minutes, asked me for a few further clarifications, then he presented to me the plan he had worked out: here, at night, cut the throat of the sentinel; then, put on his clothes; immediately after this, run over there to the power station and cut off the electricity, so the search lights would go out and the high tension fence would be deactivated; after that I could leave without any trouble. He added seriously, "If it should happen to you again, do as I told you. You'll see that you'll be able to do it."

CHAPTER 12

A Child's Garden of Science

O VER A TWO-YEAR PERIOD from 1973 to 1975, I conducted a series of interviews with the Nobel Prize–winning physicist I. I. Rabi, which culminated in a *New Yorker* profile that was published in October 1975. Rabi, who was born on 29 July 1898, in Galicia, was then in his mid-seventies. He was one of the wisest people I have ever known, and one of the things we discussed was the aging process in scientists. It is a cliché that the great scientists appear to do their best work when they are extremely young, and that many scientists seem to burn out by the time they are fifty or even earlier. I asked Rabi why he thought this was, and here is his answer:

I think it must be basically neurological or physiological. The mind ceases to operate with the same richness and associations. The information-retrieval part sort of goes, along with the interconnections. I know that when I was in my late teens and early twenties the world was just a Roman candle—rockets all the time. The world was aglow. You lose that sort of thing as time goes on. It's the sort of thing that you want to hang on to if you can. And physics is such an out-of-the-world thing. It's not like history or poetry, or even painting. In them you never really lose contact with the world—it's right there before you. But physics is an otherworldly thing. It requires a taste for things unseen, even unheard of—a high degree of abstraction and a sort of profound innate philosophy. These faculties die off somehow when you grow up. You see them in children, who are fantastically interested in making things and in asking "Why? Why? Why?" Then, at a certain age, the children just become adults and are no longer very deeply interested in anything, except in the process of making a living and in sex and power. Money. Otherwise, they're not terribly interested. Profound curiosity happens when they are young. I think physicists are the Peter Pans of the human race. They never grow up, and they keep their curiosity.

The phrase "physicists [and for "physicists," one can substitute, I think, "scientists"] are the Peter Pans of the human race" has haunted me ever since I first heard it from Rabi. I believe that it is true, but it raises another question—the question that is the subject of this essay: namely, why do certain children become scientists? What is the triggering mechanism in childhood that starts some child on the road to where he, or she, becomes an Einstein, a Feynman, or a Rabi? In short, if one looks at the lives of scientists, what was the first childhood experience that they themselves can connect to what they later became? There is, very likely, an enormous literature on this subject, of which I am blissfully ignorant. But what I have been doing for the past thirty years is to ask many of the scientists I have interviewed just this question; and where, as in the case of Einstein, I had no opportunity to ask this question myself, I have tried to find out the answer by reading autobiographical statements. This has led me to read the first chapters of an awful lot of autobiographies.

One conclusion I have come to is that there appears to be a clear distinction between mathematically oriented scientists and the rest. The triggering experiences of, say, experimental physicists are so diverse that they do not seem to fall into any obvious pattern. I will give a few examples later. But of mathematicians, there seems to be a universal law I can summarize with a slight distortion of that celebrated bit of dialogue from *Die Fledermaus*. My version reads, "So young and already a mathematician." (The late Wolfgang Pauli—a Viennese noted for his acerbic wit, which was often applied to his fellow physicists—once remarked apropos of one of them, "So young and already so unknown." The original, in case one has not heard it recently, was *"So jung und schon ein Prinz."*) I really believe, having observed a good deal of it, that mathematical genius—even high talent—is "hard-wired." I do not have the foggiest idea where in the brain, or how, this hardware is hooked up—after all, brain scientists do not even know where, if anywhere, in the brain memory is located. But I am sure it is there. We can all learn algebra, and many of us can learn calculus, but we cannot be taught to be Euler, Gauss, or Von Neumann. Even *they* cannot be taught to be Euler, Gauss, or Von Neumann.

Let me give a few examples of early mathematical experience that involve people I have spoken to myself. When I asked Hans Bethe, one of the premier contemporary mathematical physicists, whether he had any early mathematical memories, he answered:

Oh yes—many. I was interested in numbers from a very early age. When I was five, I said to my mother on a walk one day, "Isn't it strange that if a zero comes at the end of a number it means a lot but if it is at the beginning of a number it doesn't mean anything?" And one day when I was about four, Richard Ewald, a professor of physiology, who was my father's boss, asked me on the street, "What is .5 divided by 2?" I answered, "Dear Uncle Ewald, that I don't know," but the next time I saw him I ran to him and said, "Uncle Ewald, it's .25." I knew about decimals then. When I was seven I learned about powers, and filled a whole book with the powers of two or three.

Not long ago I asked the same question of the late Stanislaw Ulam. Ulam, who was born in Poland in 1909, spent most of his working life at Los Alamos. This distinguished mathematician invented, among many other things, what is called the "Monte Carlo method" of doing approximate numerical calculations. (Ulam, along with Edward Teller, discovered what is known as the "secret of the hydrogen bomb.") He told me that when he was about ten he began attending lectures on the theory of relativity. In his delightful book *Adventures of a Mathematician,* he writes, "I did not really understand any of the details, but I had a good idea of the main thrust of the theory. Almost like learning a language in childhood, one develops the ability to speak it without knowing anything about grammar." (There is a well-known school of thought that claims, and I think correctly, that grammar is also "hard-wired"; but that is a subject for another essay.) Ulam concluded: "I understood the schema of special relativity and even some of the consequences without being able to verify the details mathematically."

A little later in this chapter of his book, Ulam writes:

I had mathematical curiosity very early. My father had in his library a wonderful series of German paperback books—*Reklam,* they were called.

One was Euler's *Algebra*. I looked at it when I was perhaps ten or eleven, and it gave me a mysterious feeling. The symbols looked like magic signs; I wondered whether one day I could understand them. This probably contributed to the development of my mathematical curiosity. I discovered by myself how to solve quadratic equations. I remember that I did this by an incredible concentration and almost painful and not-quite conscious effort. What I did amounted to completing the square in my head without paper or pencil.

The computer scientist and artificial-intelligence expert Marvin Minsky told me that many of his earliest memories are mathematical. At some very young age he learned that there were both positive and negative numbers. "I thought to myself," he said, "that is very nice, but maybe there are three kinds of numbers—a, b, and c. I tried for days to find a number system with three bases that looked like arithmetic. Many years later I realized that there isn't one. At the time I didn't have the courage to add a fourth base number that works and gives you the complex number system."

I once asked Freeman Dyson if he could recall *his* earliest mathematical memories. He told me that, among them, was a time when he was still being put down for naps in the afternoon—he was not exactly sure of the age, but less than ten—and he began adding up numbers like $1 + \frac{1}{2} + \frac{1}{4} + \frac{1}{8} + \ldots$ and realized that this series was adding up to 2. In other words, he had discovered for himself the notion of the convergent infinite series.

To these examples I would like to add a few more that I have culled from various biographies and autobiographies. Emilio Segrè wrote a lovely biography of his lifelong friend and colleague Fermi, called *Enrico Fermi, Physicist*. Early in the book, Segrè writes:

> Fermi never told me how he first became acquainted with mathematics; it is possible that a friend of his father introduced him to the subject. . . . Fermi told me that one of his great intellectual efforts was his attempt to understand—at the age of ten—what was meant by the statement that the equation $x^2 + y^2 = r^2$ represents a circle. Someone must have stated the fact to him, but he had to rediscover its meaning by himself.

Some time ago, I heard an interview that Richard Feynman, perhaps the most brilliant theoretical physicist of his generation, gave on "Nova." Asked about his earliest memories, he replied:

When I was just a little kid, very small in a high chair, [my father] brought home a lot of tiles, little bathroom tiles—seconds of different colors. . . . We played with them, setting them out like dominoes, I mean vertically, on my high chair . . . so they tell me this anyway . . . and when we'd got them all set up I would push one end so that they would all go down. Then after a while I'd help to set them up in a more complicated way . . . two white tiles and a blue tile, two white tiles and a blue tile . . . and when my mother complained, "Leave the poor child alone, if he wants to put a blue tile, let him put a blue tile," he said, "No, I want to show him what patterns are like and how interesting they are as it's a kind of mathematics."

And so it is.

Einstein never thought of himself as much of a mathematician, although by almost any standards he was as powerful a mathematician as he needed to be when it came time to invent the general theory of relativity. Einstein created, or re-created, the so-called tensor calculus, a highly nontrivial affair. But the earliest scientific memory he recalled, for the purpose of his wonderful *Autobiographical Notes,* was not mathematical at all. When he was four or five years old, he remembered being shown a compass. He was fascinated by the way the compass needle behaved, especially that it pointed north: "That this needle behaved in such a determined way did not at all fit into the nature of events, which could find a place in the unconscious world of concepts (effect connected with direct 'touch'). I can still remember—or at least I believe I can remember—that this experience made a deep and lasting impression upon me. Something deeply hidden had to be behind things."

This sort of trigger experience—the experience of wanting to know how something mechanical or electrical actually works, often to the point of wanting to re-create it by building it oneself—is, as far as I can make out, characteristic of the less mathematically inclined scientists. Many scientists, of course, and Einstein is one, have both sorts of early memory. (Einstein invented a proof of the Pythagorean theorem by himself when he was twelve.) It is interesting to me that the nonmathematical trigger experience of Einstein involved magnetism, since electromagnetism was to play so important a part in his early creative life. I was also interested to learn that Ernst Mach, whose *The Science of Mechanics* had such an influence on the young Einstein, had a triggering experience that was mechanical. This is the story as recounted in John T. Blackmore's biography *Ernst Mach:*

There was a turning point in my fifth year. Up to that time I represented
to myself everything I did not understand—a pianoforte, for instance—as
simply a motley assemblage of the most wonderful things, to which I as-
cribed the sound of the notes. That the pressed key struck the chord with
the hammer did not occur to me. Then one day I saw a windmill.

We [Ernst and his sister Octavia] had to bring a message to the miller.
Upon our arrival the mill had just begun to work. The terrible noise
frightened me, but did not hinder me from watching the teeth of the shaft
which meshed with the gear of the grinding mechanism and moved on one
tooth after another. This sight remained until I reached a more mature
level, and in my opinion, raised my childlike thinking from the level of the
wonder-believing savage to causal thinking; from now on, in order to understand the unintelligible, I no longer imagined magic things in the background but traced in a broken toy the cord or lever which had caused the
effect.

Before I comment on this passage, I would like to give one more
example, and this from Isaac Newton. As far as I know, it is not known
what Newton's first scientific intimations were. I am not aware, for
example, that he showed any special fascination for numbers when he
was a child, although in adult life, as we all know, he became a prodigious mathematician. One of Newton's younger contemporaries, William Stukeley, collected information about Newton that he published in
a memoir. He, like Newton, was from Lincolnshire; and in the preparation of his memoir, published in 1752, twenty-five years after Newton's
death, he visited Newton's boyhood home, including the study where
Newton did his great work when he came down from Cambridge in the
plague year of 1665. Stukeley reports in his memoir:

Every one that knew Sir Isaac, or have heard of him, recount the pregnancy
of his parts when a boy, his strange inventions, and extraordinary inclina-
tion for mechanics. That instead of playing among the other boys, when
from school, he always busied himself in making knick-knacks and models
of wood in many kinds. For which purposes he had got little saws, hatchets,
hammers, and a whole shop of tools, which he would use with great dexter-
ity. In particular they speak of his making a wooden clock. About this time
a new windmill [shades of Mach!] was set up near Grantham, in the way
to Gunnerby, which is now demolished, this country chiefly using water
mills. Our lad's imitating spirit was soon excited, and by frequently prying
into the fabric of it, as they were making it, he became master enough to

make a very perfect model thereof, and it was said to be as clean and curious a piece of workmanship as the original. This sometimes he would set upon the house-top where he lodged, and clothing it with sail-cloth, the wind would really take it; but what was most extraordinary in its composition was, that he put a mouse into it, which he called the miller, and that mouse made the mill turn round when he pleased.

So young and already a mechanic.

What are we to make of all of this? It would appear that all children, to various degrees and with various aptitudes, go through this "scientific phase," but that few of them become scientists. The reasons for the latter are clearly many, not the least of which have to do with environmental opportunities. An Isaac Newton born in a mountain village in Nepal might well have grown up to be the village curiosity, or even a great religious figure, but would, one can safely assume, be unlikely to have invented the law of universal gravitation. But many children are exposed to similar environments, and some of them grow up to rob banks and some to own them.

Perhaps some clue about what makes certain children scientists is to be found in the quotation from Mach. He had, he tells us, this sudden realization as a child that causal explanation could make the unintelligible understandable. In his *Autobiographical Notes* Einstein describes the tension created when some experience causes us, quite spontaneously, to "wonder" about its meaning and cause. He speaks of this as a "conflict," and writes, "Whenever such a conflict is experienced hard and intensively it reacts back upon our thought world in a decisive way. The development of this thought world is in a certain sense a continuous flight from 'wonder.' "

"Flight" here is a strong word. It suggests, at least to me, that these scientific children learn early that causal explanation is a great aid and comfort in the constant flight we all make from the unintelligible. Causal explanation helps us to flee from the terrors of the unknown, and these terrors can loom large in the mind of a child. In this respect, here is what Rabi told me when I asked him if some childhood experience turned him toward science: "Yes," he said, "a very profound one. One time, I was walking down the street—looked right down the street, which faced east. The moon was just rising. And it scared the hell out of me! Absolutely scared the hell out of me." Not long afterward Rabi began reading through—in alphabetical order—all of the books in the children's section of the Brooklyn Public Library branch near his home. First he began with fiction, reading from Alcott through Trowbridge. Then he came to the science shelf and began with astronomy—a little book on astronomy—which changed his life. Of this, his first encounter with scientific explanation, he told me, "When you have the astronomical explanation, the rising of the moon becomes a sort of non-event."

Having Fun with Tom Lehrer

When they see us coming, the birdies all try an' hide,
But they still go for peanuts when coated with cyanide.
The sun's shining bright,
Ev'rything seems all right,
When we're poisoning pigeons in the park.
—Tom Lehrer

I_N 1948, my sophomore year at Harvard, I decided that, no matter what I might do in life, differential calculus would come in handy. So I dutifully enrolled in Mathematics 1, a giant course that was taught in small sections. As it happened, I had a friend who was also taking the course, and one day he showed me his corrected homework. His section man, a graduate student, had made some remarkably funny comments on the paper, and my friend told me that this was characteristic. I asked what the name of the section man was, and my friend told me that it was Tom Lehrer. At the time I made this inquiry, my friend and I were both eighteen. Although I did not know it then, Lehrer was nineteen and already in his third year of graduate school, having entered Harvard in 1943 at the age of fourteen and finished in three years.

I did not get to meet Lehrer until a few years later, when I began taking graduate courses in mathematics. Lehrer was still a graduate student, a status he happily retained, on and off, until 1965. By the time I met him, he had already acquired a sizable reputation around Harvard both for his singing and for several inspired pranks. In 1951, shortly after the completion of the new graduate center designed by Walter Gropius, with its Richard Lippold "world tree"—a stainless-steel statue that vaguely resembled a tree—Lehrer and a small band of associates organized two ceremonies in honor of the "tree." The first occurred on the vernal equinox, during which some of the group, a few dressed up as bulls and several others as "virgins," were sacrificed. This was followed by an Arbor Day ceremony, during which "world seeds" (ball bearings) were planted under the tree and a metal "world bird" was placed in its branches.

I graduated from Harvard that year and was in charge of the entertainment for our senior dinner at Eliot House. I managed to engage the late Al Capp, the creator of L'il Abner, and a family friend, and Tom Lehrer. Capp was so impressed by Lehrer's songs that he hired him, more or less on the spot, for a television engagement on a weekly satire program that Capp then had in the Boston area. As it happened, the program only lasted for four weeks, but it was the first time Lehrer had been let loose on the general public. Incidentally, Lehrer sang a song about television on the program, which had, as I recall, the lines

On Tuesday nights we choose between
Milton Berle and Fulton Sheen.

I left Harvard in 1957 and lost personal contact with Lehrer, although, like most people of my generation, I did follow his extraordinary career. Then in 1965 he disappeared; and from that day to this, except for a few fund-raising appearances, mainly for liberal political candidates, he has never again performed in public. Indeed, I often wondered whether he was still among the living. But in the summer of 1980, I came across an item in a local Colorado newspaper that had the headline "Tom Lehrer Makes London Encore." Upon closer examination, I discovered that the item referred to a retrospective musical called *Tomfoolery,* which consisted entirely of Lehrer songs sung by a cast of three men and a woman. Lehrer did not sing, and the London show's master of ceremonies noted that "he's fifty-two now but so fears old age that he prefers to think of himself as eleven centigrade." Lehrer did make a brief curtain call, but he said nothing.

When it became clear that *Tomfoolery* was heading for this country, I thought it might be a good excuse to renew my ancient contact with Lehrer and to find out what he had been up to and, indeed, why he had, more or less, vanished from the public scene. I managed to track Lehrer down in Cambridge, where he lives for half the year (the other half he spends in California). He said he would be coming to New York, and we decided to get together. At the appointed hour, early in the afternoon, Lehrer appeared at my apartment. The first thing I noticed was that, for all intents and purposes, he looked exactly as he did when I had seen him some twenty years earlier. Whatever else he had been up to, he seemed to have found some way of defeating the aging process, perhaps by remaining a bachelor. As it turned out, neither of us had eaten, so we went to a nearby delicatessen and brought back two tuna-fish sandwiches and a couple of apples and settled in for an afternoon of conversation.

I thought it might be a good idea to begin at the beginning, since it was never entirely clear to me how Lehrer got started in his singing career at Harvard. "As you know," he said, "I majored as an undergraduate in mathematics. I was good at it, but I was also very lazy, which is probably why I majored in it. It had the least requirements. I was going to be an English or a chemistry major, but when I looked at the list of requirements, I said, 'Forget it.' The mathematics department required taking a few courses—and that was that. I had entered Harvard in 1943, at fourteen, so I guess I was a semiprodigy. The New York public schools at that time believed in allowing students to skip grades, which is why I graduated so young. But everyone in college was young then because of the war, and everyone who was not young was in the army. We had three terms a year then, so I was accelerated and got out of Harvard in three years. I began teaching in my first year in graduate school because they were desperate for teachers.

"As a kid I took piano lessons, which, at the time, meant classical piano. I never really liked that, and I spent my spare time picking up popular songs on the piano. My parents, thank heaven, instead of forcing me to continue doing something I didn't want to do, found me a popular-music piano teacher, which was rare at that time. Today it is quite common to study popular music, but in those days the usual thing was to study classical music and then to pick up popular music on your own. Having a popular-music teacher worked out very well for me. I began writing tunes when I was about seven or eight. But I was in college when I began writing parodies of popular songs—for any occasion. The only one of those songs that eventually made its way into my repertory was 'Fight Fiercely, Harvard,' which was written in 1945 and shows it. The Harvard band still plays it."

When I was an undergraduate, nearly everyone had memorized:

Fight fiercely, Harvard,
  fight, fight, fight!

Demonstrate to them our skill.
Albeit they possess the might,
  nonetheless we have the will.

"I started singing those songs at parties," Lehrer continued, "but never with the intention of their becoming commercial. That is why when somebody comes to me and says, 'I write songs and how can I get started in the business? What can I do?' there's no way I can give them any advice, because I did not set out to do it myself. I just assumed that no one would like my songs, except a few of my friends. My performing career began in 1950. The Harvard Law School, for some reason, had a quartet contest—any four people could get together and sing. I entered with four other people—we were a quintet, but that didn't matter since we were the only contestants. A representative of the Harvard freshman smoker, an annual event that featured entertainment, was at the contest. The smoker committee was always looking for free local entertainment, and so we did the Harvard freshman smoker, sharing the bill with Sally Rand, who was appearing at the Old Howard in Boston. It was a memorable night."

The original members of the group were: Lewis Branscomb, who was then a graduate teaching fellow in physics and later became the director of the National Bureau of Standards and a vice president and the director of scientific research for the IBM Corporation; David Robinson, the executive vice president of the Carnegie Corporation; Robert Welker, a professor of American civilization at Case Western Reserve; and Munro Edmonson, a professor of anthropology at Tulane. Branscomb had the inspired idea of having the quintet give the last "lecture" in his freshman physics course. Entitled "The Physical Review," in honor of our professional physics journal, it was given in the large lecture hall in the Jefferson Laboratory—a gala occasion, which I attended. Among other things, the group sang Lehrer's song on the elements, which begins:

There's antimony, arsenic, aluminum, selenium
And hydrogen and oxygen and nitrogen and rhenium,

and, after a breathtaking recitation of all the elements, ends:

These are the only ones of which the news has come to Ha'vard
And there may be many others, but they haven't been discavard.

It was not long afterward that the group made its "world tree" appearance, for which Lehrer wrote the parody "Trees." This was published in the *Harvard Crimson*—the first verses of Lehrer's to find their way into print. The item was picked up by *Time* magazine in a story about Gropius; the verses were given, but without attribution. When Lehrer wrote to *Time* to complain, he was told to settle matters with the *Crimson*.

"The Physical Review" was repeated the following year. "The members of the group got their degrees, and most of them scattered to the hills," Lehrer noted. "But people began asking me to sing at dance intermissions and smokers and things like that, which I would do for minimal pay. After about two years of this, I got tired of it—tired of singing the same songs. Then I thought, 'Hey, I've got these songs. I'll make a record.' It was a case of the right technology at the right time. By then there were LPs you could ship yourself. With the old 78s this would have been impossible. I figured that if I made a record, I could sell three hundred of them. A lot of calculation went into that. Each time I sang somewhere, I asked for a show of hands as to how many people would buy a record. Adding up those people plus my relatives came to three hundred. I figured out how many I could order so that I could break even at three hundred, and that turned out to be four hundred."

At this point, Lehrer munched on his apple and recalled, "I looked in the Yellow Pages under 'Recording.' There were two places listed where you could record 'Happy Birthday, Mother' or anything else. I went to both of them. One was polite to me and one was rude, so I chose the polite one. A couple of years ago, when I was going through my basement, I came across the bill for the original recording session. The total cost of everything—studio, tape, engineer, microphone, piano, everything—was fifteen dollars. Well, anyway, I ordered four hundred records, and they sold out very fast. I had a friend design the album cover according to my instructions, and I wrote the liner notes and took the whole thing to the printer who printed up the jackets. Then they shipped them to the presser who made the records. I got the cardboards and envelopes and handled all the mail orders myself, at least for the first few months. In fact, for a while I sold most of the records in the local Harvard dining halls or in record stores in Harvard Square. But then I began to get a whole bunch of orders from San Francisco. It turned out that the music critic of the San Francisco

Chronicle had devoted a whole column to the record and not only had praised it to the skies but had given the price and the box number where you could write for it."

Lehrer's original record sold for $3.50, and a slightly later version, which I have, for $3.95. It was a ten-inch affair, and on the cover sits a diabolical Lehrer at a grand piano. The liner explains, "Tom Lehrer, longtime exponent of the *derrière-garde* in American music, is an entirely mythical figure, a figment of his parents' warped imagination. He was raised by a yak, by whom he was always treated as one of the family, and ever since he was old enough to eat with the grownups he has been merely the front for a vast international syndicate of ne'er-do-wells." Ultimately the record sold some *three hundred and fifty thousand* copies and, needless to say, was no longer sold out of Lehrer's home. Eventually it was distributed by RCA, which took the orders from the original recording firm.

It was now 1953, and the Korean War was on. Lehrer was of draft age and not eager to take part in the hostilities, so he took a job at a firm called Baird-Atomic in Cambridge, which specialized in electronics and optics, work considered essential for the war effort. He remained at Baird for a year until he thought that "nobody was going to shoot me and I wouldn't be called upon to shoot anybody else," and then surrendered to the draft board. Of his army experience he once commented, "I think it paid off. America is free today."

"I didn't let on," Lehrer told me as we were finishing lunch, "that I had any entertainment abilities, because I figured they'd put me into special services and send me off to Alaska or some place to entertain the troops." In fact, he spent two years in Washington in the National Security Agency doing top secret work that made use of his mathematics. Just before going into the army, Lehrer had made his first nightclub appearance, at the Blue Angel in New York. "They hired me for the Christmas show," Lehrer noted, "figuring that I would attract the college kids home for vacation. I was on the bill with Orson Bean, among others. There was a reviewer from the *New Yorker* who, I was told, didn't like me at all. But he had the kindness not to mention me when he reviewed the rest of the show. When I got out of the army, popular concerts were just starting. There was no real concert circuit; the Kingston Trio started all that. If you said that you were going to do a concert, people assumed that you were going to play the piano or something. The only humorous concerts then were given by Anna

Russell or Victor Borge. The idea of a George Carlin or a David Steinberg giving a concert just didn't exist. I did my first concert in 1957 at Hunter College in New York."

After his Hunter College concert, Lehrer spent three years touring much of the English-speaking world doing concerts. In 1959, he put out a second record, a concert recording entitled *An Evening Wasted with Tom Lehrer,* which sold more than two hundred thousand copies here and abroad. "I didn't want to put the record out until I was ready to retire from performing. I figured that if the record was out, who would want to come and hear me? I would just be doing my whole act on record. Doing comedy is not like being a pop singer, where audiences want to hear what they've already heard a thousand times on the record—they want to hear Sophie Tucker in person sing 'Some of These Days.' So I put the second record out—it was recorded at Harvard—as a farewell. I went back to graduate school and did five more years at the Harvard Graduate School."

Altogether, Lehrer spent eleven years in graduate school, ten at Harvard, and one at Columbia. This in itself is a rare achievement, especially in scientific fields, where students are pushed out the door as rapidly as decency will allow. In my day at the Harvard Graduate School in physics, it was considered extremely bad form if one spent more than four years there. I asked Lehrer about it. "I'm not really a mathematician," he explained. "I'm a *teacher* of mathematics. I have been teaching it for as long as I can remember. Everyone seems to have a certain level in mathematics. I know a lot of people who do wonderfully in high school, but when they get to the calculus, they find that it is a whole other ball game and they're lost. I think that is true for almost everybody at a certain level. For some people it's subtraction. I did hang on with it. When I was about half way through, I switched to statistics because that was more my style. I could handle that better. But I got to a certain level and found that, although I was doing it—that I *could* do it—I didn't internalize it. This is something that is difficult to explain to a nonmathematician. I think that the graduate school would have been happier if I had gotten through; but I wasn't taking up any space particularly, so they didn't mind.

"Of course, by the time I went back in 1960, I was the same age as the junior faculty—so I wasn't exactly a kid any more. It was a more friendly, treated-like-equals kind of situation. I was mostly auditing courses, since I had satisfied all of my requirements for a Ph.D., written the minor thesis, and even started on my dissertation. Finally, in 1965, I decided that I wasn't going to make it. It wasn't something I wanted. I kept saying to myself that if I ever get this dissertation written, I will never have to do any research again. Then I realized that I must be telling myself something, so I decided enough is enough. There was a lot of guilt in all that—all those years invested—so to deal with that, I began teaching at MIT. I taught quantitative courses in the political science department—statistics and mathematical models—from 1962 to 1971. That's another reason why I can't say that I am a mathematician. I've never held an appointment in a mathematics department. I have been in the Harvard Business School, where I taught calculus in 1961; in the Harvard Education School, where I taught geometry for high school mathematics teachers from 1963 to 1965; and in the psychology department at Wellesley, where I taught statistics in 1965. In fact, in 1965, I had three appointments simultaneously—at Harvard, Wellesley, and MIT."

In 1964, NBC imported the British television program "That Was the Week That Was," which had been a great success in England. "I didn't think that the American version was very good," Lehrer went on, "but it was the only game of its kind in town. They seemed to be using material from everywhere, so I sent in some songs, which they used. Some of them were good and some of them weren't, but by 1965, when the show ended, I realized that I had enough songs to make a record. I particularly wanted to do it because somehow they had managed to take out the best line in each of my songs and replaced it with something vapid. I wanted some sort of record of how the songs were supposed to be. My earlier songs were mainly takeoffs on popular song forms. There wasn't much political content in them. There was one called 'The Wild West Is Where I Want to Be' that was inspired by a summer I had spent at Los Alamos in 1952. It was about the atmospheric testing of atomic bombs, but it was really intended to be a 'Home on the Range,' jokey kind of send-up. But in "That Was the Week That Was," there were specific topics in the news each week that I wrote about.

"I didn't sing on the program. Most of the songs were sung by a woman named Nancy Ames. I had the fantasy that she was a gorgeous robot who had been programmed to pronounce English correctly— that is, phonetically. She had marvelous diction, but she didn't quite understand, as far as I could tell, what the jokes were. It was better when they were sung by a comedian like Steve Allen or Buck Henry. That was another reason why I wanted to do them myself. So I called the hungry i in San Francisco, where I had appeared a couple of times in the fifties, and asked if I could do a couple of weeks there to try the songs out and to polish them up for recording. I wanted to see if the laughs really were there. So I did two weeks, and then a third when Dick Gregory couldn't appear. (He was picketing somewhere.) Warner Brothers offered to do the record, and I signed a contract with them and did a fourth week a month later to make the record. At the end of it, I was finally convinced that I had no desire to be a performer. When I went back in 1965, after not having performed for five years, various people said to me that maybe I would like it and want to begin to perform again—that people would start applauding, and that would make me want to resume my career. But after the second week, I realized that I was not cut out to be a performer. It requires more than the ability to do it. You have to have the desire."

With a few rare exceptions, most of them abroad, that was the last time Lehrer appeared in public. He did not write any new songs until 1970, when he was contacted by the Children's Television Workshop, which was in the process of producing "The Electric Company" for public television. "It was the first time," Lehrer continued, "that any-body had asked me to write songs other than the kinds of songs that I had already written. These new songs were just for kiddies. They weren't supposed to be satirical or political or anything like that. They were just meant to teach reading.

"Before that, every once in a while, somebody would come up with some idea for a satirical song he wanted me to do. But it was always the same thing over again. I remember that one lady called me up and said that she loved my songs. She told me that she thought the main problem in America was materialism, and that I should write a song making fun of materialism. I told her that of course I would do it—if she paid me enough money. I couldn't resist saying that, but she was very serious and didn't think it was as funny as I thought it was.

"When 'The Electric Company' writers contacted me, it was the first time that somebody had wanted me to use my craft rather than just to repeat what I had already done. I thought it was a great idea, and I managed to write ten songs for them. One of them is called 'Silent E,' and it tries to teach kids about silent *E*'s. It still appears on reruns of 'The Electric Company.' I am amazed by how many college students, who were kids in 1970 and 1971, when the song first appeared, know it without knowing that I had anything to do with it. I didn't get any credit on the show. It was my voice, but I didn't get any particular credit. Nor did I want any. It was just fun, and 'The Electric Company' songs are the last songs I have written."

By 1971, Lehrer had been teaching at MIT for nine years. "It began to be less fun," he remarked, "and I decided that I was too old not to have fun. So I tried to think of a place where I could continue to teach, in a different kind of atmosphere. They had begun to take it all very seriously at MIT, and then they made my course compulsory for graduate students. That was the last straw. In compulsory courses, you get those people who are just sitting there, and you know they would rather be somewhere else—anywhere else. That's not how I want to teach. MIT was taking it much too seriously. There were a lot of people there who seemed to think that political science is, in fact, a science, and therefore one should pay attention to quantitative approaches to it. I don't have anything against any of them personally. Personally, they were fine. But it just became less fun—and, furthermore, they moved us to a new building on the MIT campus. That destroyed all communication whatsoever. So I started looking around. I had heard of Santa Cruz through magazine articles, and it sounded like the kind of place I would like to try. I wrote them out of the blue, just getting names out of their catalogue, to see if I could teach my math course there. They said OK, so I gave a year's notice to MIT and went out there to try it. I loved it, and I have been doing it ever since."

At first, Lehrer went out to California for only the three months in the winter quarter. "I had decided that, not only was I too old not to have fun, but that I never wanted to shovel snow again. I didn't want to be very cold. That's a sign of old age, but that's fair enough. In Cambridge, I had been a member of a play-reading group. We would read plays once a week for our mutual entertainment. Then someone got the idea that we should do a musical. That caught on so well that each year we did a musical. So when I got to Santa Cruz and saw that there was a play-reading course, I thought that we could have a musical-reading course, too. A number of students were interested in musicals, but there was no outlet for them. So I proposed my course, and it was accepted. Now I teach my math course for one quarter and the course on musicals for the other. I am there for six months."

The idea for doing *Tomfoolery* also came to Lehrer out of the blue from Cameron Mackintosh, who had co-produced the show *Side by Side by Sondheim,* a successful retrospective of Stephen Sondheim songs. "I had been approached by other people before," Lehrer said, "but never by somebody with a track record, who had such a definite plan and the idea for a first-class production." It took almost two years from the time Mackintosh first contacted Lehrer in 1978 until the show first opened in London on 5 June 1980, at the Criterion Theatre. It ran for a year. A Canadian production began touring Canada in November 1980, and there have also been productions in South Africa, Australia, Ireland, and Hong Kong. Two American productions ran in 1981, and Pantheon Books brought out *Too Many Songs by Tom Lehrer with Not Enough Pictures by Ronald Searle,* which is, as one might imagine, an illustrated songbook containing most of the Lehrer classics.

"I went over to London in the spring of 1980," Lehrer told me, "and spent a few weeks in the rehearsals and tryouts in Brighton and went to the opening in London. It was delightful, and I was very pleased with the whole idea. I think that ten years ago that kind of humor would not have worked the way it seems to now. People were too serious then. I rewrote a few things for the London performance to de-Americanize them. One thing I had to rewrite really surprised me. You may remember that in 'Poisoning Pigeons in the Park,' there is a line that goes 'and maybe we'll do in a squirrel or two.' Here, in this country, there was always a laugh there, but in London, there was nothing. I couldn't figure out why. I kept asking if I was pronouncing *squirrel* right, and if they knew what a squirrel was. Everyone said I was and they did. Finally I figured out that they don't have squirrels in their parks. Squirrels, to them, are like foxes and belong in forests. So I changed *squirrel* to *sparrow* and got the old laugh back again."

Just before Lehrer left my apartment, I asked him whether he had written any songs in recent years. "No," he replied, with no apparent regret, "except for a few I have done for birthdays or special occasions—not for public consumption."

"Do you ever have any urges in that direction?" I asked him. "No. No, I don't. In the old days the ideas would just come to me, and the next time I was at a piano I would work them out. Now the ideas don't particularly come. Maybe it's because I don't find the times as funny as I used to. Maybe it's the times themselves, or maybe it's senility. I never thought of myself as a composer anyway. I am amazed by how nice the songs sound when they are played by a five-piece orchestra, like the one we had in *Tomfoolery*. Now I see that I am often referred to as 'the late Tom Lehrer.' I have a small file of clippings like that, which I cherish, because people assume that I am dead. At the time, in the fifties and sixties, when I was writing the songs, I was not really aware of the idea that they would be presented to an audience—at least, not in the beginning. So I wasn't self-conscious about them. That's what happens when you are young. You do things like a kid without going through all those layers of self-censorship. I was just saying in those songs what I was thinking. Now if I wrote a song, I would think, 'How will this go over with an audience?' I couldn't help thinking that. When I first wrote them, they were for my own amusement, and it turned out, much to my delight, that not only did they sell, but they are still selling—something that was totally unforeseen. Who at that time would have thought that thirty years later people would still be interested in them?"

And he said, putting on his coat, "I don't know what it means, but it's probably not good."

CHAPTER 14

A Woman's Place

Not LONG AGO, I was browsing through a collection of Einstein's essays and aphorisms which was published in 1931 under the title *Cosmic Religion.* A section headed "Miscellaneous" contains both truisms (like "Youth is always the same, endlessly the same") and more challenging observations. One of them reads: "In Mme. Curie I can see no more than a brilliant exception. Even if there were more women scientists of like caliber they would serve as no argument against the fundamental weakness of the feminine organization." Since no context is given for this observation, it is not clear whether Einstein meant it literally or as some sort of ironic joke. His last assistant, who worked with him from 1950 until his death in 1955, was a woman—the mathematician Bruruia Kaufman, who eventually emigrated to Israel. None of his other assistants were women, and it is a fact that the proportion of women who work in abstract mathematical fields is very small.

The arguments as to why this is so are endless. Is it environmental prejudice? Is there an innate sexual difference? I do not know the answer, and I doubt whether the answer is simple. One of the things I would keep in mind before trying to make any judgment, is the historical record of the Jews. Throughout this century, Jews have played a important role in the abstract sciences: Einstein himself is the most obvious example. But if one looks into the history of these fields prior to the nineteenth century, it is difficult to identify any great Jewish contribution. I cannot think of any Jewish physicist of any significance around, say, the time of Newton. That can certainly be traced to the prejudicial atmosphere in which Jews lived. In the ghettos, only certain professions were allowed, and it is hard to see how a Jew born into a ghetto family could have obtained the least scientific education. It was only after the professions were opened up that Jews began playing a role in science. A historian of science writing in the eighteenth century might well have been tempted to comment that the pronounced absence of Jews in physics could be traced to a "fundamental weakness of the Jewish organization."

This issue becomes especially interesting with regard to a biography I have been reading of a woman, Sophia Kovalevsky, who is universally acknowledged to have been the greatest woman mathematician prior to the twentieth century. The book, by Don H. Kennedy, is called *Little Sparrow*, an affectionate nickname given to Sophia by a nurse when she was a child. Kennedy makes it clear in his foreword that his wife, Nina, who is evidently related to Sophia, had childhood impressions of her:

> As a schoolgirl struggling with arithmetic, for which she had no liking, Nina was bedeviled by parental efforts to inspire her by frequent references to her collateral relation whose mathematical genius startled the academics of Europe; and not surprisingly, Nina grew up with a distinct aversion to that distant Sophia, that paragon for imitation. Nina's mother had learned her first arithmetic under the dedicated man who had been Sophia's first tutor.

Later, Mrs. Kennedy became fascinated by Sophia after reading her *Recollections of Childhood*, written in 1890 when Sophia—who died the next year—was forty. In preparation for this biography, Mrs. Kennedy translated hundreds of pages about Sophia from Russian into English for her husband.

Sophia Kovalevsky was born in Moscow on 15 January 1850. Her father, General Vasily Vasilevich Korvin-Krukovsky, was a nobleman who, on the eve of Sophia's birth, had lost so much money at cards that he had to pawn his wife's jewelry to settle his debt. The general was then fifty-one, and his wife, Elizabeth, whom he had married seven years earlier, was thirty. Even apart from his loss at cards, Sophia's father did not consider her birth an especially happy event. He wanted a male heir—a son, Feodor, was born five years later; and his disappointment was, it seems, so great that Sophia's mother took an instant and lasting dislike to Sophia; a sister, Aniuta, six years older, was her mother's favorite. In her *Recollections,* Sophia tried to re-create this aspect of her childhood:

> Sometimes I feel an inclination to caress mama, to climb upon her knees; but, somehow or other, these attempts always end by my hurting mama through my awkwardness, or tearing her gown, and then I run away and hide myself in the corner with shame. For this reason I began to develop a sort of shyness with mama, and this shyness was further augmented by the fact that I often heard my nurse say that Aniuta and Fedya were mama's favorites, and that mama disliked me. I do not know whether this was true or not, but nurse always said it regardless of my presence.

From the age of eight until she was eighteen, Sophia lived on her family's two estates at Palibino, a village in White Russia close to what is now the border with Latvia. Kennedy does an excellent job of suggesting not only what young Sophia's very constrained life as the daughter of a nobleman was like but also what the life of the Russian nobility—in the case of Sophia's father, rather like that of the British gentry—was like. On the two estates, there lived some three hundred serfs who worked the land, keeping a small percentage of the production for themselves. This was only part of the retinue. Kennedy describes the rest:

> The family had twenty-five to thirty household servants, all being serfs except the tutor, the governess, the seamstress, the estates' steward, and the special chef from Petersburg. The General had Ilia, his valet-butler and general household factotum; his wife and daughters their personal maids; Feodor his nurse; also there were Daria the housekeeper, Yakov the coachman, the dishwasher, the footmen, about ten general maids, the carpenter, the gardeners, the stable hands, and the night watchman.

These comfortable arrangements changed abruptly on 19 February 1861, when Czar Alexander II emancipated the serfs. The emancipation produced financial chaos in Sophia's family and, in one way or another, haunted her for the rest of her life.

As far as I can judge from Kennedy's account, Sophia did not show any of the signs of mathematical precocity we have learned to expect from such geniuses. Though her tutor, one Joseph Ingatevich Malevich, wrote at the age of seventy-five a romantic account of his "discovery" of her abilities, in her *Recollections* she gives him short shrift; and it is clear that his own mathematical education was so poor that he probably could not have recognized real precocity. She recalls that in her early teens she studied algebra secretly at night while her governess slept behind a screen in the same room. When she was about sixteen, a neighbor who was a physicist brought her father a new text in physics, which Sophia began to study. Although her background was limited, she managed to understand enough of the book to impress the neighbor profoundly; and he, in turn, persuaded the general to hire a real mathematician, whom Sophia could visit in Petersburg. This tutor, Alexander Strannoliubsky, a professor at the naval academy, was astonished by the ease with which she learned the differential calculus—almost as if she had seen it somewhere before. In fact she had: when she was very young, one of the rooms the children used at Palibino was covered with a temporary "wallpaper" that, for some reason, consisted of sheets of lithographed lectures on the calculus, which her father had studied in his youth. Although Sophia had understood neither the symbols nor the text, she had memorized them. When she saw the symbols again, she realized their connection to her childhood.

At about this time—when Sophia was fourteen—she and her sister came to know Feodor Dostoevski. Aniuta, who was beautiful and blond, had begun a secret career as a writer. It had to be secret because, as far as the general was concerned, writers—and female writers, above all— belonged to the demimonde. Dostoevski—who had already been sentenced to be shot for political activity but had, instead, managed to serve five years in Siberia followed by four more in the army as a common soldier—was editing a literary magazine entitled *The Epoch*. He accepted two of Aniuta's stories and began a correspondence with her, writing in care of a trusted housekeeper. The general intercepted the letter containing the acceptance of the second story and three hundred rubles in payment for both stories. He was so horrified by this discovery that he took to his bed. After a week, he consented to have Aniuta read her story aloud to him. It seems he was favorably impressed, and agreed to let her correspond with Dostoevski, provided that he see all the letters. Even more important, he sanctioned a meeting between the sisters and Dostoevski, who was then forty-three, provided their mother was present. The meeting was a disaster, largely owing to Dostoevski's rude behavior; but a second meeting, arranged secretly and with only the two sisters present, was a success. Dostoevski was greatly taken by the two young women and not long afterward proposed marriage to Aniuta. Though she accepted, the engagement was short-lived because Dostoevski had a fit of jealousy during a family reception at which another potential suitor was present. For a while, Dostoevski persisted, but to no avail. However, he did become a good lifelong friend to Sophia. It has been suggested that in *The Idiot* Dostoevski based the character of Alexandra on Aniuta and that of Aglia on Sophia.

In 1868, when Sophia was eighteen, the family moved to Petersburg. This was at a time when all university education was officially closed to women in Russia. Almost the only way a woman could manage to get a higher education was to leave Russia, and the only way to do that, at least in her social circle, was to marry. The sisters decided that they would attempt to arrange what Kennedy calls a "nihilistic" marriage, into which a couple would enter with the explicit understanding that they would be married in name only. The idea was Aniuta would so marry and then chaperone her younger sister on their joint venture abroad. For the role of husband, they found a young political radical named Vladimir Onufrievich Kovalevsky; though educated in jurisprudence, he went on to become one of the founders of the new Darwinian science of evolutionary paleontology. He was not, it turned out, interested in Aniuta but soon afterward proposed a nihilistic marriage to Sophia. Thus began—in 1869—a communal life of such complexity that it would require a Dostoevski to do it full justice.

Much of Kennedy's book deals with this stormy relationship, which lasted until Vladimir's suicide in 1883. The marriage was eventually consummated; and in 1878, a daughter was born and christened Sophia, though known first as Fufu and later as Sonya. (Sophia Kovalevsky herself is generally known to mathematicians as Sonya—a name she used for much of her adult life.) From the point of view of the history of mathematics, the great thing this odd marriage achieved was that it allowed Sophia to study in Europe.

The decisive professional relationship of Sophia's life began in 1870, when she first met the German mathematician Karl Theodore William Weierstrass. Anyone who studies somewhat advanced mathematics inevitably encounters aspects of Weierstrass's work; his influence is still very much with us. When Sophia met him, in Berlin, he was a fifty-five-year-old bachelor and lived with his two middle-aged sisters. A photograph of him in Kennedy's book makes him look like the middle-aged Bach. (Photographs of Sophia make her look stunning.) He was adamant that Sophia, as a woman, could not attend his university lectures; probably to get rid of her, he agreed to tutor her privately, providing she was able to solve several problems so difficult he assigned them only to his most advanced students. A week later, she came back with the solutions. Weierstrass had the great good sense, and the generosity of spirit, to realize that Sophia was something extraordinary indeed; and for most of the rest of her life, he functioned as her mentor, both in her mathematical work and in all aspects of her career and personal life.

From Kennedy's description, he sounds like a perfectly marvelous man. By 1874, Sophia had completed three research papers under Weierstrass's guidance. In one of them—her thesis and probably the most important piece of mathematics she ever did—she generalized some work done by her great contemporary, the French mathematician Augustin Cauchy; the so-called Cauchy-Kovalevsky theorem is a basic element of the theory of partial differential equations. Having finished her degree, she returned to Russia to live with Vladimir and, despite constant remonstrations from Weierstrass, gave up creative mathematics for some seven years. The fact that there were no university positions open to women in Russia must certainly have played a role in this—but, as Kennedy writes, "the plain fact was that at the age of twenty-four Sophia had wearied of mathematics." What she might have done if she had continued to work during this period, no one, of course, can say.

By 1880, there was a rift in Sophia's marriage; although she and Vladimir were never divorced, the marriage was, for all practical purposes, over. Sophia left Russia in that year and returned only as a visitor thereafter, leaving Fufu behind in the care of friends. In 1883, Sophia finally found a teaching position—at the University of Stockholm. It was, at least in part, Weierstrass's doing. From 1874 until 1876, she had stopped answering his letters. Very concerned, he had dispatched to Petersburg another of his mathematical protégés, the Swede Gosta Mittag-Leffler, to find out what had happened to her. When Mittag-Leffler was appointed to the University of Stockholm, he arranged to have Sophia appointed, first to a nonsalaried lectureship and then, in 1889, to a life professorship.

It would be nice to report that from the time she arrived in Stockholm she lived happily ever after. It is clear from Kennedy's book that Sophia was an extremely complex woman whose restlessness never really allowed her to derive much contentment from anything—either in her work or in her personal relationships—for long. She had mixed feelings both about living in Sweden and about spending the rest of her life doing mathematics. One of her many internal conflicts concerned whether she wanted to be a mathematician or a writer. In 1876, she had begun writing and, after moving to Stockholm, wrote not just several novels but—in collaboration with Mittag-Leffler's sister Anne Charlotte—an ambitious play, "The Struggle for Happiness," as well. While all this was going on, she won—in 1888, for her paper "On the Rotation of a Solid Body Around a Fixed Point"—a prestigious prize in mathematics awarded by the French Academy of Sciences. She also fell in love with Maksim Maksimovich Kovalevsky, a distant relative of her husband. According to Kennedy, this affair was quite as stormy as her marriage. It seems that she and Maksim might have married, but Sophia died suddenly of pneumonia in Stockholm, on 10 February 1891. She was just forty-one. Mr. Kennedy tells us that her last words were "Too much happiness."

Different morals have been drawn from Sophia Kovalevsky's life. Some people see in it an argument for what women can accomplish in an abstract field like pure mathematics, given the opportunity for an appropriate education. They are certainly right. During the few years when Kovalevsky actually focused on mathematics, her accomplishments were great. But her problem was focusing. She lacked for most of her life the singlemindedness necessary to produce in mathematics consistent work of the first rank. One thinks especially of the almost seven years after her first contact with Weierstrass, when she returned to Russia and spent most of her time engaging in schemes of financial speculation with her husband—schemes that turned out disastrously and were a factor in his suicide.

Before rushing to attribute this to—in Einstein's words—a "fundamental weakness of the feminine organization," one might contemplate Einstein's evaluation of his best friend, Michele Besso. Though Besso was male, his career was in some ways similar to Sophia's. An engineer Einstein met while in the Swiss Federal Polytechnic Institute in Zurich at the turn of the century, Besso not only went to work with him in the patent office in Bern but is the only person acknowledged in Einstein's 1905 paper on the special theory of relativity. They kept up an intimate correspondence for fifty-two years until Besso's death in 1955.

The correspondence has not yet been translated into English but is available in French and German as part of the *Collection histoire de la pensée*. Besso's younger sister, Bice, married the Florentine count Rusconi, whose daughter Laura married the novelist Niccolò Tucci. In 1947, Tucci and his mother-in-law went to visit Einstein in Princeton, and Tucci wrote the visit up as a "Reporter at Large" for the *New Yorker*. Here is a bit of the conversation:

> "Herr Professor," she [Bice] asked . . . , "this I really meant to ask you for a long time—why hasn't Michele made some important discovery in mathematics?"
>
> "*Aber,* Frau Bice," said Einstein laughing, "this is a very good sign. Michele is a humanist, a universal spirit, too interested in too many things to become a monomaniac. Only a monomaniac gets what we commonly refer to as results."

Einstein's words suggest that it is difficult to be both a scientist and a humanist, a specialist and a "universal spirit." If we add to this the burden of being a woman in a world so heavily dominated by men, it becomes apparent that we must take a somewhat different perspective on Sophia's failure to focus. Women—in the sciences or any profession—have only recently been encouraged, even allowed, to focus. Becoming intensely committed to any serious subject was formerly thought a masculine trait; the time, energy, and talents of women were better spent ministering to the needs of such devotees. Further, the education of women discouraged focusing; it was thought better for them to learn a little of this, a little of that, but nothing too completely. Now that these barriers are coming down, we are, for perhaps the first time in history, in a position to confront the question raised by Einstein: namely, are there gender-related differences when it comes to the ability to think abstractly? What Kennedy's excellent and sensitive book shows, I believe, is that this gift is equally rare for both men and women.

Who Was Christy Mathewson?

I HAVE LONG FELT that the very best popular-science writing must come from scientists. For them, science is a part of everyday experience—their skin and bones—and this feeling is what emerges when a really good popular book is written by a scientist. But if this is to happen, several criteria must be met. In the first place, the scientist not only must have the ability to write but must really *want* to write. Then, the scientist must be working in a field that has broad social and intellectual ramifications and must recognize them. As someone said, God loves the details. But if popular-science writing consists only of details, no one will read it. I first became aware of the writing of Stephen Jay Gould some years ago, when I began reading his column "This View of Life" in *Natural History*. Everything about these pieces seemed right to me. There was the enthusiasm of a young and gifted scientist at the height of his powers. The problems he discussed—involving evolutionary biology—were of wide interest and could be made generally understandable, and the writing was full of fun, totally without pretentiousness, and absolutely clear. Many of these pieces have been collected in such of his books as *Ever Since Darwin* and *The Panda's Thumb*. One wondered what would happen when Professor Gould—he teaches geology, biology, and the history of science at Harvard—turned his energies to a single major subject and addressed the general reader. Now one knows. *The Mismeasure of Man* is a really extraordinary book.

The Mismeasure of Man is a devastating and often extremely angry attack on the notion that "intelligence" is a "thing"—like temperature—to which can be attached a single number; and that, furthermore, this number is an intrinsic characteristic of a person, somehow independent of all environmental influences. One might call this the "fallacy of misplaced reification." It is beautifully characterized by John Stuart Mill in a quotation given in Professor Gould's book: "The tendency has always been strong to believe that whatever received a name must be an entity or being, having an independent existence of its own. And if no real entity answering to the name could be found, men did not for that reason suppose that none existed, but imagined that it was something peculiarly abstruse and mysterious." In fact, the dispute between the "realists," who believe that behind a name there must be a "real" essence, and the "nominalists," who believe that names refer only to particular things, has had a long and honorable history in philosophy. If all that was at stake here were an academic metaphysical dispute, there would be little reason to get exercised over it. But that is not what is at stake. Professor Gould argues that because of the false reification of intelligence, hundreds of thousands—perhaps millions—of people's lives have been circumscribed or even ruined. He writes, "We pass through this world but once. Few tragedies can be more extensive than the stunting of life, few injustices deeper than the denial of an opportunity to strive or even to hope, by a limit imposed from without, but falsely identified as lying within."

It will probably come as no surprise to read that the notion that black people are mentally inferior was pervasive in American society from the very beginning. Thomas Jefferson wrote, "I advance it, therefore, as a suspicion only, that the blacks, whether originally a distinct race, or made distinct by time and circumstance, are inferior to the whites in the endowment both of body and of mind." Probably the Founders *had* to feel this way if they were to use blacks in slavery. And it will come as no surprise to read that, with the development of science in the nineteenth century, scholars used "scientific" methods to "prove" what most Europeans and Americans felt to be true anyway. Professor Gould, in the first part of his book, has re-examined the "proofs" on their own terms. The major preoccupation of these scholars was the size of brains. It was taken as a given that large brain size was correlated to intelligence, and measurements were done to confirm this "fact." In the mid-nineteenth century, Paul Broca, who was a surgeon and the founder of the Anthropological Society of Paris, felt able to announce, "In general, the brain is larger in mature adults than in the elderly, in men than in women, in eminent men than in men of mediocre talent, in superior races than in inferior races. . . . Other things equal, there is a remarkable relationship between the development of intelligence and the volume of the brain." Broca was a conscientious scientist, and he was nearly upended by his own data, for he discovered that Eskimos, Lapps, Malays, Tatars, "and several other peoples of the Mongolian type would surpass [in brain size] the most civilized people of Europe." But not to worry, for West African blacks, Kaffirs, Nubians, Tasmanians, Hottentots, and Australian aborigines had, Broca discovered, smaller brains. What Broca did not take sufficiently into account is that there is a correlation between brain size and body size. He did take this into account in the case of women but concluded that it was not relevant, since women were inferior regardless: "We are therefore permitted to suppose that the relatively small size of the female brain depends in part upon her physical inferiority and in part upon her intellectual inferiority." (Some of the later workers in this dismal enterprise did try to take into account body size, or something like it; and when one of them, Léonce Manouvrier, subtracted the effects of what he termed "sexual mass," he came to the conclusion that the corrected brain size of women was actually greater than that of men.)

There is, by the way, a legitimate and fascinating study of brain size, which is still being carried on, and is due largely to the pioneering work of Harry J. Jerison. Professor Gould touched on Jerison's work in *The Panda's Thumb*. For many years, Jerison has been measuring the size of the brains of animals, both extant and extinct (the latter through fossils). He finds that within a given class—reptiles, say—brain size increases, as one would guess, with body size, but not as rapidly as body size. Gould notes that "brains grow only about two-thirds as fast as bodies." A theory that might account for the "two-thirds" is that the animal brain may have evolved in size in response to sensory stimulations. These would be received from the surface of the body, which, roughly speaking, increases in magnitude as an area, while "body size" is really a measure of volume. (The surface area of a sphere, for example, increases with the square of the radius, while the volume of a sphere increases with the cube of the radius.) James A. Hopson, of the University of Chicago, has shown that the much-maligned dinosaurs fit very nicely on the reptile curve. While there is certainly no simple relation of brain size to intelligence, there is no reason to think that the dinosaurs perished because they were anomalously dumb. Interestingly, humans are totally off the scale on these curves. It might be expected that human growth would not follow this pattern, since much of our brain does not respond merely to sensory stimuli: we think about ourselves.

The heart of *The Mismeasure of Man* is Professor Gould's analysis of the use and misuse of I.Q. tests. The originator of the modern intelligence test was the French psychologist Alfred Binet. He emerges as one of the few heroes of Gould's book. In 1898, Binet began, in the tradition of Broca, by measuring heads. After three years of work, he decided that any interpretation of whatever differences in size there were—and they were minuscule—between the heads of bright and poor students might well reflect his own a-priori bias about how such students should score on tests. "The idea of measuring intelligence by measuring heads seemed ridiculous," he wrote. In 1904, he was commissioned by the French Minister of Public Education to develop techniques for picking out children who might be having learning difficulties. By 1908, he had got the idea of assigning an age level to each of a variety of tasks—the earliest age at which an average child should be able to complete the task. The age level of the most advanced task a child could perform was said to be his or her "mental age." When this mental age was subtracted from the child's true age, a number could be assigned to the child's so-called intelligence. In 1912, a German psychologist, Louis William Stern, concluded that it would be more satisfactory to divide the mental age by the chronological age; and hence the notion of an "intelligence quotient" was born. Binet, unlike the people who followed him, had absolutely no idea of arriving at a single number that would give a definitive measure of something called "intelligence." Indeed, he wrote, "For the sake of simplicity of statement, we will speak of a child of 8 years having the intelligence of a child of 7 or 9 years; these expressions, if accepted arbitrarily, may give place to illusions." And, above all, he did not intend that his scale be used to stigmatize a child. Professor Gould notes, "Of one thing Binet was sure: whatever the cause of poor performance in school, the aim of his scale was to identify in order to help and improve, not to label in order to limit. Some children might be innately incapable of normal achievement, but all could improve with special help." Professor Gould has no quarrel with this use of I.Q. and other achievement tests. He writes, "Speaking personally, I feel that tests of the I.Q. type were helpful in the proper diagnosis of my own learning-disabled son. His average score, the I.Q. itself, meant nothing, for it was only an amalgam of some very high and very low scores; but the pattern of low values indicated his areas of deficit." What he does quarrel with—and *quarrel* is much too mild a word, since this part of his book is a brilliantly acerbic polemic—is the evolution and corruption of Binet's work, especially in the United States, where I.Q. testing became, and still is, literally and figuratively, an industry. Along with this came the notion that if something can be tested, it must correspond to something in reality; and the further notion—which, according to Gould, is a "home-grown American product"—that such "intelligence" is hereditary. Not only could an individual be condemned to a life of lessened expectations on the basis of I.Q. tests, but so could his or her offspring.

Lest one imagine that all this is some sort of academic exercise, Professor Gould gives a concrete example: the case of Carrie and Doris Buck, two sisters in Virginia. On the basis of a variant of Binet's test, the mother of Carrie and Doris Buck was judged to have a mental age of seven. Carrie, on the basis of the same test, was awarded a mental age of nine. She was the mother of a child who was also judged to be "feeble-minded," so the State of Virginia decided that both Carrie and her sister Doris should be sterilized. In 1927, this became a Supreme Court case—*Buck* v. *Bell;* and Oliver Wendell Holmes, Jr., delivered the decision, which upheld the sterilization law, stating, "Three generations of imbeciles are enough." Under this law, several thousand people were sterilized in Virginia from 1924 to 1972, when the practice apparently stopped. Doris Buck, who, like her sister, would not be considered even mentally deficient by present standards, was not informed of what had been done to her. She later said, "They told me that the operation was for an appendix and rupture." She and her husband, Mathew Figgins, tried for years to have a child before they found out it was impossible. When she learned that, she said, "I broke down and cried. My husband and me wanted children desperately. We were crazy about them. I never knew what they'd done to me."

Professor Gould rips apart both the tests that led to this kind of result, and the atmosphere in which such tests were often given. The originator of one series of tests was Robert M. Yerkes. Yerkes was a professor in the Psychology Department at Harvard when, in 1915, as Gould puts it, he "got one of those 'big ideas' that propel the history of science: could psychologists possibly persuade the army to test all its recruits?"

Yerkes did manage to persuade an often reluctant military to test nearly two million men. The tests were of two types—Alpha and Beta—administered according to the recruit's degree of literacy. Here is a sample of the Alpha multiple-choice questions, which supposedly tested the *intrinsic* intelligence of the recruit:

Crisco is a: patent medicine, disinfectant, toothpaste, food product

The number of a Kaffir's legs is: 2, 4, 6, 8

Christy Mathewson is famous as a: writer, artist, baseball player, comedian.

The Beta tests were reserved for nonliterates, many of whom had never used a pencil prior to the test. The Beta tests required associating, among other things, a rivet with a pocket knife, a filament with a light bulb, a horn with a phonograph, a net with a tennis court, and a ball with a bowler's hand. The recruits were rushed through the tests with examiners shouting orders at them. Professor Gould gave the Beta test to one of his classes at Harvard under very benign conditions. Of fifty-three students, thirty-one scored A and sixteen B; six got C, which meant that they were fit only for the duties of a buck private. (I remember being required to take such a test at the time of the Korean War and being confronted with all sorts of weird diagrams involving tools like awls. God knows how I did on the test, but, in the event, I was not sent to Korea. The atmosphere under which the test was given was such that I am not sure I could have spelled my own name correctly.) Yerkes was convinced that blacks were innately stupid. He ignored the fact that the better-educated Northern blacks did better than the mean for whites from nine Southern states. He believed that an I.Q. was a genetically determined quantity, like blue eyes; he was not able to recognize that his own data proved that the strongest factor in this kind of testing is environmental.

Using these tests, Yerkes came to the remarkable conclusion that the average mental age of white recruits was 13.08 years. (This use of statistics, like several others that Professor Gould cites, reminds me of the disease that struck only men of fifty: there were two known cases—one a boy of two and the other a man of ninety-eight.) Yerkes's result so alarmed him and some of his colleagues that they began to seek the cause. Since they subscribed to a "hereditarian" doctrine of intelligence, they felt that the cause could lie only in the degeneration of

American genes; and this, they reasoned, must have to do with the dilution of "American" stock by immigration—or, at least, by the wrong kind of immigration. In 1923, a disciple of Yerkes named Carl C. Brigham, a psychology professor at Princeton, published one of the most insidious books on this subject that has ever been written—*A Study of American Intelligence.* Brigham concluded, on the basis of the Army tests, that recent immigrants to America were polluting the gene pool for intelligence. That his argument was taken seriously seems, in retrospect, almost unbelievable. The tests showed that each five-year period of residency in this country brought an increase in the immigrants' test scores; hence, any immigrants who had lived here five years or more were more "intelligent" than new arrivals. He dismissed the obvious explanation—the environmental bias built into the tests (Christy Mathewson was likely not a household name in a Polish *shtetl* or a Macedonian hamlet)—and concluded that the recent immigrants were intrinsically less intelligent. This was readily explained, he felt: there were fewer Germans, Scandinavians, and Britons among them. The recent immigrants were mainly Italians, Greeks, and Poles, along with Jews, whom Brigham classified as "Alpine Slavs." All this might simply be considered funny except that it was widely accepted and led to the Immigration Restriction Act of 1924, which devised a quota system to keep out the groups that had scored poorly on the Yerkes tests. Whether, as Professor Gould maintains, this was the primary cause of the death of an enormous number of Jews who could not immigrate to this country in the 1930s is debatable. My own guess is that, considering the anti-Semitism that was part of the fabric of American life at that time, this "scientific evidence" of racial inferiority simply allowed some people to do with better conscience what they would have found a way to do anyway. It is remarkable that some six years after Brigham's book led to the quota system, he described the army tests on which it was based as absolute nonsense: "One of the most pretentious of these comparative racial studies—the writer's own—was without foundation." By that time, the damage had been done.

It would be good to report that all this belongs to some "medieval" past. But, as Professor Gould makes clear, and as we all know, the spirit of Yerkes and his ilk persists. It is, in my view, important to keep certain things in mind when one reads that a race or a sex has some differential factor of intelligence. Even taken on their own terms, the phenomena— if they are phenomena—that such reports deal with are always buried beneath statistics. Real scientific phenomena usually stand out like a sore thumb. It did not take, for example, a hair-raising and controversial statistical analysis to convince people that pulsars exist. A few good nights at the radio telescope were enough. (It is this, by the way, that has always made the reports of extrasensory perception in the guessing of cards and the like seem so dull to me. At least, Yuri Geller, the famous Israeli magician who "bent" spoons, put on a good show.) Two things do stick out like a sore thumb. One is how little genetic variation there is—how similar the genes are—among all the races of the earth. Professor Gould quotes his colleague Richard Lewontin: "If the holocaust comes and a small tribe deep in the New Guinea forests are the only survivors, almost all the genetic variation now expressed among the innumerable groups of our four billion people will be preserved." The second is how numerous the genetically expressed variations are *within* any racial group. One can find a person of one's own race or of a different race who is better at just about any given task than one is oneself. These are differences that we live with every day and, if we are mature, come to accept and even enjoy. What Professor Gould's book makes clear is how dangerous race prejudices are. It also makes clear how subjective and neurotic they are. If one insists on being a racist, science is no place to come for support. Whatever racism may be, it is not science.

CHAPTER 16

Science Education for the Nonscientist

ALTHOUGH I HAVE BEEN teaching physics and related subjects for some thirty years, it has never occurred to me to think of myself as an educator. An educator, I have always thought, is either a dean or someone who has taken at least one course in education. While I did once get an offer to become a dean—to which, incidentally, I replied that I was either too old or too young to become a dean—I have never taken a course in education. For better or worse, physicists, like most scientists, are simply set adrift in the classroom, and one hopes for the best. The results, needless to say, are mixed; but since we are dealing, in large part, with apprentice physicists, we can probably safely assume that their interest in the field will carry all of us through. I. I. Rabi once remarked to me that nascent physicists seem to be able to survive any amount of bad teaching. Rabi never had, at least until he received his Ph.D., anyone he can recall who was a good teacher. Einstein's only favorable recollections of *his* teachers dated back to the year he spent in a progressive high school in Switzerland. When he went to college in Zurich, he simply cut most of his classes, figuring, correctly in his case, that he could teach himself more, and better, physics than he could acquire in the classroom. This attitude was not lost on his teachers, who seem to have thought that he was—although the phrase was not yet current—something of a "flake."

Some years ago, however, under the auspices of the Phi Beta Kappa

Visiting Scholar Program, I visited a half-dozen college campuses located in the eastern part of the United States. Apart from offering formal lectures, one of the most significant aspects of this program was the opportunity for local scholars to discuss with the visitor problems in education. At first, when these problems were presented to me, I felt a little like a eunuch in a seraglio who is being interviewed about the sexual proclivities of the several ladies therein. But being a reasonably social animal, I felt that I should give the matter sufficient thought so that I could say *something*. After some time elapsed, I decided—in what the French call *l'esprit de l'escalier*—to put down on paper all of those things I had meant to say, but had been too slow-witted actually to say when the questions were raised. It used to be pointed out that the French army was perfectly prepared to fight the previous war. I am now more or less prepared to respond to the questions that were asked of me over a decade ago.

ALL of these questions concern how to teach science to the nonscientist. This is not exactly a novel concern, and what I have to say about it may not be novel either; but perhaps I can articulate some of the problems and opportunities. In my view, before one can discuss *what* to teach the nonscientist, one must ask oneself *why bother* to teach nonscientists science at all. In thinking about this, I was led to reread C. P. Snow's celebrated Rede Lecture, which he delivered in 1959. It was in this lecture that Snow introduced his much-debated notion of the "two cultures." Snow was, of course, perfectly aware that there are not simply *two* cultures. This obvious point has often obscured the arguments he was trying to present. Practitioners of medieval French and of cognitive psychology have engaged in heated arguments—some of which I have witnessed—that they, too, represent "cultures" that should be a part of every student's intellectual baggage. For some reason, whenever I have heard these discussions, I have been reminded of a definition of Unitarianism that a mathematician once told me. "Its practitioners," he said, "believe that there is, at *most*, one God." There are at least two cultures: that of the scientifically literate and that of the scientifically illiterate, and the question that concerns me is how to take from the former and add to the latter.

Snow's reasons, I found after rereading him, are not, in my view, entirely adequate. He seems to have had two concerns. The first I might describe by the term *cultural deprivation*. Snow spent a good deal of his time among nonscientists who, according to him, gave "a pitying chuckle at the news of scientists who have never read a major work of English literature." Since he does not name these unfortunates, they are safe in their Neanderthal anonymity. But Snow, dear man, rose to their defense. "Once or twice," he writes, "I have been provoked and have asked the company how many of them could describe the Second Law of Thermodynamics. The response was cold: It was also negative." The first thought that occurred to me upon reading this was, "So what!" Put on this level, is it really more important that, say, a Cambridge classics don be able to define entropy than, for example, that P. A. M. Dirac be able to read the Upanishads in Sanskrit? (The late J. Robert Oppenheimer *was* able to read the Upanishads in Sanskrit; but that is another matter.) If we had the time and the capacity, we would all probably be pleased if we could read Sanskrit. But no college administrator whom I have ever heard of has proposed making this a compulsory requirement for getting an undergraduate degree.

The precise question I am raising is why, then, are these administrators in apparently unanimous agreement that one, or more, science course should be compulsory? Snow's second concern, as I read him, was that unless science is more widely taught, there will be a shortage of qualified scientists and technicians in many countries. While this may indeed be true, it is also beside the point, if the point is the teaching of science to people who have not the slightest intention of becoming either scientists or technicians. What, then, is the point?

I think that there are basically three points. The first is what seems to me to be the simple fact that many nonscientists have a real curiosity about science. This fact, which is evident to those of us who write about science for the general public, did not seem to occur to Snow. One gets the impression that he felt that science is something that should be rammed down the reluctant gullets of classics majors because it is good for them, just as the learning of Latin was considered good for one when I went to high school. It never seems to have entered Snow's head that his nonscientist friends might have the same sort of curiosity about the origins and destiny of the universe as the very scientists who created, for example, the theory of the Big Bang.

In fact, something that has always bothered me about Snow is his remoteness from real science, which is evident in nearly everything he wrote and especially in his unfortunate, posthumously published book *The Physicists*, which is so full of mistakes of detail that, in reading it, one does not know whether to laugh or cry. Even in his Rede Lecture, the very lecture in which he laments the breech between scientist and nonscientist, he reveals that, when it came to contemporary physics, he did not really understand what he was talking about.

For example, at one point Snow discusses the impact of the discovery made in 1956 that nature does not respect parity symmetry—the symmetry between left- and right-handedness. Apart from the fact that he never explains what this discovery was, he attributes it to an experiment—an *experiment!*—done by T. D. Lee and C. N. Yang at Columbia University. It is true that Lee was at Columbia, but Yang was at the Institute for Advanced Study at Princeton, and neither man had done an experiment since they had been in graduate school. (Yang's encounters with experimental apparatuses as a graduate student in Chicago inspired a local rhyme: "Where there's a bang, there's Yang.") Lee and Yang suggested a whole class of experiments, some of which were done at Columbia, some at the University of Chicago, and some at the National Bureau of Standards, and none of which are described by Snow.

Here was a golden opportunity, if there ever was one, to explain some deep science to the layman, an opportunity Snow let slip away. One wonders whether Snow himself understood the physics of Lee and Yang's discovery. In fact, at the time, these experiments were front-page news, and the physicists who performed them had their hands full explaining them to an excited and curious general public. But then, to repeat, the first reason for teaching science to nonscientists is that many of these nonscientists have a genuine desire to learn about science, and this, after all, is the best reason for teaching anything to anyone.

The second reason is what I myself call *technological bewilderment*. Most of us, myself included, are increasingly surrounded by objects that we use daily but whose workings are a total mystery to us. This thought struck me forcibly about a year ago. One day, for reasons I can no longer reconstruct, I was looking around my apartment when it suddenly occurred to me that it was full of objects I did not understand. A brief catalogue included my color television set, a battery-operated alarm watch, an electronic chess-playing machine, and a curious fountain pen that tells the time. Here I am, I thought, a scientist surrounded by domestic artifacts whose workings I don't understand. I then began asking several of my colleagues in theoretical physics whether they had the same feeling. (I didn't ask the experimenters I know because *those* people really do understand how things work.) They, too, reported similar feelings.

My first impulse was to try to build something—say, a radio—with the hope that, if I could actually put it together with my own hands, I might understand it, so to speak, on its own terms. I went so far as to order an electronics kit from a large scientific mail-order house in New Jersey. Following directions, I managed to make several radios, one of which actually worked. The only problem was that the components of the kit were so modular that I couldn't understand them either. A few of my friends have actually designed and built small computers. I envy them this ability. It then occurred to me that an entire course could be taught on how one nontrivial thing—say, a small computer—actually works. I don't mean how to program a computer (a skill that is now readily being acquired by elementary school students), I mean actually building one—designing the logic circuits and the rest. If such a course were taught for laypeople, I would take it myself.

The third reason for teaching science to nonscientists is what I call *technological necessity*. It is a fact of modern life that all of us are confronted by decisions, largely taken on our behalf by others, that have a significant technological component. Two obvious examples are the decisions related to energy and to nuclear weapons. It is crucial, in my view, that as many people as possible have enough of a technical background to be able to separate the purely technical aspects of these decisions from the political and moral ones. No one should be afraid of participating in making such decisions just because some "expert" says that there are technical factors involved that are beyond the layperson's understanding. I do not believe, for example, that there is in the general energy question a single technical element beyond the capacity of anyone who will familiarize himself or herself with the issues and learn to add and multiply large numbers. The latter may sound absurd, but if I had been at those gatherings where Snow had badgered his fellow guests with arcane matters involving entropy, I would have changed the discussion by asking questions like, How many gallons are in a barrel of oil? and, Is it true, as Max Frisch claims in his novella *Man in the Holocene*, that if the Arctic ice melts owing to the so-called greenhouse effect—which might become serious if we insist on burning more coal—then "New York would be under water"? These are matters that can affect the way we live now and the way in which our descendants will live in the future.

Lest I be accused of raising scientific and technical questions without answering them, let me comment briefly on the two questions I have raised. They are prototypical. The reason it is important to know what a barrel of oil is, is that the barrel is the arbitrary unit by which quantities of oil are measured. Oil is, in fact, shipped or stored not in barrels but in tanks or drums, which hold amounts measured in barrels. The standard barrel is a concept that dates back to the early fifteenth century. Henry VI of England decided that a barrel of eels should be thirty gallons, but his successor, Edward IV, raised this to forty-two gallons. After the first discovery of oil, in Titusville, Pennsylvania, in 1859, there was general chaos about how many gallons were in the standard barrel. This matter was settled in 1916 by an act of Congress that declared that the standard oil barrel was to be forty-two gallons. A gallon of oil, incidentally, supplies enough energy to keep 130 one-hundred-watt light bulbs burning for one hour. (A barrel of whiskey, which is probably enough to keep a large number of us lit for many hours, is usually 30½ gallons.)

We use something less than six billion barrels of oil a year in this country; so the next time one reads of a well that produces a thousand barrels a day—a very, very substantial well—one can use one's pocket calculator and figure out how much of a dent this makes in solving our oil problem. Knowing this scarcely requires a Ph.D. in physics—but without knowing it, how can one even begin to think quantitatively about the general energy question?

Felix Rohatyn, the physicist turned investment banker, whose clear thinking and determination pulled New York City through its fiscal crisis in the 1970s, and who is a master at dealing with just the kind of politico-technical problem that the general energy question presents, once told me that the key element in all these matters is to bring things down to choices. "Once," he noted, "you bring it down to choices, it really gets reasonably simple." That is just what the energy problem is—a question of choices. One begins with a total figure for the amount of energy we need for transportation, heating, electricity, and the rest and then begins to list the choices for supplying that energy, and their consequences. In doing this, one must manipulate large numbers—trillions, for example—and have the appropriate numbers to manipulate. Isn't this just the sort of thing we should be teaching nonscientists? If we don't, how are we going to arrive at sensible decisions? People will be at the mercy of any energy huckster who happens to have a loud voice and ready access to a television studio.

Max Frisch's confusion can be settled by taking an ice cube and putting it in a completely full glass of water and watching what happens. After the water spills—due to sticking in the ice cube—*nothing* happens. The ice cube melts, and the water it has displaced gets replenished with no change in the surface level of the water in the glass. This is characteristic of floating ice such as the ice in the Arctic. If it melted—leaving Greenland aside since the ice there is *not* floating—the level of the oceans would not rise at all. No one is quite sure what would happen to Greenland if the temperature in the Arctic rose enough to begin melting ice. The climate might change so drastically that, in fact, the ice on Greenland might get thicker. But of one thing everyone who has studied the matter is sure, and that is that a warming of a few degrees in Antarctica would be a collective disaster. The Antarctic ice is attached to the continent and is not floating. A recent Department of Energy report indicates that if we keep burning coal and other hydrocarbons at something like the present rate, or greater, the global temperature could rise five degrees in considerably less than a century. This would come about because the burning of these hydrocarbons produces carbon dioxide, which traps the heat that is reradiated from the earth after the sun heats it. There is no possible technology that can stop carbon dioxide from being formed when, say, coal is burned. That formation is simply part of the burning reaction. Given this, and given the other pollution problems caused by burning coal, how much of the stuff can we afford to burn; and if we decide that we had better be cautious about burning all we have, what then are the choices? Here, again, is a matter that nonscientists had better learn to think about before we are all drowning in the approximately 150-foot rise in sea level that would occur if all the ice in Antarctica were to melt.

HAVING offered three reasons to teach science to non-scientists—curiosity, technological bewilderment, and technological necessity—I would now like to offer some ideas on how courses addressed to these reasons might be taught. Some of this I have already hinted at. It is, I think, clear that the three kinds of courses I have in mind are quite different, and would serve differing needs and interests. The curiosity course is, by now, of a fairly familiar kind. My own interest in physics was aroused by just such a course, taught by the late Philipp Frank in the spring of 1948, when I was a freshman at Harvard. I doubt that anyone, before or since, has taught a better one. But nowadays "Physics for Poets" courses are fairly ubiquitous. Gerald Feinberg taught such a course at Columbia University for several years. The last time he taught it, it had an enrollment of over two hundred students—some of them, presumably, poets, and none of them scientists. Feinberg had a good deal of experience lecturing and writing for lay-people, so he was able to lead his charges expertly through a thicket of quarks, relativity, gluons, black holes, and the rest, with relatively few casualties. He was surprised, and pleased, to discover just how much his students were able and willing to absorb. Before it was over, in fact, a few of them decided that they might want to major in physics.

The present generation of students has been exposed to television programs such as "Nova" and "Cosmos" which, as bad as the latter was, drew the largest audience ever to watch a public television series. I do not really have any special words of wisdom about teaching a curiosity course, except that it clearly takes someone to teach it who is actively engaged in science. To be good, it must come from someone who is really on top of the material. Otherwise it simply becomes a digest of other people's popularizations. That can be done, but it is a little like eating Wonder bread: it won't do you much harm, but it is not very exciting either.

I have never heard of anyone who has tried to teach a technological bewilderment course. Since I am as nearly bewildered as anyone else, I certainly have never tried to teach one myself. I think that I would likely electrocute myself the first day. On the other hand, I have taught something very like a technological necessity course, and I would like to describe a bit of it, as well as to describe a remarkable course I witnessed and participated in during one of my Phi Beta Kappa visits.

In the spring of 1980, I was a visiting professor at Princeton University, where I taught a course under the auspices of the Humanities Council in a program called the "Literature of Fact." The nominal subject of the course was science writing for scientists. All fourteen of my students, ranging from sophomores to graduate students, were science majors of some kind. Only a small number were physicists. I decided early in the game that the only way a course like that could work was if we all learned some new science and wrote about it. I decided that a subject that we might learn about was energy. Since I had a small budget for outside lecturers, I was able to invite a variety of my colleagues to be interviewed by the students, who then wrote up these interviews as part of their course work. A final ten-thousand-word essay was required to answer the question, How would you solve the energy problem? It was to be written in a style appropriate for a magazine article.

The first day of class, I asked the students a few things about their views on energy. In particular, I asked them how many were in favor of using nuclear power. I was not surprised when no hands were raised. I then asked how many of them understood how a nuclear reactor works. I was again not surprised when no one raised a hand. Most physics majors never learn how an actual nuclear reactor works, since this is considered to be nuclear engineering. I then invited four experts on nuclear power to talk to my class: David Rossin, a nuclear engineer who is a leading spokesman for the use of nuclear power; Henry Kendall, the founder of the Union of Concerned Scientists, who vehemently opposes nuclear power; Norman Rasmussen, the MIT professor whose reactor safety study is still the basis for most reactor safety estimates; and Ted Taylor, who had then just finished serving on President Carter's Three Mile Island commission investigating the near-disaster at the Three Mile Island nuclear power plant in Pennsylvania in 1979. I invited them on different weeks since I was not interested in having a live debate, but rather a series of thoughtful interviews.

The students at first must have found this somewhat bewildering. I think they were especially impressed by Rasmussen, whose competence and integrity are obvious the minute he begins speaking, and by Ted Taylor, who is not an advocate of nuclear power, to put it mildly, but who told the students that he could find no scenario, however far-fetched, that could have turned Three Mile Island into any more of an accident in terms of threats to human life than it was—which was, essentially, no threat. I took no position in any of these discussions and simply let the students boil around in their own intellectual stew. The net result was that, in their final reports, *every* student said, however reluctantly, that nuclear power was an essential short-term part of the solution to the energy problem. During the course, we had had an opportunity to examine all of the possible choices of power sources, including solar and wind power. It had come down to a matter of choices; and while no choice was perfect, the students decided that nuclear power, on the basis of what they had learned, was an acceptable imperfect choice. Perhaps another group of students would have reacted differently to what was presented to them. That these students were science majors is not, I think, relevant to the workability of a course like this. When we began, none of them knew much, if anything, about the actual details of the general energy problem. The students—and their teacher—learned about it as they went along.

THE other example of a technological necessity course is one that was designed specifically for nonscience majors. I encountered it on my Phi Beta Kappa visit to the University of Delaware. I am reluctant to attempt to give credit to any particular individual for creating the course, since I do not know the details, but my tour guide and host was the astronomer H. L. Shipman. On the day I visited, he was teaching it in collaboration with a biologist and a philosopher. The three teachers were present in the classroom. The subject that day was world hunger. In previous classes, I gathered, the biologist had explained the facts about hunger and had made it clear what the resources were. On this particular day, the discussion, led by the philosopher, had to do with choices—specifically: Whom shall we choose to feed? This is, obviously, an agonizing question. The moral dilemma is clear. Feeding people raises health standards, especially the health standards of children. Hence, it produces a growth in world population, which, in turn, lowers the standard of living for everyone. The discussion got quite personal. Individual students were asked if they were willing to lower their standards of living—for example, to reduce their consumption of meat, which is a notoriously inefficient way to use both food and energy—in order to feed people they did not know. What are our moral and ethical obligations? How do we balance our self-interests against what is possible and what is right? These are immensely difficult questions, and the students were, rightly, deeply serious about them. The discussion affected all of us—and, one would like to think, helped the students to think about a future that is, after all, theirs.

We live in a complex, dangerous, and fascinating world. Science has played a role in creating the dangers, and one hopes that it will aid in creating ways of dealing with these dangers. But most of these problems cannot, and will not, be dealt with by scientists alone. We need all the help we can get, and this help has got to come from a scientifically literate general public. Ignorance of science and technology is becoming the ultimate self-indulgent luxury.

Some Things I Did Not Write

As I mentioned in the introduction, my profile of Lee and Yang ran in the *New Yorker* on 12 May 1962. In the previous January, I had signed the first of some thirty annual agreements with the magazine. In between the two dates, I had decided that I was not going to be a full-time professional writer. The opportunity was certainly there. I had, by then, published book reviews in the *New Yorker* and elsewhere, and begun writing fairly regularly for the "Talk of the Town." I had also begun to think of myself as a writer-physicist rather than as a physicist who occasionally wrote. During this time, however, I reached the conclusion that I was heading in the wrong direction. There were two reasons for this change: one I will call intellectual; and the other, moral. The intellectual reason is pretty simple to explain. I loved physics. I knew by that time, age thirty, about where I stood in the field. I knew that I was not going to make any great breakthroughs. I had been around really good physicists—the best—enough to understand that I was not one of them—not a Feynman or a Bethe. I was not bitter about this. I felt that I had other compensating abilities and enough ability as a physicist to continue to make decent contributions. I knew that I got more joy from doing and understanding physics than from any other intellectual activity. I was not about to give that up, and I never have. There has not been a year since 1962 when I have not published at least one paper in a significant physics journal.

The second reason for my not making the switch I have called "moral," for want of any better term. I hope that I don't sound self-righteous, but it is the simple truth. By the spring of 1962, I was earning more money than I had ever seen in any one place in my life. I think that I had gotten paid twelve hundred dollars for my first *New Yorker* article on Corsica. For me, this was a very large sum of money. I had been living on fellowships for nearly a decade, and these paid about four thousand dollars a year. In fact, until I began writing for the *New Yorker*, I had never had a bank account; I had so little money that it seemed hardly sporting to open one. Now that I actually had some money, I decided to buy a few things I had always wanted. The first thing I bought was a blue Sunbeam Alpine convertible. I loved that car. Everything about it, from the smell of the leather to the sound it made when I started it, was a sensual delight. I rode all over eastern Long Island around Brookhaven that spring with the top down, feeling like a lord.

Sometime during that spring, there was, in a small town not far from the laboratory, an occurrence that deeply reverberated in the rest of my life—my writing life. A boy of about ten fell down a well. He could not get out. His parents could not get him out, nor could the firemen and police get him out. It was a desperate situation and covered by both local and national news. After a few days, the Brookhaven National Laboratory got involved—whether because the community asked it or someone there offered its services, I do not know. In any event, an experimental physics colleague of mine named George Collins devised a method for getting the boy out. Though I have searched my memory, I can't for the life of me remember what it was. Whatever it was, it worked. The boy was rescued. That also was national news. It seemed to me that if anything qualified as "science as experience," it was this episode. I brought it to Mr. Shawn's attention, and he encouraged me to go ahead and try to write about it.

The first step was to track down the family. That was not hard. I had their name and the nearby town they lived in. I called them. I had given some thought to what I would say. I did not want to see them under false pretenses. I wanted to make clear that I was *both* a writer for the *New Yorker and* a staff member of the Brookhaven National Laboratory. I wanted to make it clear to them that it was my intention to write an article about them for the magazine. I think that I spoke to the boy's mother. I told her my story. I could tell from the tone of her voice that she was not enthusiastic about seeing me but, because of her gratitude for what the laboratory had done, was willing to do so. I decided to accept this in the spirit in which it was being offered. I arranged to see the family in the early evening after the working day.

On the afternoon of the appointment I set off in my Sunbeam Alpine, the top down and the radio playing some delightful music. I was happy and rather full of myself. I soon found myself, however, driving in a part of eastern Long Island that I had only read about in John O'Hara stories. This is the part far from the ocean resorts of East Hampton or Quogue. It is the terrain of subsistence dirt farmers, of towns with bowling alleys and diners. Prosperous New Yorkers commuting to the other Long Island would see this one only if their cars broke down.

After about an hour's driving, I found the family's house. It was pretty run-down. There was the hulk of a rusting car in the back. My Sunbeam Alpine stood out like a tiara. I knocked on the door. The family, the three of them, were dressed in what I suppose was their Sunday best. The man from the *New Yorker* was visiting. The boy looked as if he had been dunked in a barrel of soap. His hair was slicked like the boys in a Norman Rockwell painting. I didn't like him much. We began to talk, and I took out my notebook. But I didn't write anything, because by then I knew that I was not ever going to write anything about this tragedy for the *New Yorker*. I recognized what I was doing for what it was: pure exploitation. I was going to trade on what had been a desperate experience for this poor family in order to write something that, if accepted, would have earned me more money than any of these people had seen in a very long time, if ever. I couldn't even justify it on the grounds that there was any real science involved.

I got back into my Sunbeam Alpine and drove slowly back to the laboratory. I realized that it had been a close call. I had come very close to becoming something I did not want to be. I also realized a corollary to this. I would never, if I could help it, allow myself to be in a position where I *had* to do this kind of writing to support myself. I would never let myself be anything but a professional physicist who also writes. And that is what I became.

Bibliography

Bell, J. S. *Speakable and Unspeakable in Quantum Mechanics*. New York: Cambridge University Press, 1987.

Blackmore, John T. *Ernst Mach: His Work, Life, and Influence*. Berkeley: University of California Press, 1972.

Brigham, Carl C. *A Study of American Intelligence*. Princeton: Princeton University Press, 1923.

Camon, Ferdinando. *Conversations with Primo Levi*. Marlboro, Vt.: Marlboro Books, 1989.

Clark, Ronald W. *Einstein: The Life and Times*. Chicago: World Publishing, 1971.

The Dictionary of Scientific Biography. 7 vols. New York: Scribner, 1980.

Einstein, Albert. *Autobiographical Notes*. Trans. and ed. by Arthur Schlipp. La-Salle, Ill.: Open Court Publishing, 1979.

————. *The Collected Papers of Albert Einstein: The Early Years, 1879–1902*. Ed. by Dr. John Stachel. Princeton: Princeton University Press, 1987.

————. *Cosmic Religion, with Other Opinions and Aphorisms*. New York: Covici-Friede, 1931.

————. *The Meaning of Relativity*. 2d ed. Princeton: Princeton University Press, 1945.

Euler, Leonhard. *Elements of Algebra*. Trans. by John Hewlett. New York: Springer-Verlag, 1984.

Feynman, Richard P. *"Surely You're Joking, Mr. Feynman!"* New York: Norton, 1985.

Frank, Philipp. *Einstein: His Life and Times*. New York: Alfred A. Knopf, 1985.

Frisch, Max. *Man in the Holocene*. New York: Harcourt Brace Jovanovich, 1980.

Gamow, George. *My World Line*. New York: Viking Press, 1970.

Gould, Stephen Jay. *Ever Since Darwin*. New York: Norton, 1977.

———. *The Mismeasure of Man*. New York: Norton, 1980.

———. *The Panda's Thumb*. New York: Norton, 1980.

Gregory, Richard L., ed. *The Oxford Companion to the Mind*. New York: Oxford University Press, 1987.

Hawking, Stephen. *A Brief History of Time*. New York: Bantam, 1988.

Herzberg, Gerhard. *Spectra of Diatomic Molecules* (1950). Melbourne, Fla.: Krieger, 1988.

Hodges, Andrew. *Alan Turing: The Enigma*. New York: Simon & Schuster, 1983.

Kennedy, Don H. *The Little Sparrow: A Portrait of Sophia Kovalevsky*. Athens, Ohio: Ohio University Press, 1983.

Kepler, Johannes. *Kepler's Dream*. Madison, Wis.: Wisconsin Press, 1967.

Kilmister, C. W., ed. *Schrödinger: Centenary Celebration of a Polymath*. London: Cambridge University Press, 1987.

Kovalevskaia, S. V. *Recollections of Childhood* (1890). Trans. and ed. by Beatrice Stillman. New York: Springer-Verlag, 1978.

Laue, Max Theodor Felix von. *Das Relativitätsprinzip*. Braunschweig, 1911.

Lehrer, Tom. *Too Many Songs by Tom Lehrer with Not Enough Illustrations by Ronald Searle*. New York: Pantheon, 1981.

Lenin, V. I. *Materialism and Empirio-Criticism*. International Publishers, 1927.

Levi, Primo. *Dialogo*. Princeton: Princeton University Press, 1989.

———. *The Drowned and the Saved*. New York: Summit, 1988.

———. *The Mirror Maker*. New York: Schocken, 1989.

———. *The Periodic Table*. New York: Schocken, 1989.

———. *The Reawakening*. New York: Collier, 1987.

———. *Survival in Auschwitz*. New York: Collier, 1961.

Levi-Montalcini, Rita. *In Praise of Imperfection: My Life and Work*. Trans. by Luigi Attardi. New York: Basic Books, 1988.

Levy, Steven. *Hackers*. New York: Anchor Press/Doubleday, 1984.

Luria, S. E. *A Slot Machine, A Broken Test Tube*. New York: Harper & Row, 1984.

Lyell, Charles. *Principles of Geology* (1830). Johnson Reprint Corp., 1969.

Mach, Ernst. *History and Root of the Principle of the Conservation of Energy*. Trans. by Philip E. B. Jourdain. Chicago: Open Court Publishing, 1911.

———. *The Science of Mechanics*. 6th ed. Trans. by Thomas J. McCormack. La Salle, Ill.: Open Court Publishing, 1960.

Maimonides, Moses. *The Guide for the Perplexed*. 2d ed. New York: Dover Books, 1956.

Manuel, Frank E. *A Portrait of Isaac Newton*. Cambridge: Belknap/Harvard University Press, 1968.

Moore, Walter. *Schrödinger: Life and Thought*. New York: Cambridge University Press, 1989.

Moritz, Michael. *The Little Kingdom: The Private Story of Apple Computer.* New York: William Morrow, 1984.

Newton, Isaac. *Mathematical Principles of Natural Philosophy.* Chicago: Encyclopaedia Britannica, 1955.

Pais, Abraham. *Niels Bohr's Times: In Physics, Philosophy, and Polity.* New York: Oxford University Press, 1991.

———. *Subtle Is the Lord: The Science and Life of Albert Einstein.* New York: Oxford University Press, 1982.

Schrödinger, Erwin. *Collected Papers on Wave Mechanisms.* London and Glasgow: Blackie & Son, 1928.

———. *My View of the World.* Cambridge: Cambridge University Press, 1966.

———. *Nature and the Greeks.* Cambridge: Cambridge University Press, 1954.

———. *Space-Time Structure.* Cambridge: Cambridge University Press, 1963.

———. *Statistical Thermodynamics.* 2d ed. Cambridge: Cambridge University Press, 1952.

———. *What Is Life?* Cambridge: Cambridge University Press, 1964.

Schwarz-Bart, André. *The Last of the Just.* Princeton: Princeton University Press, 1960.

Segrè, Emilio. *Enrico Fermi: Physicist.* Chicago: University of Chicago Press, 1970.

Snow, C. P. *The Physicists.* Boston: Little, Brown, 1981.

Speziali, Pierre, trans. *Albert Einstein, Michele Besso: Correspondence, 1903–1955.* Paris: Hermann, 1972.

Stukeley, William. *Memoirs of Sir Isaac Newton's Life* (1752). Ed. by A. Hastings White. London: Taylor and Francis, 1936.

Turing, Sara. *Alan M. Turing.* Cambridge: W. Heffer, 1959.

Ulam, Stanislaw M. *Adventures of a Mathematician.* New York: Scribner, 1976.

Watson, James. *The Double Helix.* New York: Atheneum, 1968.

Weinberg, Steven. *The First Three Minutes.* Rev. ed. New York: Basic Books, 1988.

Welchman, Gordon. *The Hut Six Story: Breaking the Enigma Codes.* New York: McGraw-Hill, 1982.

Wensberg, Peter C. *Land's Polaroid: A Company and the Man Who Invented It.* Boston: Houghton Mifflin, 1987.

Acknowledgments

Grateful acknowledgment is made to the following for their permission to reprint previously published material:

"How Can We Be Sure That Albert Einstein Was Not a Crank?" originally appeared in the April 1991 issue of *MD* Magazine. Reprinted with permission.

"The Chemistry of Primo Levi" originally appeared in the August 1990 issue of *MD* Magazine. Reprinted with permission.

"A Woman's Place" is reprinted by permission of the editors of *The Gettysburg Review*, in whose pages it first appeared.

"Niels Bohr's Times" is reprinted with permission from *The New York Review of Books*. Copyright © 1991 Nyrev, Inc.

"I Am a Camera" is reprinted with permission from *The New York Review of Books*. Copyright © 1988 Nyrev, Inc.

The following pieces originally appeared in *The New Yorker*: "Who Was Christy Mathewson?", "A Portrait of Alan Turing," "Einstein When Young," "Cosmology," and "Feet of Clay."

The following pieces originally appeared in *The American Scholar*: "Ernst Mach and the Quarks," "The Merely Personal," "A Child's Garden of Science," and "Having Fun with Tom Lehrer."

Index